INFLATION AND STABILISATION IN LATIN AMERICA

St Antony's/Macmillan Series

This new series contains academic books written or edited by members of St Antony's College, Oxford, or by authors with a special association with the College. The titles are selected by an editorial board on which both the College and the publishers are represented.

Titles already published or in the press are listed below, and there are numerous further titles in preparation.

INFLATION AND STABILISATION IN LATIN AMERICA

Edited by

Rosemary Thorp
and
Laurence Whitehead

in association with
St Antony's College, Oxford

First published 1979 by
THE MACMILLAN PRESS LTD
London and Basingstoke
Associated companies in Delhi
Dublin Hong Kong Johannesburg Lagos
Melbourne New York Singapore Tokyo

Filmset by Vantage Photosetting Co. Ltd
Southampton and London
Printed and bound in Great Britain by
Redwood Burn Limited
Trowbridge & Esher

British Library Cataloguing in Publication Data

Inflation and stabilisation in Latin America
   1. Latin America – Economic policy
   2. Latin America – Economic conditions – 1945–
   3. Economic stabilisation
   I. Thorp, Rosemary   II. Whitehead,
   Laurence   III. St Antony's College
   330.9'8'003   HC125

   ISBN 0–333–25596–8

Contents

List of Tables and Figures

TABLES

FIGURE

Acknowledgements

This book is the final product of a collaborative effort, which began with a series of seminars in Oxford in early 1978, and continued with several further meetings to review and discuss the papers. Each contributor would like to acknowledge his debt to the group. We would also like to thank the other members of the seminar for their participation. Michael Kuczynski and Alan Angell made extensive and helpful comments. The Oxford Inter-faculty Committee for Latin American Studies provided finance and the Latin American Centre, Oxford, provided facilities.

Notes on the Contributors

GUIDO DI TELLA is an associate of the Instituto Torcuato di Tella in Buenos Aires, and has been a Visiting Fellow at St Antony's College, Oxford, and Professor of Economics at the University of Buenos Aires.

HENRY FINCH is Lecturer in Economics at the University of Liverpool.

VALPY FITZGERALD is Assistant Director of Development Studies, Faculty of Economics and Politics, University of Cambridge, and a Fellow and Tutor of St Edmund's House, Cambridge.

ROSEMARY THORP is a Fellow of St Antony's College and Lecturer in Latin American Economics at the University of Oxford.

JOHN WELLS is a Lecturer in the Department of Applied Economics, Cambridge, and a Fellow of King's College, Cambridge.

LAURENCE WHITEHEAD is a Fellow and Senior Tutor of Nuffield College, Oxford.

1 Introduction

ROSEMARY THORP and LAURENCE WHITEHEAD

The issue of inflation and stabilisation policy in Latin America attracted considerable debate and research during the 1960s. In the early years of the 1970s the debate largely died out, for reasons which, as we explain below, are closely related to international developments. But today the issue is reviving as a focal point of controversy, in reaction to further significant changes in the international economy. This is the motivation for the case studies drawn together in this book: what new light can be thrown on these difficult policy issues by reviewing the reactions of six countries to the major adjustment problems thrust upon them since the early 1970s? What can the comparison show us both about the internal structures of those countries and about the *modus operandi* of different stabilisation techniques?

It is clearly important that these policies are being attempted in a context distinctly different from that of a decade earlier. It is the task of this Introduction, first, to define the differences both in the international economy and in Latin America itself, and, second, to attempt to define the issues – which, we shall argue, have also shifted somewhat in the intervening years.

LATIN AMERICA, THE IMF AND THE WORLD ECONOMY

Since the 1960s major developments in the international economy have led to the collapse of the old Bretton Woods system. We must therefore outline briefly what that system meant for Latin America and how the continent was affected by its disintegration. It was in 1944 at Bretton Woods that the IMF and the World Bank were founded (with dual membership) as fruits of the Allied victory in the Second World War. Of the forty sovereign members enrolled by the end of 1946, no less than eighteen were Latin American republics, but this by no means reflected the true realities of international power at that time. More significant was the fact that the Latin American members were expected to contribute no more than 6 per cent of the Fund's initial resources, and that the headquarters of both organisations were located in Washington. Some notable potential member states failed to join as they were unwilling to send confidential information about the state of their economies to the American capital or to accept the restrictions on their freedom of economic policy-making that membership required. Thus, not only the Soviet Union, but also Argentina remained outside the IMF (until after the downfall of the Perón regime in 1955). Likewise China never contested the representation from Taiwan, Poland withdrew and Czechoslovakia was expelled in the 1950s, and Cuba withdrew to avoid expulsion in 1964. Clearly, then, the Bretton Woods system was underpinned by the political and economic power of the USA and membership did not offer the same attractions to that country's enemies as to its friends. (However, Cambodia, Laos and Vietnam have retained at least nominal membership since 1975.) Even for the majority of Latin American republics (those which were well-behaved allies of the USA and enthusiasts for the American economic system), membership of the Fund was not in itself a great attraction, since it involved accepting a series of conditions and disciplines which were likely to be relatively onerous for capital-scarce economies with high exposure to international trade cycles. For them the main attractions of Bretton Woods were the prospect of benefiting from a stable and open trading system, and the hope of receiving large inflows of development finance on favourable terms. In the event, however, it was trade between the more developed countries that showed the greatest dynamism under the Bretton Woods system and, although world trade flourished during the 1950s and 1960s, Latin America's share of the total sharply declined. Similarly, at least until 1961 (when the USA responded to the Cuban revolution by launching the ill-fated Alliance for Progress), Latin America was regarded as a politically secure base area which therefore ranked rather low among geographical regions as a claimant for official financing.

The benefits of the Bretton Woods system reached Latin

America relatively slowly and weakly. By contrast, its disciplines arrived early and with full force. To avoid payments restrictions the system provided that the currencies of member countries should be freely convertible (at least on current account transactions) and should be maintained at fixed parities to one another, to avoid the competitive devaluations of the 1930s. In the event of a 'fundamental' disequilibrium members were allowed to devalue, while temporary disequilibria were to be financed by resources provided by the IMF, with conditions attached to ensure that the recipient country's balance-of-payments deficit was in fact temporary. The practice of attaching economic policy conditions to the provision of Fund resources was gradually developed during the 1950s, mainly using Latin American economies as the testing ground for these techniques.[1] But in general the less developed members of the Fund had relatively little influence in its policy-making councils, which, as Susan Strange has recently suggested, may help to explain why they were favoured targets for Fund supervision.[2]

The asymmetries in the Bretton Woods system are most apparent when the role played by the USA is considered.[3] The dollar, backed by the strength of the American economy and the USA's huge stocks of gold, provided the effective reserve currency for the whole system. The President of the World Bank has always been an American, effectively nominated by Washington, as has the Deputy Managing Director of the Fund, and the US government also enjoys a veto on such important matters as changes in the Fund's membership and in the price of gold. Although the original Keynes-White plan of 1943 envisaged an international system in which the burden of adjustment would be shared equally by surplus and deficit countries, in the event capital-scarce and deficit-prone countries have been the only ones whose autonomy of policy-making has been sacrificed to the stability of the system as a whole. None of this is to deny, of course, that in order to preserve an open international trading system it is necessary to have a lending agency of last resort with powerful sanctions at its disposal and a clear commitment to the maintenance of confidence in the system as a whole, even where the consequences for individual member states are quite painful. The point has rather been to emphasise the central role of US power in defining the content and the boundaries of the Bretton Woods system, and to point out that it has not necessarily been those countries whose economic policies cause the greatest strains to the system who have felt the main weight of its sanctions.[4]

We have stressed the central role of the US in this system; it was inevitable that, as that power waned, so the system would be shaken to its foundations. The events of 1971, which finally undermined the credibility of the dollar as a sound reserve currency, were only the culmination of profound long-term changes in the world economy. The rise of rival economies to challenge US pre-eminence was a key development affecting the whole system. Throughout the preceding generation the US government had been engaged in extremely ambitious programmes of defence expenditure, combined with overseas investment and aid commitments. To maintain the international role of its currency implied credit restraint and relatively deflationary economic policies at home. But of course its international strength also depended upon a reasonable growth of domestic investment, rising incomes and relatively full employment. Critics of the reserve currency system had long argued that it would prove inherently unstable, as the country providing the reserve currency took advantage of the freedom this system conferred. In the event the surplus of dollars held outside the USA grew rapidly during the 1960s, and correspondingly foreigners' willingness voluntarily to hold dollars as their main reserve asset went into decline. From the mid-1960s the process was accelerated by US expenditures on the Vietnam War and a more rapid decline in the purchasing power of the dollar.

The outflow of dollars during the 1960s began to generate a new private international financial market – the euro-currency market – which from the viewpoint of the developing countries was to prove one of the most immediately significant aspects of the new developments. In general about three-quarters of the funds in the euro-currency pool have been dollars held outside the USA. The net euro-currency market grew from an estimated $9 billion in 1964 to $44 billion in 1969, $80 billion in 1972 and $210 billion in 1975, and perhaps double that again by 1978. Until the late 1960s Third World governments were as likely to be lenders as borrowers on this market, but as its size increased private bankers became increasingly interested in seeking out new clients. Bank lending to the more resource-rich and credit-worthy developing countries became increasingly fashionable (and profitable) in the early 1970s.[5] Whereas initially the funds may have been tied to specific development projects, after a while they became in practice available for unconditional balance-of-payments financing – thus temporarily freeing borrowing governments from dependence on the IMF. In this respect, as in various others, the abandonment of Bretton Woods rules after August 1971 facilitated a rapid and co-ordinated but unsustainable upswing in economic activity all round the world, which culminated with the commodity boom of 1973:

> Price fluctuations on world commodity markets were wider between 1972 and 1975 than at any other time since the end of World War II. Real commodity prices increased from 1972 to 1973 more than twice as much as they did from 1953 to 1954 . . . They also declined in 1975 by more than twice as much as they did in 1971 when the steepest annual fall since World War II occurred.[6]

Latin America was powerfully affected by this process, as can be seen from the abrupt movements in the terms of trade for our six countries, shown in Table 1.1. As the essays in this volume show, many Latin American economic policy-makers responded to this temporary abundance of finance and upsurge of demand for their exports by over-borrowing and perhaps committing themselves to major development projects that were soon, in the ensuing recession, to prove distinctly unremunerative.[7] It should not be assumed, however, that their misjudgements were more irrational than the policy decisions of many other governments or private credit institutions that were caught up in the euphoria of 1973. In fact, from a global perspective, the ability and willingness of non-OPEC developing countries to sustain heavy increases in their external indebtedness was of considerable benefit in minimising the severity of the ensuing recession. Indeed, their willingness to continue importing from the industrialised countries, despite the fall-off in demand for their exports, helped to sustain aggregate demand in the developed economies.[8] By means of this counter-cyclical financing the Latin American region as a whole has won commendation from the World Bank and the Inter-American Development Bank for its success in maintaining a positive growth rate while much of the world was in recession.[9]

As we have indicated, the brief burst of prosperity and freedom from Bretton Woods restraints was quickly and necessarily fol-

TABLE 1.1   Export and import prices and terms of trade for the six countries, 1968–76

Indices 1970 = 100, US$

	Argentina	Brazil	Chile	Mexico	Peru	Uruguay
Export prices						
1968	88	86	83	91	83	89
1970	100	100	100	100	100	100
1971	101	97	80	112	91	97
1972	122	109	78	119	92	118
1973	180	150	111	142	169	169
1974	196	189	156	188	189	168
1975	170	196	113	201	160	130
1976	179	229	n.a.	234	176	133
Import prices						
1968	94	n.a.	92	93	104	98
1970	100	100	100	100	100	100
1971	96	104	102	104	104	90
1972	104	111	109	107	112	88
1973	166	139	134	115	132	113
1974	272	214	177	134	134	228
1975	239	217	193	164	185	243
1976	256	219	n.a.	168	196	230
Terms of trade						
1968	110	n.a.	91	99	80	90
1970	100	100	100	100	100	100
1971	105	93	78	107	88	107
1972	117	99	72	110	83	134
1973	109	109	83	123	128	150
1974	72	88	88	140	113	74
1975	71	91	59	123	87	53
1976	70	105	n.a.	139	90	58

Source: Country chapters and United Nations *Yearbook of International Trade*.

lowed by a sustained spell of global demand-deficiency, while the rise in commodity prices, and in particular the price of oil, fed through to costs in the centre countries to produce 'stagflation' followed by a sharp reversal of terms of trade for Latin America (Table 1.1).[10] The result was currency turmoil, generalised loss of confidence in the stability of the world economy, and severe balance-of-payments disequilibrium for many Latin American governments.

It is at this point that our case studies take up the story, in a context significantly different from that of the 1950s and 1960s.

Perhaps the key change, from the point of view of stabilisation policies, is that the IMF is less clearly in a position of solid authority than was the case in earlier years. It remains the pivotal source of last-resort conditional finance for countries facing acute balance-of-payments disequilibria, but the nature of its prescriptions elicit more controversy, and the international support that it can rally for its activities is now more hesitant and uncertain. Before we discuss further the near-crisis of identity thrust on the IMF by the decline in the hegemony of the USA, the upheaval in currency systems and the loss of confidence among Western economic policy-makers, we need to review briefly the changing scene in Latin America.

In Latin America the 1960s was still the 'euphoric' stage of import-substituting industrialisation, which was to provide an escape route from balance-of-payments vulnerability and a stimulus to growth independent both of exports and the internal market. But even by the mid-1960s it was very clear that the consequence of the way such a route had been followed was, if anything, increased rigidity in the balance of payments, as imports became concentrated in industrial inputs and raw materials, while, as possibilities for further substitution became limited and no breakthrough to exporting manufactures occurred, the rate of growth again became basically determined by traditional exports. Further, the multinationals played a larger role than had been anticipated in the industrial expansion, so reducing the balance-of-payments gains and making the management of the new import structure even more difficult. As the import-substituting route became less rewarding, so attention was directed towards two possible routes for further progress in the 1970s — routes by no means mutually exclusive in terms of economic theory but which were to prove so in terms of political economy. One was that more state planning was needed to advance import substitution rationally to its next stage, and closely related to this was the desire to implement more successful control over the multinationals. The other was that more weight should be given to market efficiency in order that non-traditional exports might rescue the model. Both these solutions lay behind the intentions of the Andean Pact. For a brief period in the early 1970s, with the governments of Allende in Chile, Velasco in Peru and Torres in Bolivia, and similar tendencies in Ecuador and even Venezuela, it appeared that state intervention and stronger control over international capital might be the dominant themes, at least for some West Coast republics. The quasi-radical military government of Peru was hailed as the start of a new trend, developmentalist and nationalist at the same time. But rather rapidly fundamental political change brought a different and more familiar style of military government to all major Southern Cone countries; with the new conservatism came also 'market efficiency' and 'openness to market forces' as the new conventional wisdom. These moves were a response fundamentally to internal shifts in the balance of class forces, but international events also played a not insignificant role: the early days of improving terms of trade and increasing freedom of capital movement strongly favoured a move to 'openness',[11] while the collapse of the fixed exchange rate system made a move to flexible exchanges entirely acceptable. That the shift reflected deeper forces, however, is evident from its survival once conditions changed, as the case studies will show.

We are now in a position to consider why the position of the IMF today is both so strikingly different from the early 1960s and so critical. The context of balance-of-payments crises of the late 1950s and early 1960s was, as we have explained, one of credit scarcity and domination of lending to less developed countries by official agencies. This meant that such agencies, and the IMF in particular, had extraordinary power as credit rationers. Further, the solution required within the system, of tight monetary and fiscal control, was in no way against the interests of the major private investors who also looked to the IMF 'seal' of good behaviour: their interests were still in primary sectors, or perhaps in new import-substitution lines whose rate of growth was still independent of the local market.

Since the early 1970s, with the increasingly uniform right-wing complexion of the governments in the region, many countries have been engaged in major policy changes of which the internalisation of orthodoxy is an integral part. In these cases the role of the IMF has been less central, since stabilisation has been part of a much wider shift in the model of development.

Then, in general during the 1970s, international liquidity has remained abundant. Hence any country conforming closely enough to the rules of the international community in regard to foreign capital, inspiring sufficient confidence in its policy management, and/or carrying enough weight as a debtor, can hope to continue commercial borrowing. This has offered a major incentive to governments in the region to persevere with their 'market efficiency' economic strategies.

All this implies that in Latin America during the 1970s, in contrast to earlier periods, few governments have had IMF-type stabilisation policies imposed upon them from outside – namely those who have tended to borrow for unorthodox needs rather than to support private capital and whose weight in the banks' total debt is not that of Brazil or Mexico. So the IMF is liable to exert maximum pressure in those countries where there is least internal base for the policy, which are also where the policies previously adopted were of a particularly unorthodox variety – at least in the eye of international creditors. Further, under the old system, the Fund had a clear and necessary role to play as 'lender of last resort', with its sanctions a central part of the maintenance of a system of fixed exchange rates and full convertibility against the dollar. With the decline in the hegemony of the USA and the upheaval in currency systems, there were bound to be major implications for the role of the Fund, and, not surprisingly, such rethinking has not been instantaneous. Between 1971 and 1973 the Fund devoted most of its attention to somewhat unsuccessful attempts to stabilise exchange rates on a new basis, and to reform the world monetary system. The adjustment problems of developing countries received relatively little attention. However, by the end of 1973 financing the deficits of the non-oil developing countries suddenly became an urgent task.

Managing-Director Johannes Witteveen has explained the Fund's initial reaction:

> At an annual average of about $29 billion, the current account deficits of non-oil producing developing countries were somewhat over three times as large in 1974–7 as during 1968–73; as between the two periods, the share of assistance provided by the Fund increased from 3 per cent to 6 per cent.[12]

This increase in assistance was possible because in 1974 and 1975 the Fund set up special credit facilities for oil-importing countries with balance-of-payments difficulties. Funds were provided in part by OPEC, but were used up by late 1976. Also, in 1975 an additional form of credit – compensatory financing – was provided for countries suffering from temporary shortfalls on their export earnings; and in 1976 the Fund began a four-year pro-gramme of gold auctions to finance a trust fund for developing countries. Clearly these moves represented no more than a mod-est and temporary contribution, while commercial banks and other official agencies provided an overwhelming proportion of the recycling finance.

However, the importance of the Fund's assistance has always consisted less in the volume of resources it could provide, than in the 'conditionality' it could attach to its assistance beyond the first credit tranche: conditions that would inspire the confidence of other suppliers of credit. Since 1976 this type of activity has once again come to the fore, as 'adjustment' has taken the place of 'recycling' in the Fund's priorities.

To avoid precipitating the whole world into a major deflatio-nary spiral the IMF must distinguish between the legitimate (or globally necessary) disequilibria that non-OPEC developing countries must be expected to experience collectively (and there-fore individually), and the 'excessive' or 'irresponsible' dise-quilibria attributable to domestic mismanagement by individual Third World governments. However, the distinction between 'recycling finance' and 'conditional credit for adjustment pur-poses' is clear enough in principle, but highly subjective (not to say political) in practice. Legitimate disequilibria tend to become simply those that the private commercial banks are prepared to finance, and the judgements of the banks in turn are not precisely the impersonal and non-political judgements of a disembodied market, as the saga of Peru's relations with the US banks, for example, makes clear.

There have been three main innovations in the area of adjust-ment finance. Whereas before the oil price rise 'standby' pro-grammes were normally for one year, since then it has been increasingly accepted that two years should be the norm. In certain circumstances a three-year time scale is allowed to ease the process of adjustment: this is the 'Extended Fund Facility' introduced in 1974 and so far used by only five members (includ-ing Mexico and Jamaica). Lastly, in April 1978 the articles of agreement of the Fund were amended to enhance the oppor-tunities for the Fund to check on the exchange rate policies of all members. This mechanism may develop into an 'early-warning system' whereby the Fund can begin to influence the policies of the more vulnerable member countries before a fully fledged balance-of-payments crisis has developed.

So far these innovations do not seem likely to produce any drastic change in the *modus operandi* of the Fund. Although its membership has more than trebled since 1945, the distribution of power remains very unfavourable to the great majority of weak debtor members. Despite a recent one-third rise in quotas, the resources available for lending remain desperately scarce and at least some of the major contributors have taken the line that they will only supply more money if there is even more strict conditionality. Even after amendment of the articles of agreement, the Fund's effective capacity to influence the economic policies of great powers and countries running disruptive surpluses is extremely slight.[13] It also lacks control, or even much influence, over the creation of international liquidity. (The Special Drawing Rights that were created in 1969 to increase the Fund's leverage here have, in practice, been completely overshadowed by other types of reserve creation.) In short, despite the innovations of the last few years the Fund still finds itself essentially disciplining the weakest economies on behalf of an international system that is no longer under much overall control.

In view of these ambiguities in the Fund's position, and of the great seriousness of the economic problems facing many of the governments with which it deals, it is not surprising that its activities have become a subject of growing controversy. In a recent speech on 'conditionality' Managing-Director Witteveen reviewed some of the criticisms of the Fund's approach, and made a few minor concessions to his critics. He admitted that in some parts of the world there had been 'an increase in the number of governments whose position was insufficiently strong to enable them to undertake difficult adjustment measures', and that 'the Fund can counsel and agree but it assuredly cannot – as is, unfortunately, so often said – "impose" policies and conditions', but he also argued that 'it is necessary to counter the belief that Fund conditionality involves policy measures that countries in balance of payments difficulties could otherwise do without'.[14] In other words the political conditions for Fund-approved stabilisation policies are in some cases almost impossible to satisfy in current conditions, and yet in the absence of such policies economic conditions will become even worse. Whatever the subjective preferences of individual officials, the clear implication of this analysis is that in some situations only a determined and authoritarian regime may be capable of carrying out the economic policies required to secure Fund support.

The growing concern with the political implications of such policies, as much as with their long-run implications for the system of accumulation, plus the increasingly clear links between the Fund and the international power structure, are the key elements influencing the definition of the issues at stake in the appraisal of policy, which is the topic we discuss in the remainder of this chapter.

ALTERNATIVE APPROACHES TO STABILISATION

As the discussion so far has stressed, we consider it to be essential to appraise stabilisation policies not merely in relation to their immediate targets – which provide the typical 'performance criteria' of international agencies[15] – but also in relation to more long-run aspects. We suggest three 'levels' of consequences. The first is the reduction of the disequilibria which both precipitate the policies and form their immediate goal: namely, the deficit in the balance of payments and rising internal prices. The second is the establishment or reinforcement of a particular system of accumulation and distribution. The third is the consolidation of the social and political bases of the resulting economic system, so that it can operate effectively over a long period. We here consider the various types of stabilisation policy typically practised in Latin America, and exemplified in our case studies, in relation to these three levels.

The orthodox approach

The best-known and most widely used approach is that of 'orthodox' or 'monetarist' stabilisation policy. The term is a convenient shorthand for the policy approach common to most conservative regimes in Latin America, and strongly backed, if not imposed, by the IMF. This brand of monetarism is typically more extreme than its more sophisticated cousin, the modern monetarism of the developed academic world,[16] has a strong ideological content[17] and a rather clear package of policy prescriptions aimed at correcting the short-term disequilibria. Its underlying philosophy leads it to advocate reductions in state expenditure (rather than increased taxation), while implicit in its policy prescriptions is a belief in the power of the price system, once this

has been restored to health. Thus, implicitly, relative price adjustments aimed at recreating a dynamic economic system will be
modest and effective. It borrows the work of 'modern' monetarism
on the role of expectations to explain why the period of 'shakeout'
may be characterised by temporary unemployment and continued price rises.[18]

Its views on the second level of consequences are already
implied in this description: the way to lay the foundation for
sustained economic growth is to restore the system to financial
sanity and to 'correct' relative prices; investment will then flour-
ish, sustained by inflows of long-term funds from abroad.[19] (Pure
monetarist theory – which refers to a full employment world
without distortions – sees growth as determined independently of
monetary factors, by forces such as productivity and thrift. The
monetarist practitioner has first to return the economy to that
world.) The third level typically receives no attention – though
the need to consider it is conceded by Emil Spitzer, in the official
history of the IMF.[20] The inability of the orthodox analysis to
confront these long-term issues is, perhaps, the basic defect of the
approach.

It is not surprising, then, given the nature of orthodox views on
the longer-term aspects of stabilisation, that short-term measures
predominate in the typical 'package'. Both internal and external
disequilibria can be restored by a combination of cuts in demand
and shifts in relative prices, the latter occurring at least in part by
the liberalisation of the economy which henceforth will allow the
price mechanism to function more efficiently. Thus, credit must
be restricted, government spending cut, and tax revenue raised,
so that the increase in the money supply can be kept within the
limits considered to be non-inflationary, given the (autonomous)
growth in real output. The cuts in expenditure are supposed to fall
on current spending, not on investment, so that growth is
safeguarded (nearly always an impossible recommendation).
Price controls are to be lifted as far as possible and subsidies
ended, both to restore incentives and because of the implications
for the government budget. A crucial relative price adjustment is
usually the exchange rate. Wage and salary restraint is stressed,
in a developed economy because of its importance in achieving the
shift in relative profitability of exports and imports. In semi-
industrial economies this effect is likely to be less pronounced, but
earnings restraint still features importantly in the programme, in

part because a monetarist still tends to believe in the efficacy of relative price adjustments, in part because it may be the only practicable way of reducing government expenditure, and in part as a tool for slowing down the inflationary spiral. In practice, its greatest significance will probably be distributional; in a monopolistic environment it may allow business to restore profitability in the face of cuts in demand.[21]

Identifying the severity of a given set of stabilisation measures is complicated by the fact that, as several of the case studies make clear, the measures often produce apparently perverse results: thus, for example, large cuts may be achieved in real public expenditure but the effect of depressed output and lower imports on tax revenues and the effect of lifting price controls on the price level may be such that the government deficit still rises. This can only be handled in qualitative terms; for our purposes here we follow the IMF practice of defining a successful *ex-post* imposition of stabilisation measures in terms of whether there is a (sufficient) fall in the government deficit as a percentage of GDP and a significant reduction in the ratio of the internally generated money supply to GDP. (Since a balance-of-payments deficit financed by an outflow of foreign exchange results in a corresponding reduction in domestic financial assets and liabilities, the overall ratio of money supply to GDP may fall without any deliberate measures of credit restriction on the part of the government). For 'successful stabilisation' to occur, in terms of our first-level goals, these measures must eventually result in some significant reduction of the rate of inflation, although our case studies show that in some cases the time lags may be painfully long.

The non-orthodox approach

As is by now well-known, the 1960s saw the evolution within Latin America of a tradition of criticism of the monetarism-in-practice which we have described here, known as the 'structuralist' school. Its adherents differ in their diagnosis of the causes of inflation, and stress that policy measures are applied not in the ahistorical apolitical world assumed by the monetarists, who are in fact theorists of liberal capitalism, but in a very destructive and unsatisfactory institutional and political context, which affects the long-term *meaning* and viability of orthodox stabilisation measures. To summarise the position of the Latin American critics of monetarism crudely, the local variant of capitalism is seen as heavily monopolistic, largely directed or controlled from abroad, directly benefiting and influencing only a limited and privileged sector within the society, and therefore lacking in legitimacy for the population as a whole. This perspective led to a rejection of the basic orthodox assumptions on the role of the price system and the free enterprise system. On the specific question of inflation, the lack of response to price signals was regarded as the primary cause of inflation, monetary factors playing only a permissive role.

Unfortunately, while making it very clear that the system operates according to principles which are not precisely those postulated by theories of liberal capitalism, these writers failed to provide an alternative theory that combined greater realism with the necessary degree of internal rigour. Their writing lacked clarity at all three levels of consequences. The most conspicuous gap was at the level of short-term policy-making. It was commonly found that at the moment of crisis the structuralists lacked a coherent and practicable alternative package to monetarist measures. This helped the monetarists to carry the day, not just cutting demand (the unavoidable step which structuralists were generally reluctant to take), but doing so without regard for the relative priority of the various expenditures to be affected. There was also a lack of clarity in the structuralist view of long run consequences: were structural reforms to produce a more legitimate and better-functioning dependent capitalism, or was the implication really a totally distinct system?

In the world of academic debate, these problems had by the late 1960s led structuralists themselves to redefine their preoccupations, as they became increasingly disillusioned with a theory that pointed to individual structural bottle-necks as the source of the problem, yet could provide no coherent vision of why the bottlenecks existed nor why the structural reforms which were the logical policy response were so impossible to carry out. But the resulting 'dependency school' proved no better at defining either short-term or long-term alternatives – despite some useful insights as to the nature of the limitations on internal policy-making resulting from the manner of integration into the international system – limitations resulting both from the way that integration closed options and from its deeper effects on class structure and ultimately the choice among options.

The barrenness of this approach for policy-makers confronted by the urgent imperative of economic management in conditions of severe disequilibrium is undoubtedly part of the reason for the increasing dominance of monetarist views. A further influence has been the nature of the new inflationary spurts of the early 1970s. As we shall see, while international events played a large role, in a number of cases the inflations were quite clearly the result of expansionary government policies often justified by reference to the urgency of structural reform. This thrust into the centre of the stage the particular structuralist argument where the distinction between monetarist and structuralist is least satisfactory: the idea that government spending is itself a reaction to 'rigidity' in public spending. This strengthened the case for policies which emphasised demand restraint.

Nevertheless, the influence of structuralism remains strong among Latin American bureaucrats – though more in Planning Institutes (which are on the decline) than in Central Banks (which are gaining in influence). The essence of their position lies in the necessity to increase public expenditure – or at least resist cuts – while controls, above all import controls, are used to handle the crisis.

What compounds the weakness of the non-orthodox position is the fact that while the orthodox view is solidly backed by banking interests – 'finance capital' – the presumed ally of the structuralist bureaucrat is the domestic industrialist, who typically is far more equivocal about where his real interests lie (protection and import controls are clearly in his favour, but 'tampering with the market' is instinctively to be feared). Domestic industrial groups have also hardly been strenghtened as a class by the spreading denationalisation of industrial sectors. But in a number of Latin American countries, the strategic state enterprises remain a powerful reduct where the structuralist position may still be defended.

It is no surprise, given the above considerations, that when we turn to consider the content of 'non-orthodox' stabilisation policy the picture is less coherent than for orthodoxy. 'Non-orthodox' approaches to stabilisation policy refer to an attempt to cure the disequilibria by methods which the theorists of 'orthodoxy' would claim aggravate the underlying distortions in the economy. These are usually price controls and import controls, but possibly include wider foreign exchange controls. Monetary and fiscal restraints will often also be used at the same time but in a less drastic fashion than in orthodox policy. A further 'non-orthodox' reaction, but hardly 'stabilisation', may be to focus on living with the inflation by indexation and such techniques (indexation may logically form part of orthodox policy too – although it typically does not). The 'non-orthodox' element is the use of indexation to soften the impact of what under orthodox policies would be sudden and brutal shifts in the allocation of resources, and to lengthen the period of time over which necessary adjustments can be phased. Clearly we have a range of phenomena here – from policies that are *almost* orthodox, but allow a little more time to ease the processes of adjustment and reduce the associated political tensions although the same final outcome is intended as under orthodox policies, to policies that only *pretend* to be attempts to stabilise, while essentially rejecting the underlying objectives of orthodox policies, perhaps in the belief that the basic orthodox analysis is too mechanistic or too overcharged with unacceptable political conditions, perhaps in the hope that if adjustment is postponed 'something will turn up'. There are some examples of relatively successful non-orthodox stabilisation (e.g. Brazil), but these have tended to be where the policy does not diverge too fundamentally from orthodox views of a realistic time scale and of the inevitability of adjustment. The more extravagant forms of unorthodoxy (Argentina before 1976?) have tended merely to postpone the evil day, without in the least mitigating the severity of its eventual impact.

CONCLUSION

We would like to conclude by suggesting a number of issues in the light of which the case studies that follow may be read. We have emphasised the frequent incoherence of the non-orthodox approaches. But we must stress that the very coherence of orthodoxy may be a danger, since there are fundamental problems associated with this type of approach. In the first place, even at the level of short-term handling of disequilibria, it *may* be both costly and inefficient: this depends on the economic and political structure of the country in question. (The Peruvian case study illustrates this.) But more important still are its rather weak position on long-run growth, and its total neglect of the third issue we mentioned at the start: the consolidation of the social and political bases of the system. Orthodox stabilisation policies are not purely a question of technical economic management, or even purely a question of the distribution of material output. As our case studies show, in Latin America they tend to involve the forceful imposition of an entire political and social system, one which was certainly neither spontaneously chosen nor gradually evolved by the people of the country themselves. On the contrary, recent experiences have been of orthodox stabilisation policies being imposed by increasingly severe repression against a workforce whose collective forms of self-expression are seen as the principal obstacle to 'sound' economic policies. Further, such policies often also tend to have far-reaching social and political consequences, aggravating the social tensions and deepening the political contradictions which have been at the root of previous upsurges of inflation (Argentina is here a key example). However, orthodox economists have prepared a division of labour with regard to the tasks of stabilisation, under which they can disclaim responsibility for the long-term social and political phenomena associated with their 'technical' prescriptions. This outlook enables them to operate within implicit or unstated assumptions about the character of Latin American societies, assumptions which their critics would regard as highly schematic and ideological. So long as these economists are operating within the context of a strong dictatorial regime, which is insulated from the response and reactions of the society at large which they are attempting to remould, their disregard for what they may see as the 'side-effects' of technically necessary policies may not hamper their effectiveness. While the stabilisation crisis remains acute, all they may need is the support and understanding of foreign creditors and the disciplined collaboration of the state apparatus. In the longer run, however, they will need to secure a wider base of public understanding and support if they are to establish the permanency of their chosen economic strategy. The narrowness of their range of vision could prove a serious obstacle to their long-run effectiveness.

In principle, practitioners of the type of economic orthodoxy prevalent in most of the case studies under review may envisage two alternative ways of making their achievements permanent. Either they may envisage the continuation of a system of political repression, capable of insulating economic policy-makers indefinitely from the demands and distractions coming from all those social groups and interests whose influence, security and welfare seems undermined by orthodox policies; or they may envisage that once the painful task of stabilisation is completed their views will command such general acceptance and approval that, in gratitude for their success in remedying the 'errors' of past policy-makers, they will be voluntarily accorded a position of lasting influence as guardians of 'sound management' in the post-stabilisation period. Their critics claim that neither of these alternatives is likely to prove viable. According to these critics, neither the international nor the internal bases exist for the indefinite persistence of repressive regimes single-mindedly committed to economic orthodoxy. Even elements of the military and the business community, not to mention the middle class, are liable to tire eventually of stifling the justifiable expression of economic grievances by the many groups who suffer from impersonal market orthodoxy, especially once a degree of economic normalcy has been restored. If this proves true, then the only way further resurgences of inflation can be averted in the future is if, after the worst of the repression has passed, the orthodox economic policy-makers can legitimise their doctrines in the eyes of the population as a whole. Frequently in the past, however, this hope has proved unfounded. According to the critics of orthodoxy such hopes will prove even more groundless in the future, for the long-term effects of the recent wave of orthodox stabilisation policies will have been to sharpen underlying social conflicts, and to render popularly negotiable variants of the existing economic system less viable than ever. It is for the reader to judge between these alternative perspectives, in the light of the case studies that follow. We offer our own assessment in the final chapter.

NOTES

1   In September 1947 'The managing director [of the IMF] had told the Governor for Chile . . . that it would be better to request a smaller amount, and also to support the request with "a clearer indication that appropriate fiscal and monetary measures were in prospect." At a further meeting . . . there was some discussion about the propriety of the suggestions thus made to Chile. One comment was that there were no provisions in the Fund agreement permitting the Fund to attach conditions to the use of its resources. As against this, it was pointed out that . . . Chile had been suffering a serious and prolonged inflation, and, unless effective measures were taken, the temporariness of the disequilibrium for which Chile was

asking assistance must be doubtful. The latter opinion prevailed' (Horsefield, 1969, p. 19). However, owing to unclarity about the nature of the conditions the IMF was entitled to demand, Brazil withdrew her first request for $15 million in 1949. It was not until 1952 that the principles governing IMF 'standby' arrangements were clearly defined.

2 'The less industrial members' were, around 1960, 'the principal targets of Fund appeals for monetary discipline ... [and] since most of them maintained Article XIV restrictions on the convertibility of their currencies they were obliged to have annual consultations with the Fund aimed at the reduction and elimination of these restrictions. The conditions attached to standby credits arranged for them were often tougher than for richer countries. The multiple exchange rates, which were the administrative device which many of them preferred for national economic protectionist purposes, were more hardly frowned upon than the no less protectionist tariffs and other barriers devised by the industrial countries. And only a small minority of them had so far been able to get much help from the Fund. One reason for this lay in the ... voting arrangements in [the Fund's] most important body, the Executive Board ... In 1960 the twenty Latin American countries elected three directors between them but held only 10.2% of the total quota votes' (Strange, 1976, pp. 32– 3).

3 Fred L. Block (1977) argues that 'the struggle of the United States to increase its freedom of action in international monetary affairs destroyed the Bretton Woods system. Step by step the United States either broke the rules of the old system or forced other countries to break them' (p. 203).

4 One example of how such pressures could work to the disadvantage of Latin America was the campaign to oblige developing countries to hold the great bulk of their reserves in dollars: 'By the mid-1960s the US Treasury had set up a division for developing countries with the special task of leaning on potential transgressors, making it clear that Congress could be expected to take a poor view of gold conversions when making its aid appropriations' (Hirsch and Oppenheimer, 1976, vol. V (2), p. 630).

5 By 1973–4, of the four heaviest borrowers from the euro-currency market among less developed countries, three feature in our group: Mexico, Brazil, Peru.

6 Goreux (1977) p. 20.

7 Diaz Alejandro differentiates here between those countries that borrowed to complement inflows of other types of foreign capital, such as Brazil, and countries that used euro-dollars as a substitute both for internal and other forms of external savings – such as Peru (Diaz Alejandro, 1976).

8 According to Holsen and Waelbrock (1976) p. 175, non-oil LDCs borrowing for balance of payments purposes of $20 billion in 1974 sustained developed country aggregate demand by 1% of GDP or $30 billion. Despite the build-up of Third World debt since 1973 and the doubtful prospects for future growth of many of their exports, the signs are that once again in 1978 the industrial countries are relying quite heavily on rising Third World demand for imports to sustain the growth of world trade.

9 *IMF Survey*, 17 April 1978, and *Finance and Development*, March 1978. Note that these figures are heavily influenced by the contributions of Brazil and Venezuela; our case studies confirm that the experience was not uniform.

10 We have selected for our case studies only countries severely affected by these events. But, as Table 1.1 shows, even here the experience was not uniform: Uruguay experienced the sharpest reversal, while Brazil and Mexico suffered least severely, Mexico with rising oil exports and Brazil because of the belated rise in the coffee price (which however was largely due to frosts in Brazil, so did not have as startling an effect on export revenues as it did on Colombia; the latter's recent strong position was the reason for her exclusion from our study).

11 'Openness' refers to the degree of reliance on international demand to stimulate growth. It therefore implies policies favouring competitiveness in international markets. See Kuczynski (1976) for a discussion of forces favouring 'openness' or 'closedness'.

12 *IMF Survey*, 22 May 1978, p. 145.

13 Interviewed about the powers conferred under the amended article, Fund officials replied: 'The Fund has a variety of what are commonly called "sanctions", but it really does not use them in its normal behaviour, because this is not conducive to good relations or good behaviour. It has one very important procedural device. That is to adopt decisions commenting on policies and conduct . . . it is called the 'mobilization of shame' (*IMF Survey*, 3 April 1978, p. 101). However, the amount of shame that can be mobilised by comments that are not made public remains to be seen.

14 *IMF Survey*, 22 May 1978, pp. 147, 149–50.

15 The Fund itself conducted a study of seventy-nine representative stabilisation programmes which activated standby arrangements in the higher credit tranches between 1963 and 1972. To study the 'success' of these programmes the Fund analysts examined quarterly data on the expansion of overall domestic credit and/or credit to the public sector for the two years prior to, and succeeding, their introduction. Overall the Fund analysts concluded that their programmes had achieved a 75·9 per cent success rate and that in only twelve out of the seventy-nine cases were the failures attributable mainly to internal causes (Reichman and Stillson, 1977, pp. 22–4).

16 Which has recently – in its softer form – become almost indistinguishable from Keynesianism. The 'new' quantity theory is seen as referring to one market only, while the price level is determined simultaneously in many markets. Monetarism as practised in Latin America often appears to adhere more to the old-fashioned form of the quantity theory.

17 How far this particular ideology is *not* inherent in monetarism, is convincingly demonstrated in a recent article by Cobham (1978), which shows how a monetarist diagnosis of the causes of inflation may be combined with a Marxist view of society.

18 See, for example, Friedman's classic article on the role of monetary policy (Friedman, 1968) where he explains Brazilian unemployment in these terms.

19 Spitzer (see next note) stresses the role of foreign capital.

20 'A prolonged inflation derives, to a large extent, from a failure to resolve by other means the conflicting claims of different social groups . . . The success of a stabilisation program in this situation depends largely on the broad acceptance of its objectives . . . by the main social, political and economic

forces in the country' (Spitzer, 1969, p. 474).

21   The many roles of wage cuts – which also further depress the market – make it clear why business reactions to the programmes are often far from unambiguous.

REFERENCES

Block, Fred L. (1977), *The Origins of International Monetary Disorder: A Study of US International Monetary Policy from World War II to the Present*, California University Press.

Cobham, D. (1978), 'The Politics of the Economics of Inflation', *Lloyds Bank Review*, no. 128, London.

Diaz Alejandro, C. (1976), 'The Post 1971 International Financial System and the Less Developed Countries', in G. K. Helleiner (ed.), *A World Divided*, Cambridge University Press.

Friedman, M. (1968), 'The Role of Monetary Policy', *American Economic Review*, March 1968.

Goreux, L. M. (1977), 'The Use of Compensatory Financing', *Finance and Development*, September 1977.

Hirsch, F., and Oppenheimer, P. (1976), 'The Trial of Managed Money: Currency, Credit and Prices, 1920–70', in C. M. Cipolla (ed.), *The Fontana Economic History of Europe*, London.

Holsen, J., and Waelbroeck, J. (1976), 'The Less Developed Countries and the International Monetary Mechanism', *American Economic Review*, vol. 66, no. 2.

Horsefield, J. Keith (1969), *'The International Monetary Fund, 1945–65*, vol. I, IMF, Washington.

Kuczynski, M. (1976), 'Semi-developed Countries and the International Business Cycle', *BOLSA Review*, January 1976, London.

Reichman, T., and Stillson, R. (1977), 'How Successful are Programmes Supported by Stand-by Arrangements?', *Finance and Development*, March 1977.

Spitzer, E. (1969), Chapter 20 of *The International Monetary Fund, 1945–65*, vol. II, by Margaret de Vries, *et al.*, IMF, Washington.

Strange, Susan (1976), *International Economic Relations of the Western World, 1959–71*, ed. A. Shonfield, *Vol. 2: International Monetary Relations*, Royal Institute of International Affairs, London.

United Nations, *Yearbook of International Trade*, New York.

2 Stabilisation Policy in Mexico: The Fiscal Deficit and Macroeconomic Equilibrium 1960–77

E. V. K. FITZGERALD*

Stabilisation policy has possibly played a greater part in Mexican economic strategy than anywhere else in Latin America over the last twenty years. Between 1955 and 1970 Mexico was held up to the world as a case of Rostovian 'takeoff' in which the skilled application of stabilisation policy had preserved macroeconomic equilibrium in a period of rapid industrialisation, thereby strengthening the growth process itself; the severe macroeconomic disequilibrium after 1970 which culminated in the massive devaluation of August 1976 (the first for nearly a quarter of a century) has been attributed both to the abandonment of monetary conservatism and to the neglect of structural reform during the previous decade.[1] This debate has a crucial importance in Mexico not only because of the need to understand the immediate past, but also because despite incipient oil wealth the strategic choice for the future still lies between a continuation of 'desarrollo compartido' and a return to 'desarrollo estabilizador'.[2]

Without wishing to duplicate the Introduction to this volume, three general points on stabilisation policy do seem to be in order. The first is that the tendency of 'structuralist' economists[3] to minimise the importance and even the relevance of monetary and financial policies, on the ground that these are 'demand oriented' while the real problem of underdevelopment is one of supply, seems somewhat misplaced. It is almost a truism that the structure of production and exchange determines the long-run de-

23

velopment of the economy, but the very external and internal dualism of the peripheral capitalist economies mean that demand disequilibria are equally crucial, although the composition of that demand (as Kalecki pointed out) may well be more important than its size. Successful stabilisation policy[4] not only involves the balancing of internal and external supply and demand through the adjustment of prices and money supply, but also the balancing of the traded and non-traded sectors within the economy. In this context, the debate between 'structuralist' and 'monetarist' approaches to the problem – to the extent that it is not really a political disagreement about the freedom of capital – can be seen as an argument about the speed of adjustment and the relative efficacy of various instruments rather than a crude distinction between the primacy of 'supply' or 'demand'.

Second, stabilisation policy elsewhere in Latin America has usually been a drastic experience, often implemented by new and reactionary regimes after periods of inflationary growth and involving substantial unemployment, real wage cuts, encouragement to foreign investors and reductions in public investment programmes as well as the familiar devaluation and credit restraint. These factors are not absent in the Mexican case, but being 'spread out' over the years they have been less unsettling – and in the 1976–7 crisis they have almost been conspicuous by their absence. This makes analysis simpler to the extent that economic and political phenomena can be distinguished from one another – in marked contrast to Argentina and Chile, for example – but more difficult to the extent that in the absence of sudden adjustment the repercussions are harder to identify. Third, it is logically impossible to operate an independent monetary, and by implication budgetary, policy if freedom of capital movement, a fixed exchange rate and inflexible tax structure all obtain at the same time. Indeed, it is not really feasible to do so if any two of these three constraints obtain. This is a classical point in macroeconomic policy analysis that is well recognised in the British tradition, for example, but is sometimes overlooked in the context of developing countries – possibly because most do not have the sophisticated money markets enjoyed by Mexico.

In this chapter we shall proceed in the following manner. First, we shall briefly outline the post-war economic development of Mexico, not just to provide a background to our analysis, but rather because we shall be arguing that it was underlying 'structural' factors in production, trade and fiscal patterns that made monetary stability possible in the 1960s but virtually impossible in the 1970s. Second, we shall look at the period of *desarrollo estabilizador* from the viewpoint of monetary analysis, suggesting that it worked in a way somewhat different from the 'received orthodox' model – a suggestion that has considerable implications for interpretations of policy in the 1970s. Third, we shall explore the 1970–5 period in some detail, arguing that the massive expansion of public sector economic activity (and consequent budget deficits in the absence of tax reform) was not the main cause of inflation or even the balance-of-payments crisis, although it certainly contributed to the macroeconomic disequilibrium. Finally, we shall put forward a tentative critique of the August 1976 float of the peso and the other elements of the 1976–7 stabilisation policy.

THE MEXICAN ECONOMY

This is clearly not an appropriate place to go into the post-war development of Mexico in any depth: the causes and consequences of the rapid growth of the Mexican economy are amply covered elsewhere.[5] None the less, it is necessary to summarise, however briefly, the main elements of the economic structure upon which a stabilisation policy is to operate.

As Table 2.1 indicates, both aggregate output and *per capita* incomes rose at an accelerating rate right up to the mid-1960s, after which the rate began to decline: this growth was accompanied by rapid industrialisation, based on the familiar import-substitution model with the usual attendant problems of foreign exchange intensity, transnational ownership, limited employment creation and regional concentration. All observers agree, moreover, that it had been the outstandingly good performance of agriculture – as the provider of foreign exchange and urban food supplies on the one hand and the sustainer of rural incomes and preventer of internal migration on the other – that underpinned the rest of the economy, a performance that was derived more from the vast state investment in irrigation and transport facilities of the 1940s and 1950s than from the land reform. But agrarian expansion decelerated in the mid-1960s to fall below the rate of population growth, mainly as the result of declining rural public

TABLE 2.1 Structure of aggregate output, expenditure and accumulation in Mexico, 1939–76

	1939–46	1947–56	1957–66	1967–71	1972–6
Annual average growth rates of:					
Gross Domestic Product	5·5	6·0	6·7	6·2	5·4
GDP *per capita*	2·8	2·9	3·3	2·7	1·9
Agricultural output	3·2	7·8	4·8	1·3	–1·3
Manufacturing output	7·1	7·2	8·5	7·4	5·8
Price level	12·7	7·6	4·3	3·6	15·9
Percentage composition of GDP					
Fixed capital formation	7·6	14·6	16·9	19·2	21·0
Stockbuilding	1·5	1·3	2·7	2·0	1·7
Government consumption	6·0	4·5	6·9	7·7	10·2
Private consumption	85·4	80·3	75·3	73·3	70·4
Exports *less* imports	–0·5	–0·7	–1·8	–2·2	–3·3
Percentage of GDP					
GFCF: Public	4·0	5·4	6·1	7·4	9·0
Private	3·6	9·2	10·8	11·8	12·0
Total	7·6	14·6	16·9	19·2	21·0
Saving: Public	3·0	4·3	3·8	4·6	1·9
Private	4·2	9·6	11·3	12·4	15·8
External	0·5	0·7	1·8	2·2	3·3
Total	7·6	14·6	16·9	19·2	21·0

	1940	1960	1965	1970	1975
Exports of goods and services/GDP	16·0	13·9	11·4	8·8	7·9
Imports of goods and services/GDP	10·2	13·6	13·9	11·6	12·5
Imports: Volume index	—	100	133	186	288
Unit value index	—	100	103	120	197
Exports: Volume index	—	100	137	163	180
Unit value index	—	100	110	135	271
Terms of trade	—	100	107	112	132

Source: Banco de México (1977); Reynolds (1970), Table 3.

investment a decade earlier. Meanwhile the industrialisation process was suffering the stagnation endemic to the later stages of import-substitution and mineral production was flagging seriously. In all three sectors of 'means of production' (agriculture, minerals and heavy industry) it appeared that massive capitalisation was clearly overdue; as the private sector was unwilling to undertake, or incapable of undertaking, this (preferring the high profits of light manufacturing, real estate and tourism) an expansion of state investment became inevitable.

The basic sectors of the Mexican economy having entered a period of deceleration in the mid-1960s, the effects were reflected in severe external disequilibrium in the 1970s. The balance of payments (see Table 2.2) reflects this clearly, with exports (mainly farm and mine products) declining as a proportion of GDP while imports (mainly industrial inputs) remained a more stable proportion. In consequence, the current account moved steadily into deficit, while on capital account the inflow of private investment – always a slender one[6] – was steadily replaced by official borrowing and short-term foreign bank credits to private firms, particularly to the subsidiaries of multinational corporations. Thus the growing external disequilibrium was closely connected to changes in the structure of the economy during the 1960s; in the 1970s export volume grew comparatively slowly, and only improving world export prices prevented the visible balance from deteriorating more rapidly than it did under the pressure of wheat and oil imports at inflated world prices and massive purchases of capital goods abroad. The Mexican economy is very 'open' indeed on both current and capital accounts, so to speak. Economic activity is clearly linked to the US business cycle, principally through fluctuations in demand for Mexican exports, but also through price levels reflected in import prices and competitive manufacturing prices on the Mexican traded goods sector.[7] The slowdown in the US economy at the end of the 1960s and rapid inflation thereafter were transmitted to Mexico, therefore. Further, the maintenance of complete convertibility of the peso and the large scale of short-term flows of foreign funds across the exchanges means that there is little control over the capital account and that this can be as seriously affected by speculative confidence as by real economic conditions.

The internal macroeconomic balance (see Table 2.1) was maintained in the face of a steadily rising rate of aggregate

TABLE 2.2   Balance of payments and external official debt of Mexico, 1950–76 (US$m)

	1950	1960	1965	1970	1975
Balance of goods	−76	−428	−431	−643	−1237
Balance of services	+108	+88	+51	−433	−178
Current account balance	+32	−340	−380	−1076	−1415
Long-term capital	+102	+120	+163	+626	+1820
'Basic balance'	+134	−220	−217	−450	+405
Short-term capital	+55	+63	−15	+55	−308
Errors and omissions	+19	+132	+191	+425	+46
'Monetary balance'	+74	+195	+176	+480	−262
Changes in reserves, etc.	+208	−23	−58	+30	+46

	1960	1967	1970	1973	1976
Total disbursed debt	816	2514	3227	5416	15923
Disbursements	351	667	781	2115	5851
Amortisation	188	397	475	794	1526
Net capital inflow	164	271	307	1321	4325
Interest payments	—	112	217	357	1024
Debt service/Exports	—	24%	25%	27%	37%

Source: IMF, *International Financial Statistics*, Washington, various years; Banco de México (1960); Programación (1977).

investment by the steady decline in the proportion of GDP devoted to consumption throughout the period 1939–76 and, given the expansion of government consumption as well as public investment in both the 1960s and 1970s, the share of private consumption fell dramatically. It is fairly clear that the high profit rates established during the 1950s[8] were maintained thereafter, and in consequence it was wage restraint which 'made room' for savings and investment out of profits. This was politically tolerable during a period of rapid growth in total national income, but when the economy slowed down even the historic co-optive power of the Partido Revolucionario Institucional (PRI) seemed insufficient to cope with labour pressure, and renewed expenditure on welfare became necessary in order to hold the social fabric together, a fabric that was also coming under increasing strain from the stubborn refusal of birth rates to follow death rates downwards and the migration of the rural unemployed towards the cities to join the ranks of the reserve army of the urban underemployed.

The public sector[9] had played a central role in the Mexican economy since the time of Calles and Cárdenas, although by the 1960s its expenditure was not as large in relation to national income as the other advanced Latin American economies such as Argentina and Brazil.[10] This was partly due to less 'legitimising' expenditure on security and grandiose monuments, but also because welfare benefits were only extended to a minority of the workforce – organised urban labour. As Table 2.3 indicates, a considerable expansion in current government outlays and fixed investment as a proportion of GDP took place in the 1960s, and in the absence of an increase in tax pressure the budgetary deficit expanded; in the 1970s – particularly between 1973 and 1976 – this trend continued as current income rose less rapidly than total expenditure in both the government and para-statal sectors. The increase in central government current expenditure, however, was mostly made up of transfers to, and payment of interest on debt incurred on behalf of, the rest of the public sector; the expansion of the state through the 1960s and 1970s was concentrated upon the public enterprises and decentralised agencies. By the mid-1960s, moreover, the share of state investment allocated to agriculture had fallen to 9 per cent (as opposed to 18 per cent in 1940–9), while that allocated to industry had risen from 14 to 39 per cent – so that the expansion in the subsequent decade took place not only in heavy industry (e.g. steel), but also in agriculture and, eventually, oil exploration and processing. None of these would result in increased returns to the treasury or the economy in any but the medium term. Overall, the current and capital expenditure of the Sector Público Federal rose from 15 per cent of GDP in 1960 to 22 per cent in 1968 and 29 per cent in 1976, without a parallel increase in income.

As Table 2.3 indicates, tax pressure (tax makes up nine-tenths of current federal government income) hardly increased at all during the two decades leading up to 1970; within this total, the almost exact balance between direct and indirect tax had hardly changed at all, either. In response to expanded public expenditure plans and a desire to increase the progressivity of taxation on the one hand, and the erosion of the tax base by corporate tax exemptions (such as those in the *Ley de Industrias Nuevas y Necesarias* of 1955) and declining import duty yields as import-substitution took hold on the other, the Lopez Mateos administration (1958–64) tried to implement a substantive tax reform. It was intended to raise federal tax pressure from 8 per cent of GDP in 1960 to 12 per cent in 1965 and 16 per cent in 1970; this was to be based on the direct taxation of property income, particularly through the aggregation of personal incomes from different sources in a single tax base to which the higher reaches of the existing schedules would then apply and the abolition of 'anonymous' forms of wealth-holding such as bearer bonds. However, by 1962 business interests had managed to block the reform and in fact under the subsequent Díaz Ordáz regime (1964–70) the direct tax burden was shifted towards earned salaries, and the targets of the Lopez Mateos reform were far from fulfilled – federal tax pressure had only risen to 9 per cent in 1970. Both the revenue and equity arguments for tax reform were greatly strengthened under the Echeverría administration; in 1972 the plans for effective property tax were resurrected more or less in their original form, based on the aggregation of incomes and the abolition of the *anonimato*. But the bill never reached Congress, having been dropped by the President under pressure not only from business groups, but also from the central bank itself on the grounds that it would lead to capital flight. In the event, tax pressure was increased to some extent, but mainly by stricter enforcement of income tax and the effect of inflation on nominal scales on the one hand, and by increases in purchase tax

TABLE 2.3 Consolidated public sector account of Mexico, 1940–76 (percentage of GDP)

	1940–9	1950–9	1960–4	1965–8	1969–72	1973–6
Federal government:						
Current income	6·5	7·7	7·2	7·8	8·2	9·8
Current expenditure	4·6	4·5	5·8	6·5	6·5	8·9
Surplus	1·9	3·2	1·4	1·3	1·6	0·9
Other public sector surplus	2·4	0·9	1·6	3·2	2·6	0·3
Total public sector surplus	3·3	4·1	3·0	4·5	4·2	1·2
Fixed investment:						
Federal government	1·7	2·1	1·7	2·3	2·2	3·2
Other public sector	2·7	3·3	4·8	5·2	5·1	6·0
Total GFCF	4·4	5·4	6·5	7·5	7·3	9·2
Public sector financing requirement:						
Internal	0·8	0·5	1·9	2·3	2·5	5·4
External	0·3	0·8	1·6	0·7	0·6	2·6
Total PSBR	1·1	1·3	3·5	3·0	3·1	8·0

Source: Methodology given in FitzGerald (1978b) – calculated on the basis of Banco de México (1970, 1976), Programación (1977), Bueno (1977).

rates on the other. The result, as in 1964, was to provide insufficient fiscal income and leave the equity issue unresolved.

The other internal source of funds, savings by the rest of the public sector, fluctuated widely, as Table 2.3 shows. These were steadily undermined after the mid-1960s by two factors. First, the prices charged by public enterprises – particularly power, steel, petroleum and transportation – were held down in order to sustain private profitability and curb inflation, while social security premia were constrained for similar reasons – and in any case, the system only covered 11 per cent of the population in 1960, a figure which had risen to only 24 per cent in 1970 and 33 per cent in 1975. Second, the parastatal sector expanded to take in such activities as price support, cheap finance, education, research and bankrupt firms (e.g. sugar mills) for 'social' reasons, all of which have involved a massive drain on the current account of the public sector without any likelihood of an economic return to the state. Thus, in spite of the subsidies from the central government (which rose from 1·3 per cent of GDP in 1950–9 to 2·3 per cent in 1960–8 and 3·4 per cent in 1973–6) the parastatal sector was increasingly incapable of financing its own investment.

The result was that the state generated a steadily falling proportion of domestic saving; while its share of aggregate investment was declining into the 1970s this was not too serious, but as it began to rise again the budget deficit (see Table 2.3) rose dramatically, too. Although this public sector borrowing requirement was potentially a serious problem in the 1960–72 period (at 3 per cent of GDP it was over double the level of the previous two decades) it had risen alarmingly to 8 per cent of GDP by 1973–6. The effect of this expansion, distributed between internal and external borrowing, is a central theme of the next two sections of this paper.

DESARROLLO ESTABILIZADOR

In order to examine Mexican stabilisation policy in the 1970s we must first go back over the previous decade, because the disequilibrium of the 1970s can only be understood in the context of the financial system built up in the 1950s and 1960s and the prolongation of these 'rules of the game' from one period to the other. The general characteristics of the financial structure and monetary policy that emerged in Mexico after the mid-1950s have been extremely well documented;[11] here we shall confine ourselves to the elements that have particular bearing upon events since 1970.

As we have noted, both national income and capital formation were rising very rapidly indeed during the 1960s, the latter requiring and the former providing for a very high level of savings without excessive recourse to foreign capital markets. As Table 2.1 indicated, most of this saving was in the private sector, mainly in the form of retained company profits,[12] a substantial part of which was channelled through the banking system (see Table 2.4). Between 4 and 5 per cent of GDP each year was acquired in new domestic liabilities (i.e. loanable funds) by the Mexican banking system in the 1960s and as a result the total of financial liabilities rose from 28 per cent of GDP in 1955 to 40 per cent in 1970. This growth of the financial system, which was stimulated by the role of the major banking houses acting as the 'nexus' for networks of firms in different productive sectors on the one hand[13] and the supply of negotiable instruments at substantial real rates of interest on the other,[14] permitted the public sector to finance its deficit without destabilising consequences. This was achieved mainly by imposing quite high marginal reserve requirements on the banking system, which shifted about one-quarter of new bank funds into the Banco de México during this period – most of which was transferred to the Treasury. In other words, the high rate of real growth in the economy and the increase in financial intermediation meant that the transactions demand for money was rising extremely rapidly.

This extraordinary expansion of the capital market[15] has been attributed to the 'stabilising' monetary policy pursued by the Banco de México and the Secretaría de Hacienda during the period and is particularly associated with the reign of Ortiz Mena in the latter portfolio. This claim is important to the critique of monetary policy after 1970, and is worth examining in some depth. It was argued[16]: that tight control over the money supply had kept down the rate of inflation and promoted high rates of saving; that reserve requirements had obviated the need for higher taxes on profits (which would have discouraged private investment) or excessive external debt by funding the fiscal deficit directly in a non-inflationary manner; that in a situation of excess

TABLE 2.4   Mexican monetary and banking survey,[a] 1955-75

	1955	1960	1965	1970	1975
Billion pesos					
1 Foreign assets	5·5	5·6	7·3	10·4	19·8
Domestic credit:					
2 Claims on government	2·7	3·6	13·6	24·7	129·8
3 Claims on private sector	4·9	14·3	20·1	35·4	67·4
4 Money	10·8	17·4	30·2	53·8	122·4
5 Quasi-money	3·0	4·9	10·0	18·2	41·7
6 Money GDP	34·9	150·5	252·0	418·7	1000·9
Percentages					
1÷6	6·5	3·7	2·9	7·5	2·0
2÷6	3·2	2·4	5·4	5·9	13·0
3÷6	5·8	3·5	8·0	8·5	6·7
(1+2+3)÷6	15·5	15·6	16·3	21·9	21·7
4÷6	12·7	11·6	12·0	12·8	12·2
5÷6	3·5	3·3	4·0	4·3	4·2
(4+5)÷6	16·2	14·9	16·0	17·1	16·4

TABLE 2.4   continued on p. 36

TABLE 2·4 Mexican monetary and banking survey,[a] 1955–75 *continued*

Percentage of GDP	Liabilities			Assets		
	1965	1970	1975	1965	1970	1975
Banco de México	5·5	5·4	5·9	3·4	11·8	16·4
Other state banks	11·4	12·8	14·6	12·1	13·2	15·0
Total public sector	16·9	18·2	20·5	21·5	25·0	31·4
Deposit banks	7·1	7·3	6·7	4·6	5·0	3·7
Savings banks	2·0	2·5	2·4	1·1	1·7	1·6
Financieras	6·1	14·5	13·3	6·5	11·8	8·7
Hipotecarias	3·1	3·8	3·6	1·0	2·7	2·5
Other	3·2	2·7	2·2	0·3	0·3	0·2
Total private banks	21·5	30·7	28·2	13·5	21·5	16·7
Total banking system	38·4	48·9	48·7	35·0	46·5	48·1

Sources: IMF, *International Financial Statistics*; Banco de México, *Indicadores Económicos*.

Note: [a] definitions in monetary survey as used in IMF, *loc. cit.*; difference between assets and liabilities of the Banco de México is the reserve requirement.

demand for funds, increases in government borrowing automatically reduced private expenditure, so that higher public investment had been balanced by lower private investment and the internal and external equilibria maintained by stabilising aggregate demand.

Taking these three points in turn, there seem to be several shortcomings in this interpretation, all of which are relevant to the experience of the 1970s. The first point, that the Central Bank could and did control the money supply through limits on fiduciary emission and marginal reserve requirements, is challenged by Brothers and Solís.[17] Their argument is that the monetary base can vary widely in response both to short capital movements over the exchanges and fluctuations in 'new' savings moving into the banks from the non-financial sector, so that if the banks had taken full advantage of this they could have varied credit far beyond the limits desired by the monetary authorities. In addition, the need to set the real rate of interest above that obtaining in New York so as to prevent a massive outflow of foreign *and* Mexican funds (the peso being freely convertible) prevented the use of the bond rate as an independent policy instrument. Griffiths[18] agrees with this, but claims that the Central Bank could always adjust its sales of treasury paper to counteract the balance-of-payments effect, although this view would seem to imply a degree of administrative flexibility in, and even strategic unimportance of, public expenditure if it is to be used merely as a means of countering short-run financial flows. Fortunately, perhaps, no large demands were made on this system in the 1960s, and in any case there is considerable evidence,[19] as one might expect in any concentrated banking system, that in reality credit control is exercised by 'moral suasion' – informal arrangements between the monetary authorities and the main bankers, half a dozen of whom account for three-quarters of the private credit in the system.

The second point is that much of the burden of public finance is borne by the banking system, a point that is extended to a major strategic problem, the so-called 'Mexican dilemma', by Vernon.[20] It is true, as Table 2.3 shows, that the public sector financing requirement (PSFR) was equivalent to half of tax income, but the offtake of funds by the public sector during the 1960s was far from large, representing as it did only one-sixth of private savings even though this was only one-half of the new funds coming into the banking system. Indeed, private savings seem to have risen steadily to accommodate domestic borrowing by the public sector. Moreover, the external debt was far from negligible: official borrowing abroad accounted for half of total external finance in the 1960s, and debt service had already used up one-fifth of export receipts by the middle of the decade. However, the main reason why the system 'worked' and the deficit was contained to within the banks' demand for money was because state expenditure was kept down in order to match limited tax revenues. This was, fundamentally, what *desarrollo estabilizador* consisted in from the financial point of view, although the control over wages through the corporate state and the exposure of the economy to US prices levels were also, as we shall argue, important determinants of price stability.

Third, the claim that the system allowed public and private investment to be automatically balanced rests on the supposition that there was a shortage of investible funds in the system. As a hypothesis, this has been deduced from the evident excess of profitability over interest rates, but there are good reasons for doubting it in practice – particularly in the 1960s. Over the period as a whole (see Table 2.1) private savings rose sufficiently to finance public borrowing and leave enough to finance private investment.[21] In the 1960s, new funds coming annually on to the capital market were equivalent to a steady 4–5 per cent of GDP, of which about a half was absorbed by public sector borrowing; however, these funds represented only one-quarter of private saving and of that the part 'on-lent' to the private sector only represented one-fifth of private investment, which was mostly financed out of retained profits or funds transferred directly between firms. In other words, as the bulk of savings took the form of retained corporate profits, Mexico did not experience a separation between a mass of small savers with fixed savings plans on the one hand and borrowing entities competing for the funds on the other[22] – rather the decision to invest (whether in capital formation or government bonds) was really one by conglomerate groups to reduce consumption (or remittances in the case of multinationals) out of profits. As a corollary of this it could well be argued that it was the banking system that was controlling government domestic borrowing (and thus spending) through control of new funds and consent to reserve ratios, rather than the other way around.

This is not to argue, of course, that non-inflationary growth was no more than 'manna from heaven', or entirely the result of structural factors. Conservative monetary policy certainly contributed to high rates of domestic saving, investment and industrialisation. With an 'open' economy, moreover, a fairly tight rein on the budgetary deficit and (in the absence of tax reform) of public spending did reduce the strain on the balance of payments by containing domestic demand. However, as savings were based on reinvested profits and constrained wages, it is not immediately obvious that the low rate of inflation stimulated private investment or savings *directly*; it would seem more convincing to argue that the manifest conservatism of the monetary and fiscal authorities (that is, the Banco de México and the Secretaría de Hacienda) inspired *confidence* in both domestic and foreign investors – a phenomenon which, when balanced against the customary populist rhetoric of the Mexican presidency, was of crucial political importance.

In sum, it would seem reasonable to argue that the Mexican monetary system during the period of *desarrollo estabilizador* relied for its success not upon the rigid control of credit and the money supply which then kept inflation and the balance of payments in check so as to encourage rapid capitalist growth, but rather upon favourable developments in the real economy and tacit agreement between the banks and the Treasury to finance a modest fiscal deficit in return for no tax reform. In other words, returning to the opening comments of this chapter, in the absence of tax flexibility and in the presence of a fixed and convertible currency, monetary and budgetary policy were *not* autonomous.

DISEQUILIBRIUM: 1970–5

We can now turn to the central theme of this book, the experience of stabilisation policies in the 1970s.[23] In contrast to the 1960s, castigated by Reynolds as 'Stabilising Development that was Actually Destabilising', the Echeverría administration (1970–6) is entitled by Solís as 'Monetary Will-o'-the-Wisp: Pursuit of Equity through Deficit Spending'. As we have already indicated, 1970–6 was indeed a period when, in the absence of an adequate tax reform or a radical reshaping of state enterprise pricing policies, the expansion of public expenditure generated enormous fiscal deficits. Further, in a period of rising inflation and a widening balance-of-payments gap, the monetary authorities were pursuing much the same 'rules of the game' as in the previous decade, while the 'planning' authorities (the Secretaría de la Presidencia[24] and the Secretaría de Patrimonio y Fomento Industrial) were pursuing the expansionary policy of *'desarrollo compartido'*. In the process the contradictions of the Mexican industrialisation model that had begun to emerge in the late 1960s became more acute, revealing both the strengths and weaknesses of stabilisation policy as a development strategy.

The last year of the Díaz Ordáz administration (1970) was one of balance-of-payments instability, but a slowdown in public expenditure created monetary restraint of the traditional kind by reducing the local borrowing requirement (and thus the monetary base) to 1 per cent of GDP as opposed to 2 per cent in the previous year; meanwhile the terms of trade were shifting in Mexico's favour and a considerable inflow of short-term private capital served to correct the problem in the short-run. However, by the middle of 1971 it had become clear that the economy was slowing down seriously in any case, and that the continued deflation while new public expenditure plans were being drawn up was leading to a depression – exacerbated by the stagnation north of the border. GDP, agricultural and manufacturing output increased by much less than the long-term trend – indeed GDP per head of population actually *fell* (see Table 2.5). Further, the continued rise in the rate of private savings meant that the banking system now had reserve funds in excess of their legal requirements deposited with the Banco de Mexico.[25] This had a double effect upon policy-making by the government: first, it removed the objection to increased government spending, even under monetarist criteria; second, and more significantly, it reduced the credibility within the administration of the monetary authorities and their demands for budgetary restraint.

The new expenditure programme was not just to be a Keynesian demand reflation, however, because (as we have already noted) it was anticipated that the new state investments would increase output and remove 'bottlenecks', being thus to some extent 'self-balancing' on the supply side,[26] while the tax reform would maintain equilibrium on the demand side. This latter[27] would have kept the fiscal deficit in check, while the rising rate of real national income would have generated the necessary private savings surplus to finance this deficit.

TABLE 2.5   Annual economic indicators, 1970–7

	1970	1971	1972	1973	1974	1975	1976	1977
Rates of change at 1960 prices:								
Agricultural output	4·9	1·8	−2·6	2·1	3·2	−0·7	−3·7	3·4
Manufacturing output	8·7	3·1	8·3	8·9	5·7	3·6	2·6	3·0
Gross Domestic Product	6·9	3·4	7·3	7·6	5·9	4·1	2·1	2·8
GDP *per capita*	3·3	−0·1	3·6	3·9	2·2	0·4	−1·5	−0·8
GDP deflator	4·5	4·5	5·6	12·4	24·0	18·2	19·5	31·2
Percentage of GDP:								
PSFR – internal	1·2	2·3	4·1	4·1	4·7	6·7	5·9	3·7
– external	0·7	—	0·3	2·1	2·2	3·5	2·7	3·1
– total	1·9	2·3	4·3	6·2	6·9	10·2	8·7	6·8
Imports of goods and services	11·6	10·8	11·1	12·1	13·7	12·5	12·4	13·4
Exports of goods and services	8·8	8·8	9·3	9·7	9·8	7·9	8·8	11·1
Current balance	−2·8	−2·0	−1·8	−2·4	−3·9	−4·6	−3·6	−2·3
Minimum wage (1970 pesos/day)	31·2	29·6	33·9	31·3	35·5	34·9	39·0	37·5
Price indices (1970=100):								
Mexico – consumer	100	106	111	124	153	176	204	264
– wholesale	100	104	107	123	151	167	204	288
USA – consumer	100	104	108	114	127	139	145	156
– wholesale	100	103	108	122	145	158	166	176
Exchange rate (pesos/US$):								
Nominal	12·5	12·5	12·5	12·5	12·5	12·5	15·4	22·6
'Real' – I	13·6	13·7	13·5	13·7	14·2	14·3	16·7	22·3
'Real' – II	12·4	12·5	12·8	13·4	14·8	15·9	17·3	20·8

Source: Calculated from Banco de México (1977); IMF, *International Financial Statistics*; Programación (1977); and Banco de México *Informe Anual, 1977*.

Note: The 'real' parities are calculated by multiplying the 'original' parity (12·5) by the ratio of Mexican to US price indices (1960 = 100); 'I' refers to wholesale price basis, 'II' to consumer prices; the 1970 values of these ratios are 109 and 99, respectively.

Public expenditure did start to rise very rapidly indeed from there on (as Table 2.3 indicates), gaining its own momentum as ambitious welfare and investment schemes were announced in 1972 and got under way in 1973. But, as we have seen, the proposed tax reform had been blocked at the end of 1972 by a combination of private business and Central Bank pressure. Tax revenues were increased to some extent through improved efficiency in collection and additional purchase taxes, while public enterprise surpluses were sustained by price revisions in 1973 (50 per cent on petroleum and 30 per cent on electricity), but these were balanced by increased government expenditure (including rising debt service and swelling subsidies on foodstuffs) and the most that could be done was to hold the rate of government saving steady. In consequence, the rapid expansion of state investment pushed up the public sector borrowing requirement as a proportion of GDP from 2 per cent in 1971 to 6 per cent in 1973 and 10 per cent in 1975.

At the same time private investment remained remarkably stable (11–12 per cent of GDP), mainly in response to the state expenditure programme. Manufacturing production, in contrast, after its recovery in 1972 and 1973, began to decelerate from then on, as did agriculture, bringing down the rate of GDP growth with them. In this situation of buoyant demand and production difficulties, continued import growth was hardly surprising, and the deficit on current account widened alarmingly in 1974 and 1975. Moreover, as early as 1973 capital flight had become a serious destabilising factor, but the presidency was apparently set against a devaluation for two reasons: first, because the experience of 1954[28] had seriously weakened the support of organised labour for the PRI, support that was considered essential in view of growing business opposition to the government; second, because it was felt (with some justification) that the short capital outflow was a merely 'political' phenomenon that would eventually be reversed. The Mexican authorities were willing, therefore, to go on borrowing to support the reserves and the continued convertibility of the peso. However, by the beginning of 1976 it was clear that drastic action would soon be necessary in order to restore the external balance and, if possible, curb internal inflation.

But before turning to the devaluation and stabilisation of 1976–7 we must examine stabilisation policy between 1970 and 1975 in somewhat more detail. In particular, we are interested in the interrelationship between the PSFR, demand expansion, inflation and the balance of payments. It is true (see Table 2.5) that between 1970 and 1975 the budget deficit expanded from 2 to 10 per cent of GDP, the rate of inflation rose from 5 to 18 per cent per annum and the current account deficit of the balance of payments widened from 3 to 5 per cent of GDP; it would be tempting to attribute this entirely to demand expansion resulting from the monetisation of government borrowing. However, during this same period (see Tables 2.1, 2.3 and 2.4) import prices rose by 58 per cent, private savings rose considerably and the money supply actually fell as a proportion of money GDP. There were other factors at work, therefore.

It might seem foolhardy to enter the quagmire[29] of the causes of inflation in Latin America, but some examination of the problem in the Mexican context must be made, albeit from the brink, particularly since for Mexico it was something of a novelty. We have already noted that private savings rose to cover a considerable part of the fiscal deficit, but this internal indebtedness (unlike external debt) becomes monetised, and forms a very important part of the increased money supply, as we shall see. But was this the cause of the inflation? First, we must examine the relative price movements in Mexico and the USA because due to the exposure of Mexico's economy to its northern neighbour, the prices of imports and exports, and to a great extent those of manufactures and foodstuffs in the two countries – that is, traded goods prices – are closely linked. Table 2.5 indicates that although Mexican wholesale[30] prices rose by 67 per cent between 1970 and 1975, US wholesale prices rose by 58 per cent in the same period. Specifically, the years of really bad inflation (1973–5) exhibited increases in the GDP deflator of 12, 24 and 18 per cent respectively, while the import price index rose by 12, 23 and 11 per cent, and US wholesale prices by 13, 19 and 9 per cent. In consequence, it would appear that the greater part of Mexican inflation in traded goods prices is attributable to external factors[31] – unless, of course, we wish to argue that US prices are determined in Mexico! The second candidate is always wage rates: while it is generally accepted that wage increases (which are negotiated centrally in Mexico) did not contribute to inflation in the past, they did not rise very rapidly during the 1970–5 period either. The minimum wage rose by only 12 per cent in real terms (manufacturing earnings rose by 14 per cent) and there is no evidence that wage rises preceded price rises in any systematic way.[32] It is true, of course, that this increase was more than that in real GDP *per capita* (10 per cent) during that period – but the difference is hardly serious.

However, although the wholesale price indices in Mexico and the USA do seem to have moved quite closely together, consumer prices diverged to a considerable extent. In the USA traded prices (heavily influenced by raw material imports) moved up faster than non-traded prices, so the wholesale index outpaced the consumer price index. In Mexico, in contrast, the consumer price index moved faster than the wholesale index as non-traded goods prices shifted rapidly upwards. There were three reasons for this: first, the Mexican economy is much more open than its northern neighbour, so that exogenous price changes 'penetrate' more deeply; second, with a high degree of monopolisation in prices and wages, traded price increases are very quickly transmitted to the non-traded goods sector;[33] third, the government revised certain key non-traded prices (such as petroleum and electricity) in 1973 and rents were moving up in response to real estate speculation. An important consequence of this was that demand was not shifted towards non-traded goods (i.e. domestic production) as import prices rose, as it would have been if non-traded prices had been held down, with destabilising consequences for the balance of payments.

Relative rates of inflation have important implications for the overvaluation of the peso, and thus for the need for devaluation, as we shall see in the next section of this chapter. As far as purchasing power parity is concerned, the comparison of wholesale prices (i.e. traded goods) would seem appropriate, in which case the overvaluation[34] of the peso ('Real – I' in Table 2.5) did increase considerably between 1970 and 1975, rising from 9 to 14 per cent. However, it might be argued that in the Mexican case that, given the proximity of the two countries and the ease of personal and capital movement between the two, the consumer price indices ('Real – II' in Table 2.5) would be relevant, in which case the peso was slightly *under*valued in 1970 but overvalued by 27 per cent in 1975.

If inflation was mainly an exogenously generated phenomenon in the 1970–5 period, how did orthodox monetary policy handle the problem of the fiscal deficit? The keystone of policy in the 1960s was to limit the public sector domestic borrowing requirement to more or less the increase in the transactions demand for money[35] – and as this was rising very rapidly in the 1970s due to the exogenous rise in prices, the leeway was considerable. Indeed if the public sector had not used these funds, reserves would have piled up in the Central Bank to an embarrassing and deflationary extent. Table 2.9 indicates how the rate of domestic fund acquisition rose from 5 to 6 per cent of GDP between 1965–70 and 1971–5; of this, the share acquired by the state banks rose from one-fifth to one-third, and in addition they obtained the bulk of foreign funds. Meanwhile, the state banks' share of credit expansion rose from one-half to two-thirds, but by pumping back funds through the rapidly expanding development banks, credit expansion to the private sector remained at a fairly stable level in relation to GDP. In other words, the 'traditional model' had been modified in two crucial respects – first, by the sudden increase in the demand for money which placed the government in a relatively strong position in relation to the private banks; and, second, by the expansion of state development banks which allowed the public sector in effect to lend to itself. Further, the political stance of the presidency itself had weakened the grip of the banks over monetary policy. In particular, the repeated raising of reserve requirements on the banking system in order to keep credit expansion to the private sector in check and finance the government between 1970 and 1975 produced an increase in the ratio of claims of the private banks on the Banco de México to their liabilities to the private sector from less than one-third to over two-fifths;[36] without this stratagem, monetary expansion would have been much greater. However, as the state banks (other than the Banco de México) were lending increasingly to state enterprises against 'reserves' of government paper, the classical model of monetary policy (based as it is on an independent private banking sector responding to a market demand for credit and restrained by reserve requirements) became almost irrelevant – the Keynesian metaphor of 'pushing on a string' springs to mind.

None the less, if we leave aside confidence in the government, which admittedly had been seriously eroded by 1975 (albeit mainly for 'political' reasons as Echeverría embarked on populist rhetoric at home and abroad) the financial policy does not seem to have worked all that badly in gaining for the public sector enormous amounts of funds without adding unreasonably to inflation. But the continuation of the traditional model of finance had, of course, another facet – borrowing abroad to make up the rest of the PSFR, as Table 2.5 indicates. In 1975, a massive US $3·1 billion were borrowed abroad, as opposed to a mere 0·3 billion in 1970, and the composition had shifted away from multilateral creditors such as the IBRD towards US commercial banks and supplier credits.

Ironically, the very slowdown of the US economy that had contributed to stagnating demand for Mexico's exports of goods and services (especially for fresh farm products and tourism), and thus to the balance of payments crisis, also meant that the US banks had surplus funds for which there was little investment demand in that country. These banks were suddenly and un-characteristically willing to lend to Latin American governments in general without imposing many conditions[37] and to Mexico in particular, because of her reputation for monetary conservatism earned in previous decades. In consequence, the Echeverría administration enjoyed what appeared to be almost unlimited foreign credit to finance its deficits and support the peso. Moreover, although the swollen external debt was contracted on progressively harder terms, the short-run 'balance of payments cost' remained at a quarter of export income[38] and the repayment burden was shifted forwards towards the end of the decade. More seriously, the eventual effect was to build up a massive 'leverage' in the hands of the US banks – which was to be deployed with effect in the 1976 crisis, as we shall see. The immediate objective was to allow the State to finance its own imports (which rose from 24 to 38 per cent of merchandise imports between 1970 and 1975) and those of the private sector without using up the reserves or generating demand inflation – but the indirect result was to effectively finance the flight of short private capital to the dollar, as Table 2.2 indicates very clearly.

The capacity of the system to absorb the increased budget deficit is underlined by the fact that the greater part of inflation is attributable to exogenous factors and the fact that while the PSFR rose by 8 percentage points of GDP between 1970 and 1978, the current balance of payments deficit widened by only 2 points. In consequence, the view of the International Monetary Fund that

> The key demand management variable in Mexico is the size of the public sector deficit. On this reasoning, with which the Mexican authorities seem to be in full agreement, that part of

> the balance of payments deficit that is attributable to excess demand pressure can be eliminated only by a corresponding compression of the public sector deficit.[39]

cannot be taken literally. However, it does contain a crucial element of truth: *if* it is assumed that tax reforms, suspension of convertibility, control over capital movements and import controls are not politically feasible or economically desirable (as the IMF does), then the budget deficit is indeed the *only* variable open to government control. But this does *not* mean that it is the only factor affecting macroeconomic stability, or even that reductions in the PSFR will necessarily bring about stabilisation. Literal interpretation of the IMF view quoted above would seem to suggest that only a quarter of the fiscal deficit was reflected in the balance-of-payments deficit, and that the 'compression' required would be correspondingly small.

We are not trying to suggest that deficit finance in the 1970–5 period was not destabilising at all, or that traditional Mexican monetary policy could handle the problem without difficulty; it clearly added to demand pressure through public expenditure uncompensated by reductions in private expenditure, and obviously built up a massive problem for the future in the form of public external debt. None the less, had the fiscal deficit been restrained to slightly lower levels by less wasteful expenditure or tax reform, it could quite possibly have been manageable. But in any case, by the end of 1975 it had become clear that drastic action would have to be taken to bring the balance of payments back into equilibrium; as it was considered politically unfeasible to impose exchange controls and the expected increases in exports (particularly oil) would only be forthcoming towards the end of the decade, a devaluation and demand restraint package was the only course open to the government, now in the last months of its term.

THE 1976/77 DEVALUATION

We can now turn to the peso 'float'[40] of August 1976, and to the accompanying deflationary measures. As the last few months of the *sexenio* wore on, public expenditure continued to rise as the various agencies attempted to complete their programmes before the presidential change. Agricultural and manufacturing production growth rates declined seriously in 1976, and aggregate output per head fell by 1·5 per cent, particularly affected by the political uncertainty verging on hysteria in business circles over the prospect of rural and urban land reform, the nationalisation of multinationals and the freezing of bank deposits – prospects that were none the less destabilising for their lack of factual foundation. Prices continued to rise, even though US prices were settling down, driven up by speculation and major wage claims. By early 1976 (Table 2.6) capital flight (registered short-term capital movements plus 'errors and omissions') had assumed disastrous proportions – over $0·5 billion left the country on capital account over that winter. At the same time, the current account deficit had increased once again, so that during those six months nearly $2·5 billion had to be found – which the authorities covered by further borrowing from the US banks and the euro-dollar market, much of it on very short terms. The massive external debt built up by the public sector was clearly causing foreign creditors considerable concern – by the end of 1976 Mexico held nearly one-quarter of all third world debt to private multinational banks[41] – although the prospect of massive oil income (net exports had started in 1974) and the Mexican record for financial probity in the 1960s meant that they seemed willing to go on lending almost indefinitely, doubtless anticipating that the US government would underwrite the debts in the unlikely event of a default.

Under considerable pressure from the political establishment, Echeverría consented to devalue the peso at the end of his term, thus leaving his Finance Minister and chosen successor, Lopez Portillo, a 'clean sheet' on current account, so to speak, and the anticipation of vast oil revenue to set against the burden of external debt on capital account. But the degree of devaluation to be adopted was not at all clear. Table 2.6 indicates that the peso was becoming seriously overvalued, by 28 per cent in August 1976 according to the relative wholesale price indicator – the one used by the policy-makers themselves.[42] Thus only a modest devaluation was apparently needed to correct the price disparity with the USA; the adjustment necessary to utilise the 'elasticity effect' in order to bring the level of imports down to that of exports in an open economy was known to be infeasible,[43] so the strategy relied on cutting bank credit and the budget deficit so as to reduce imports through the 'absorption effect'.

In view of the lack of confidence in the authorities and the need

TABLE 2.6 Quarterly economic indicators, 1976−7

	1976				1977			
	I	II	III	IV	I	II	III	IV
Visible[a] Trade (US$m.):								
Exports: Agriculture	304	323	160	399	450	407	205	315
Mining	56	78	65	79	77	81	72	66
Oil	97	167	145	148	170	238	243	265
Manufacturing	259	331	285	316	326	350	359	357
Other	22	29	23	31	37	26	17	32
	738	928	678	973	1060	1102	896	1035
Imports: Consumer goods	108	92	60	51	60	62	124	173
Raw materials	562	736	707	700	490	580	689	749
Capital goods	639	677	611	583	486	523	463	505
Other	124	152	119	108	96	135	131	219
	1433	1656	1497	1442	1133	1301	1407	1646

TABLE 2.6 continued on p. 50

TABLE 2.6 Quarterly economic indicators, 1976–7 *continued*

	1976				1977			
	I	II	III	IV	I	II	III	IV
Balance of payments (US$m.):								
Exports of goods & services	1716	1933	1677	1906	2023	2068	1875	2044
Imports of goods & services	2438	2817	2604	2417	2148	2404	2481	2757
Short capital movements[b]	−722	−884	−927	−512	−125	−336	−606	−713
Long capital: Public	−270	−258	−775	−597	134	−560	−261	−1051
Private	772	933	932	1571	317	771	949	1861
	176	186	117	−91	−159	142	134	−30
Reserves	−45	−24	−654	390	168	16	216	71
Price indices								
(increase over previous year)								
Wholesale (1954=100)	16·0	15·2	17·7	39·1	45·7	50·5	48·7	24·8
Consumer (1968=100)	13·1	12·8	12·7	24·3	29·4	31·7	33·1	22·9
Money supply[c] (bn pesos):								
Nominal	109·1	114·9	125·2	141·6	142·4	148·0	154·8	179·3
Real[d]	56·2	57·7	61·7	62·9	53·6	57·6	58·4	64·3

Sources: Computed from Banco de México, *Indicadores*, vol. VI, no. 2, 1978.

Notes: Columns may not sum to exact totals owing to rounding errors; [a] Excludes 'border transactions' and omissions'; [b] includes 'errors and omissions'; [c] '*medio circulante*' in the Bank of Mexico's definition, appears to correspond to 'M₁' in the IMF definition; [d] deflated by consumer price index (1970=100) seasonally adjusted.

to attract back flight capital, it was decided to float the peso and let it 'find its own level', which would then have a certain credibility of its own. Once the Banco de Mexico ceased to support the parity it promptly passed from 12·5 through 15 pesos to the US dollar in September, reaching 22 by the end of the year, after which it stabilised early in 1977 at around 22·6–22·8, where it has remained since. The immediate effect of the float was not to control the outflow of funds – this continued unabated, as Table 2.6 shows, and only came to a halt in mid-1978, a year after the Mexican authorities had agreed to insure 'foreign' deposits against further exchange loss.[44] As the parity drifted down, rising peso import prices were transmitted into the economy and exacerbated by protective price and wage adjustments, thereby justifying further parity decline. At no stage during this entire two-year saga do exchange controls seem to have been seriously contemplated, although the fear of such a move undoubtedly exacerbated capital flight.

In consequence, the Banco de México was forced to continue borrowing abroad. In October 1976, an agreement was reached with the International Monetary Fund to make available nearly $1 billion in the form of Extended Fund Facilities and Compensatory Financing Facilities – a move which also eased access to further foreign bank credit, but which involved the signing of the familiar 'letter of intent'. This document[45] was neither very precise nor very harsh by comparison with those signed by many debtor countries in recent years; its main elements were a reduction in the budgetary deficit, wage restraint and the eventual lowering of some import tariffs to make domestic manufacturing more competitive. The only specific commitment (apart from some quite optimistic growth projections – GDP growth up to 7 per cent again by 1980, and investment to reach 28 per cent of GDP by that date) was on the public sector deficit: this was to be cut to 2·5 per cent of GDP, public sector saving to rise to 5.5 per cent of GDP, and external borrowing to fall to 1 per cent of GDP, by 1979. The increase in public sector savings was to be achieved by raising public sector income by 2·5 per cent of GDP (taxes and enterprise prices) and cutting current expenditure by only 0·5 per cent of GDP. No drastic reduction in public expenditure, real wage cuts or sales of para-statal assets were demanded by the IMF, price controls on wage goods were to be continued, and the Mexican authorities appeared to be relying implicitly on the net effect of the devaluation plus the natural slowdown of public expenditure at the outset of a new administration as well as the evident depression in the real sectors of the economy to restore equilibrium.[46]

To evaluate the effect of a stabilisation programme of such a 'soft' nature is difficult enough, and it is made more so by the lack of data on the events of 1977 at the time of writing.[47] However, for such a programme to 'work', the terms of trade effect on imports and exports should be positive, relative prices should shift towards non-traded production, aggregate demand should be held in check (particularly by reducing the budgetary deficit and wage consumption), and credit expansion should be cut back so as to bring the supply of domestic money into line with the demand for it. These are not, of course, independent factors: for the devaluation to be effective, the 'pass-through' effect (domestic prices adjusting by the full amount of the devaluation) must be blocked by credit restraint, which in turn is very difficult without a reduction in government borrowing, while non-traded prices and wages must be constrained to make the parity adjustment at all effective.

Taking the devaluation itself first, the short-run effect[48] relies upon the terms of trade, and in the Mexican case on the relationship between US and Mexican prices. As Table 2.5 indicates, however, the immediate effect of the float seems to have been to force up the domestic price level to more or less parity with the US price level again by the end of 1976, near which it has remained since. In other words, the devaluation was effectively of only one-sixth, the rest of the parity change being nullified. Why a single parity adjustment of this order was not carried through in the first place, rather than letting speculation force the rate up to levels from which the 'ratchet effect' of induced inflation would not let it descend, is difficult to understand in retrospect. The devaluation did shift the relative price balance in the right direction, the fact that the consumer price index rose by so much less than the wholesale index indicating a relative price movement in favour of non-traded goods and thus a potential shift of domestic demand away from imports and exportables.

In contrast, the main instruments of demand restraint do not appear to have been applied with much vigour. In the first half of 1977,[49] the federal government deficit did fall to the annual equivalent of 2·4 per cent of GDP from 4·1 per cent in the first half of 1976, but public enterprise borrowing actually increased in peso terms because of the revaluation of their dollar obligations, bringing the overall public deficit for 1977 back only to the level of 1974, as Table 2.5 indicates. Moreover, the gap was reduced mainly by the customary decline in public capital expenditure at the outset of a presidential *sexenio*: this was equivalent to 10 per cent of GDP in 1977, as opposed to 12 per cent in 1976, although it was hardly a reduction compared with 1975 (11 per cent) and 1974 (8 per cent). However, the money supply was kept under fairly tight control in real terms (see Table 2.6), even if it did not actually fall, and total bank credit was cut by about 12 per cent in real terms between June 1976 and 1977 because of the withdrawal of private funds across the exchanges and their replacement by non-monetised public sector borrowing abroad. Wage restraint is the other lynchpin of stabilisation policy, and it has the added advantage of shifting income towards profits and thus hopefully restoring business confidence. The strength of organised labour in Mexico is such that substantial rises in the minimum wage (that for Mexico City in nominal and real terms is shown in Table 2.5) were awarded in September 1976 and January 1977, and price restraint on wage goods (including food subsidies and grain imports) maintained, which appear to have kept real wages nearly stable despite the massive price rises. The effect on labour was felt in terms of rising unemployment and depressed living standards for those in the 'informal' sector – but this was as much a result of a longer trend of decelerating national output and rising population (see Table 2.1) as of the stabilisation policy as such. The initial impact of devaluation on prices took some time to abate, speculation on domestic prices and the currency itself continuing for a full year after the start of the stabilisation programme, as Table 2.6 indicates. Only at the end of 1977 did prices begin to decelerate, and even in the first quarter of 1978 both wholesale and consumer prices were 18 per cent above their level twelve months before.

However, the main objective of the stabilisation programme was to achieve an equilibrium in the balance-of-payments position. At first sight, the effect seems to have been quite encouraging on the export side, but in fact much of the increase was due to oil shipments (which were growing anyway) and rising prices for manufactures (particularly processed foods) on the North American market. None the less, the physical volume of non-oil exports did rise by 11 per cent between the first halves of 1976 and 1977 –

but again, at least half of this must be attributed to natural market growth in the USA. On a conservative estimate, the net effect of the devaluation on these exports might be 5 per cent, implying an elasticity of the order of one-third – the rest coming from natural improvements such as coffee prices. Tourism does not seem to have responded to the devaluation at all: the number of visitors stayed stable at about 1·5 million in the first halves of 1976 and 1977, while dollar income actually dropped.

On the import side, in contrast, there was a much more marked effect, the 22 per cent fall between the first halves of 1976 and 1977 being shared fairly equally by the public and private sectors on the one hand, and raw materials and capital goods on the other. It is difficult to see how public sector imports would be price-sensitive in this way (being financed in dollars), and in fact much of the cutbacks are accounted for by reduced government imports of wheat and steel consequent upon improved domestic production on the one hand and lower state investment on the other. In the private sector, the determinant factor was probably the deceleration of manufacturing, for which most imports are in fact inputs. This implies, of course, that the effect was probably temporary, to be reversed once production recovered – a view sustained by the fact that imports were already declining before the devaluation: in dollar terms from US\$6·6 billion in 1975 to US\$6·0 billion in 1976, and in physical terms since 1974.

The capital account of the balance of payments did eventually show some improvement as long-term private capital began to move back across the exchanges in the second quarter of 1977, mainly in the form of *'operaciones con valores'* (bonds). Meanwhile, however, the authorities were still borrowing heavily abroad in order to sustain the new parity: the total official external debt, which had reached US\$16 billion in 1976, approached 18 billion by the end of 1977; in the last quarter of 1977 alone, Mexico placed bonds worth \$1·2 billion on the euro-dollar market.

In sum, the impact of the massive adjustment of the parity – from 12·5 to 22·5 pesos to the dollar – was mostly nullified by the 'pass-through' effect, and the deflationary measures, while supportive, could hardly be described as drastic. The balance of payments did show some improvement in the short-run, but more as the result of continued economic stagnation and the political posture of the new administration than of stabilisation policy as such. This outcome was made possible, of course, by the continued credit-worthiness of Mexico, based now not so much on the financial rectitude of the past, as on the prospect of oil wealth to come.

CONCLUSIONS

The IMF certainly seems to have believed that the stabilisation policy had been a success, despite its heterodoxy.

The evaluation of the causes of the imbalance in the Mexican economy does seem to have varied, for in 1976[50] it was stated that

> over the past two years the Mexican economy has been adversely affected by domestic and foreign economic developments. At that time, Mexico was not in a position to benefit from the buoyant foreign demand because bottlenecks developed ... later on, the economy was adversely affected by the recession in industrial countries ... the combination of inflation and recession abroad, and the financial costs of the efforts made to strengthen key sectors of the economy and their effects on the level of domestic prices had an inverse impact on the balance of payments. Mexico's international position was further eroded by a wage policy which led to domestic price increases in excess of those abroad. Recently speculation against the Mexican peso brought new pressures to bear on the balance of payments.

With the exception of the wage problem (for which we have suggested there is no firm evidence – certainly the IMF offers none) this seems to be broadly consistent with the position outlined in this chapter. However, by 1978,[51] the Fund was arguing that

> beginning in 1972, Mexico's financial and economic position steadily deteriorated, largely because of rapidly mounting public sector deficits. In 1974 and 1975 this deterioration was aggravated by shocks to the world economy; and the growing financial imbalances, together with the unfavourable external environment, created strong pressures on domestic prices and the balance of payments. During 1975–6, these adverse developments were compounded by substantial outflows of private short-term capital due to exchange rate uncertainties ...

[but] the results of [the stabilisation] strategy have already been striking . . . the balance of payments continued to recover very rapidly and recorded a large overall surplus in 1977. The current account improved to 2·5 per cent of GDP, largely as a result of the success of the Government's demand and exchange rate policies in reducing . . . pressures on available resources and in restoring international competitiveness, but also because of increasing petroleum exports and favourable world prices for some important primary exports . . . The combination of fiscal, monetary and balance of payments management contributed to the decline in domestic price increases. The success of these policies also explains the moderation of wage demands in 1977, a moderation on which the attainment of the Government's objectives was crucially dependent. The success on the wage front was also encouraged by a program to keep down the prices of basic consumer goods. This program, which required the collaboration of business, appeared to have been effective despite its possibly moderating effect on profits. By mid-year, the annual rate of inflation had been brought down to under 15 per cent, compared with some 60 per cent in the last four months of 1976. This unusual adjustment was made while average real wages in 1977 remained at their high level of 1976, a level that was reached through large but unsustainable increases in previous years.

In addition to the evident shift in emphasis, the IMF view on Mexico (which certainly deserves fuller exploration than we have given it here) seems somewhat ambiguous:[52] the Fund's monetarism appears to be sullied by an almost Keynesian approach to real wage pressure on the one hand and an almost structuralist regard for the effect of the US business cycle on the other. Our own interpretation, while in agreement on the significance of these factors (although giving them a different weight), has been rather different; we have stressed the 'political economy' aspects of the problem of resource acquisition for an expanded state rather than seeing it as one of demand management. The Mexican experience of stabilisation policy during the past two decades is a complex one, and the depth of our analysis is probably insufficient to allow us to draw any definite conclusions. None the less, there are two general observations that we can make by way of a summary of our argument.

First, three 'real' economic factors made stabilisation through monetary policy that much easier during the 1960s and that much more difficult during the 1970s: the balanced and rapid growth of the economy during the former period as opposed to its imbalance and deceleration during the latter; low public investment, budget deficits and taxes in the former period in contrast to the high public investment rates and budget deficit in the latter; and the openness of the economy to US markets throughout. In the period of *'desarrollo estabilizador'*, rising supply growth held domestic inflationary pressure down while the balance of payments was kept stable despite rapid industrialisation by the strength of agricultural exports; but by the 1970s these conditions no longer held, while the recapitalisation of the natural resource base was needed at the same time as (and precisely because) the growth rate was declining and the balance of payments was running into structural disequilibrium. In the 1960s it was possible to maintain low taxes, low public investment rates and low fiscal deficits because of earlier *étatist* reforms, but this conservatism led in its turn to a need for much greater investment in the 1970s, and, in the absence of tax reform, a greater budget deficit. The openness of the economy to US markets helped to keep the price level stable, maintain the growth of exports and supply foreign funds in the 1960s, but in the 1970s this exposure raised the rate of inflation, slowed exports down and allowed massive capital flight. Under these circumstances, it is hardly surprising that the traditional instruments of monetary policy could not maintain stability in the economy – the surprising thing (and a tribute to the strength of the Mexican system) is that they had any effect at all.

Second, three 'non-economic' factors on various planes made stabilisation through monetary policy easier during the 1960s and very difficult during the 1970s. At the 'management' level, the 'understanding' between the private banks and the monetary authorities, consisting in the willingness of the latter to permit the former to determine the level of the fiscal deficit (and thus that of public expenditure) during the 1960s, did not obtain during the 1970s, when the government was attempting to drain off far more funds than the private banks were really prepared to relinquish – and in consequence the voluntary system of credit restriction was abandoned as well. At the 'political' level, the confidence of Mexican liquid asset-holders in the essential conservatism of government in the 1960s permitted full convertibility of the peso without debilitating consequences for the balance of payments, but the populist reformism of the Echevarría administration shattered this confidence and led to capital flight and self-justifying speculation against the peso. Again, at the 'policy' level, the inherited impossibility of imposing tax reforms or exchange controls meant that the only policy instrument left to a government determined to carry through its expenditure plans was a large budget deficit and continuation of orthodox monetary policy *ad absurdum*. Finally, at a 'strategic' level, it could be argued that the Mexican state was undertaking a programme designed to renew the natural resource base, revive industrial progress and recapture the support of organised labour, but that domestic capital (particularly its financial fraction) was not willing to support such a programme despite the fact that the result would be in their own interests in the long-run – in other words, the state could not obtain the 'relative autonomy' necessary in order to restructure productive capital and sustain industrialisation.[53]

Whether the Mexican state can now implement its public investment strategy, and work out a new stabilisation policy consistent with it, remains to be seen.[54]

NOTES

*   I am indebted to the Overseas Studies Committee (Cambridge), the Ministry of Overseas Development (London) and the Secretaría de Programación y Presupuesto (Mexico City) for their support, without which this paper (and the research project of which it forms a part) would not have been possible. The responsibility for errors and misinterpretations is mine alone, of course.

1   The first point of view is represented in Solís (1977) and IMF (1976), the second by Reynolds (1977) and Bueno (1977).

2   These two terms, of common currency in Mexico, refer to the period of rapid growth without inflation between 1956 and 1970 (*desarrollo estabilizador*) and the attempt to reduce social inequality and restructure the economy between 1970 and 1976 (*desarrollo compartido*); 'stabilising development' is particularly associated with Secretary Ortíz Mena (Finance Minister between 1958 and 1970), and 'shared development' with President Echeverría (1970–6). See also FitzGerald (1978c).

3   Often associated with the 'ECLA school'; Solís (1971) has a good exposition of this debate in the Mexican context.

4   One of the better expositions of modern stabilisation theory is Findlay (1973), especially Chapters 10 and 11.

5   See, for example, Davis (1967), Solís (1970, 1971, 1973), and Reynolds (1970). For good surveys of more recent events, see Reynolds (1977), Solís

(1977), Bueno (1977). For a quasi-official version of economic policy during the Echeverría administration, see Gribmont and Rimez (1977). The arguments in this section are given at greater length in FitzGerald (1978d).

6 According to the IMF *International Financial Statistics* direct foreign investment net of amortisation averaged US$131 million per annum in 1957–66 and $225 million in 1967–76, but the average annual outflows of profits and royalties were $139 million and $453 million respectively, leading to net drains on the balance of payments; the contribution on visible trade account was little different to that by similar Mexican firms – see Jenkins (1978).

7 Reynolds (1970, pp. 238–51) and IMF (1976). The USA accounted for three-quarters of Mexican imports and exports in 1960, and still for two-thirds in 1976 despite attempts at market diversification. Further, according to Sepúlveda and Chumacero (1973, p. 124), 79 per cent of all foreign investments in Mexico belonged to US corporations in 1970.

8 There are no reliable data on the functional distribution of income, but Reynolds (1970) argues convincingly for a considerable shift towards profits after the 1954 devaluation, an argument which is corroborated by the deterioration of the distribution of personal income for the period. It is probable that a shift back towards wages took place during the 1972–6 period, but this does not seem to have affected savings out of profits, as we shall see.

9 The remainder of this section is drawn from FitzGerald (1978b), the main data sources for which are Banco de México (1970) and Programación (1977).

10 See FitzGerald (1978a); for the 1960s, the ECLA calculates that the ratio of general government expenditure and public investment to GDP was 32 per cent in Chile, 29 per cent in Brazil, 23 per cent in Argentina and 17 per cent in Peru – as opposed to 19 per cent in Mexico.

11 See, for example, Brothers and Solís (1966), Goldsmith (1966), Basch (1968), Griffiths (1971), Eckaus (1974) and Fernández (1976).

12 For a discussion on the division of private savings into household and corporate savings – a distinction that is in any case ambiguous due to the fact that the bulk of personal savings come out of profit income in Mexico – and preliminary estimates, see FitzGerald (1977).

13 See Gómez (1975) and Eckaus (1974) on bank concentration and the organisation of ownership groups.

14 According to Banco de México (1970) the nominal rate of interest on most bonds was around 10 per cent during the 1960s when inflation ran at about 4 per cent. In addition, these bonds were redeemable at par, making them almost perfectly liquid: see Griffiths (1971).

15 The Mexican market is really a 'money market' rather than a 'capital market', due to the liquidity of instruments (see Note 14) and the fact that very few equities at all are traded. Also, it should be noted that we do not use the term 'financial *development*' in the sense of Gurley and Shaw (1960) because there is no convincing evidence that the Mexican private banking system has assisted the flow of funds between productive sectors or that it has mobilised small savings.

16 The claim is set forth in many places: in general terms in Ortíz Mena's address to the 1969 Annual Meeting of the IBRD and IMF ('Stabilising

Development – a Decade of Economic Policy in Mexico') but more precisely in Solís (1971) and Ghigliazza (1972); the best formal model of the process is given by Koehler (1972).

17   Brothers and Solís (1966) p. 125.
18   Griffiths (1971) p. 76.
19   See Sanchez (1976); the 'Radcliffe' view of the British system is an obvious parallel.
20   Vernon (1965) p. 55.
21   For a more complete statistical analysis of this process, see FitzGerald (1977).
22   This assumption underpins all models where the stability of the savings function produces a 'crowding-out' effect if the government increases its borrowing from the domestic money market – by reducing private investment or forcing the private sector to borrow abroad. For a recent survey, see von Furstenberg and Malkiel (1977).
23   Comparatively little of note has been written as yet on the period, but see Gribmont and Rimez (1977) for an apologia, Solís (1977) for a critique from within the government, IMF (1976) for a conservative view from outside, and Ayala (1977) for a radical view.
24   This planning role was strengthened by the creation of the Secretaría de Programación y Presupuesto (SPP) by Lopez Portillo, although the split in policymaking powers is continued because although all expenditure decisions are vested in the SPP, the Treasury is still responsible for taxation and borrowing; see FitzGerald (1978c).
25   The *Informe Anual* of the Banco de México for 1971 revealed excess reserves of 2·6 billion pesos.
26   A point of view particularly associated with Horacio Flores de la Peña, the Secretario de Patrimonio at the time and the doyen of progressive Mexican economists – see Flores de la Peña (1976).
27   See Solís (1977) pp. 95–103 for an excellent discussion of these proposals and their downfall. Solís himself was a key architect of tax reform, as chief economic adviser to the Presidency at the time. Even the World Bank acknowledged the need for a considerable increase in tax pressure (IBRD, 1976, pp. 41–3) but somewhat equivocally because it also held that 'the context of the tax reform should be consistent with the encouragement of private savings and investment'.
28   Reynolds (1970) pp. 231–6, and Buira (1976).
29   Where even angels tread with some trepidation – see Thorp (1971).
30   We are using the wholesale price index as a proxy for traded goods, and the consumer price index as a composite of traded and non-traded prices.
31   That is, the 'unified market hypothesis' essential to the 'monetary approach to the balance of payments'; econometric support for this is given in Wilford (1977). The case of Canada provides an interesting parallel, where prices also appear to be largely determined exogenously – see Beare (1973).
32   Griffiths (1971), Buira (1976). The minimum wage (for Mexico City in Table 2.5) is a crucial indicator in Mexico because it is negotiated centrally and explicitly forms the basis for other wage scales. Examination of quarterly data does not yield any detectable lagged relationship – but then even if one found that prices preceded wages, it could be argued that

oligopolistic sectors raise prices in anticipation of the regular national wage agreements. The problem, as ever, is one of identification.

33 See Bulmer-Thomas (1977) for an interesting analysis of this transmission mechanism in Costa Rica.

34 1960 is taken as the base year as it is widely agreed that the 1954 devaluation left the peso seriously undervalued – see Bueno (1974). Of course, the parity is also *structurally* supported by tariff protection – Bueno (1970) estimates that overall nominal protection in 1960 to have been 22 per cent and the effective rate to have been 25 per cent (35 and 42 per cent on manufactures) and this has been augmented by higher tariffs and import controls since that date, sustaining the higher degree of overvaluation in the early 1970s.

35 Gomez (1976) estimates the money demand function for 1940—73 as exhibiting a unitary elasticity with respect to money GDP but a small and unreliable coefficient with respect to the cost of holding money itself.

36 IMF (1976) p. 39.

37 See the discussion in the Introduction to this volume.

38 The 'economic cost' of extra debt can only be assessed in terms of a long-run growth model – see Loser (1977).

39 IMF (1976) p.7: this is a crucial source because it is the supporting document to the IMF support for the 1976/77 stabilisation package.

40 Referred to by Mexicans as *'flotar como una piedra'*.

41 IBRD, *Debt Tables*.

42 Programación (1977).

43 Clavijo and Gómez (1977) and Bueno (1974) seem to agree that the price-elasticity of import demand is very low (around one-fifth) but suggest that the price elasticity of export supply is rather higher, at around 0·3—0·5.

44 Referred to as *dolarización* – 'foreign' in this context including, of course, funds belonging to Mexicans deposited with nominees in New York.

45 IMF (1976). See also the *IMF Survey* for 1 November 1976: here it is pointed out that the Compensatory Financing Facility 'provides balance of payments assistance when needed for member countries experiencing shortfalls in export earnings below the medium-term trend of exports when such shortfalls are attributable to circumstances largely beyond their control' (p. 333).

46 See the press conference of the Minister of Finance (31 August 1976) and the address to the Mexican Congress by the President (1 September 1976), both reproduced in the *Trimestre Económico* vol XLIV, 1 (1977).

47 May 1978; but see note 53 below.

48 The long-run effect should be more substantial in theory (i.e. the response to the elasticities would be greater) but the extent of the 'pass-through' effect on prices that has already taken place, and the pressure of renewed economic growth on import demand may well leave matters much as they are now – and in any case the oil income will presumably rectify the position by the end of the decade. Official estimates (considered conservative by *The Economist*) are of proven reserves of 20 billion barrels of oil and gas as at mid-1978, with probable reserves of 37 billion, and potential reserves of 200 billion barrels. The forecast for 1982 is an offtake of 2·2 million barrels a day – which could add up to $8 billion a year to Mexican exports.

49 Programación (1977); see also note 53 below.

50   *IMF Survey* for 1 November 1976 (p. 333).
51   *IMF Survey* for 14 April 1978 (pp. 119–21).
52   As evinced by the conflicting interpretations of the causes of the imbalance in the two *IMF Survey* articles just quoted, or between the quotation on pp. 46–7 and the granting of Compensatory Financing Facilities. It has been suggested to the author that the main interest of the IMF was to 'get in on the Mexican action' in order to exercise some control over not only Mexico but also the US banks that were lending to her – this at least would help to explain the leniency of the terms and the vagueness of the diagnosis.
53   A recent account of economic policy in the 1970s by a central political figure has a similar political analysis to ours – particularly of the 'blocking' role of the banks – but the economic analysis is somewhat too structuralist, underrating the potential of demand management in support of state capital accumulation: see Tello, C. (1979).
54   The data available by early 1979 in the Banco de México *Informe Anual 1978* indicate that the explicit IMF targets for the stabilisation programme were not met in that year. The PSFR was 6·4 per cent of the GDP and the deficit on current account of the balance of payments equivalent to 3·0 per cent. In fact, this latter deficit had widened from 1977 to US$2·46 billion, because although exports rose by 31 per cent (mostly oil), imports increased by 38 per cent as the economy was allowed to expand under the pressure of renewed consumer credit and GDP itself rose by 6·6 per cent in real terms; the public sector was forced to borrow another US$4·06 billion in 1978 in order to cover both this deficit and the continued outflow of short-term funds – although by the last quarter of the year the outflow of private funds appeared to have stopped, there were no signs of backflow. Meanwhile, wholesale and consumer prices rose by 16 per cent in 1978, bringing the overvaluation of the peso to 10 per cent with respect to the US dollar, but growing confidence (in oil rather than the Lopez Portillo admininstration) kept the parity steady. On the prospects for demand management in the medium term, see FitzGerald (1978c).

REFERENCES

Ayala, A. (1977), 'Auge y Declinación del Intervencionismo Estatal, 1970–76,' *Investigación Económica* vol. XXXVI, 3.
Banco de México (1970), *Manual de Estadísticas, 1970.*
Banco de México (1977), *Estadísticas de la Oficina de Cuentas de Producción 1960–1976*, Banco de México, Subdirección de Investigación Económica y Bancaria.
Basch, A. (1968), *El Mercado de Capitales en México*, Centro de Estudios Monetarios Latino-Americanos, Mexico.
Beare, J. B. (1973), 'Wage and Price Change Relationships in Post-war Canada', *Canadian Journal of Economics*, May 1973.
Bravo, L. (1977), 'La Política Impositiva', in G. Bueno (1977).
Brothers, J., and Solís, L. (1966), *Mexican Financial Development*, Texas University Press, Austin.
Bueno, G. (1970), 'The Structure of Protection in Mexico', in B. Belassa *et al.*,

The Structure of Protection in Developing Countries, Johns Hopkins Press, Baltimore.

Bueno, G. (1974), 'La Paridad de Poder Adquisitivo y las Elasticidades de Importación y Exportación en Mexico', *El Trimestre Económico*, vol. XLI, 2.

Bueno, G. M. (ed.) (1977), *Opciones de Política Económica Después de la Devaluación*, Editorial Tecnos, Mexico.

Buira, A. (1976), 'Causas Principales y Efectos Internos de la Inflación', in E. Fernández, (1976).

Bulmer-Thomas, V. (1977), 'A Model of Inflation for Central America', *Oxford Bulletin of Economics and Statistics*, vol. 39, 4.

Clavijo, F., and Gomez, O. (1977), 'El Desequilibrio Externo y la Devaluación en la Economía Mexicana', *El Trimestre Economico*, vol. XLIV, 1.

Davis, T. (ed.) (1967), *Mexico's Recent Economic Growth*, Texas University Press.

Eckaus, R. S., 'The Structure and Performance of the Mexican Banks and Financieras', *Working Papers no. 142*, Department of Economics, MIT.

Fernández, E. (1976), *Cincuenta Años de Banca Central: Ensayos Conmemorativos 1925–75*, Banco de México y Fondo de Cultura Económica, Mexico.

Findlay, R. E. (1973), *International Trade and Development Theory*, Columbia University Press, New York.

FitzGerald, E. V. K. (1977), 'Patterns of Saving and Investment in Mexico, 1939–76', *Working Papers Series no. 30*, Centre of Latin American Studies, Cambridge.

FitzGerald, E. V. K. (1978a), 'The Fiscal Crisis of the Latin American State', in J. F. J. Toye (ed.), *Taxation and Economic Development*, Cass, London.

FitzGerald, E. V. K. (1978b), 'Patterns of Public Sector Income and Expenditure in Mexico', *Technical Papers Series*, Center for Latin American Studies, Texas University.

FitzGerald, E. V. K. (1978c), 'Mexico: a New Direction in Economic Policy?', *Bank of London and South America Review*, vol. 12, 10.

FitzGerald, E. V. K. (1978d), 'The State and Capital Accumulation in Mexico', *Journal of Latin American Studies*, vol. 10, 2.

Flores de la Peña, H. (1976), *Teoría y Práctica del Desarrollo*, Fondo de Cultura Economica, Mexico.

Ghigliazza, S. (1972), 'Programación Financiera a Corto Plazo: Reciente Experiencia de México', in ILPES, *Discusiones Sobre Programación Monetario-Financiera* Mexico, Siglo XXI.

Goldsmith, R. W. (1966), *The Financial Development of Mexico*, OECD, Paris.

Gomez, A. (1976), 'La Demanda de Dinero en México', in E. Fernández (1976).

Gomez, N. (1975), 'Estructura Financiera, Rentabilidad y Crecimiento Económico en México', *Comercio Exterior*, vol. 25, 6.

Gribmont, C., and Rimez, M. (1977), 'La Política Económica del Gobierno de Luís Echeverría (1971–6): Un Primer Ensayo de Interpretación', *El Trimestre Económico*, vol. XLIV, 4.

Griffiths, B. (1971), *Mexican Monetary Policy and Economic Development*. New York: Praeger.

Gurley, J. G., and Shaw, E. S. (1960), *Money in a Theory of Finance*, Brookings, Washington.

IBRD (1976), *An Updating Report on the Economy of Mexico* (1110-ME) IBRD, Washington.

IMF (1976), 'Mexico – Recent Economic Developments' and 'Mexico – Use of Fund Resources', *Executive Board Papers*, IMF, Washington.

Jenkins, R. O. (1978), 'Manufactured Exports – Development Strategy or Internationalisation of Capital', *Bulletin of the Society for Latin American Studies*, no. 28, April 1978.

Koehler, J. E. (1972), 'Economic Policymaking with Little Information and Few Instruments: The Process of Macro-control in Mexico', *Rand Papers no. 4764*, Rand Corporation, California.

Loser, C. M. (1977), 'External Debt Management and Balance of Payments Policies', *IMF Staff Papers*, vol. XXIV, 1.

Programación (1977), *Información Económica y Social Básica*, Secretaría de Programación y Presupuesto, Mexico.

Reynolds, C. W. (1970), *The Mexican Economy: Twentieth Century Structure and Growth*, Yale University Press.

Reynolds, C. W. (1977), 'Why Mexico's "Stabilising Development" was Actually Destabilising (with some implications for the future)', *Sub-Committee on Inter-American Economic Relationships Hearings*, Washington: Congress of the United States.

Sanchez, L. (1976), 'Instrumentos de Política Monetaria y Crediticia' in E. Fernández (1976).

Sepúlveda, B. and Chumacero, A. (1973), *La Inversion Extranjera en México*, Fondo de Cultura Económica, Mexico.

Solís, L. (1970), *La Realidad Económica Mexicana*, Siglo XXI, Mexico.

Solís, L. (1971), 'Mexican Economic Policy in the Post-War Period: the Views of Mexican Economists', *American Economic Review*, vol. 61, 3, Part 2.

Solís, L. (ed.) (1973), *La Economía Mexicana*, Fondo de Cultura Económica, Mexico.

Solís, L. (1977), 'A Monetary Will-o'-the-Wisp: Pursuit of Equity through Deficit Spending', *Discussion Paper no. 77*, Princeton University Press.

Tello, C. (1979) *La Política Económica en Mexico 1970–1976*, Siglo XXI, Mexico City.

Thorp, R. (1971), 'Inflation and the Financing of Economic Development', in K. Griffin, *Financing Development in Latin America*, Macmillan, London.

Vernon, R. (1965), *The Dilemma of Mexico's Development*, Havard University Press.

von Furstenberg, F. M., and Malkiel, B. G. (1977), 'The Government and Capital Formation: A Survey of Recent Issues', *Journal of Economic Literature*, vol. XV, 3.

Wilford, D. S. (1977), *Monetary Policy in an Open Economy: Mexico's Experience*, Praeger, New York.

3 Inflation and Stabilisation in Chile 1970 – 7

LAURENCE WHITEHEAD

INTRODUCTION

During the 1970s Chilean society has been wracked by a political and ideological conflict of great intensity. In the course of these struggles the rate of inflation, which had long been endemic at annual levels of 20–30 per cent, accelerated to levels unprecedented in the history of the republic (see Table 3.1). It remained above 100 per cent for about five years (briefly running above 500 per cent at the peak), and even with the most draconian-looking programme of stabilisation several years were needed to bring the rate of inflation back into the previously accepted range of tolerance. Comparing the state of the economy at the end of the period with its condition at the beginning, one observes that after all the drastic structural changes – first in a socialist, then in a capitalist, direction – almost no net investment or growth has occurred. The labour force has increased by 18 per cent (see Table 3.9 below), a great deal of skilled human capital has been lost through emigration, unemployment levels that would have been considered a disgrace in the 1950s are now considered a matter for congratulation, and the distribution of income, after a marked shift towards wage earners in the early years, has become more regressive than ever.

Of course these bald statements about the economy fail to express the more subjective, but also more profound, changes that have occurred in Chilean society over the same period. Chile has been transformed from a bourgeois democracy with strong welfare state and socialising tendencies into a reactionary dictatorship, relying on market forces to promote efficiency and

TABLE 3.1 Chile indicators of inflation, 1968–77. (Year-on-year percentage increases)

	(1) GNP deflator	(2) $ exchange rate	(3) Wholesale prices (a) Imports	(4) Wholesale prices (b) All goods	(5) Retail prices (a) Food	(6) Retail prices (b) All goods	(7) (c) Corrected all goods	(8) Private sector money supply (M₁)	(9) Private sector M₁ as % of GDP
1968	30·3	36·0	38·7	30·5		26·6	27·7	30·7	7·9
1969	37·8	33·8	37·4	36·5		30·6	31·9	41·5	7·7
1970	38·8	28·1	34·4	36·1		32·5	34·1	52·5	8·1
1971	26·3	7·5	22·1	17·9	23·8	20·1	29·9	100·1	12·2
1972	86·2	58·2	56·2	70·0	115·2	77·8	107·4	98·4	13·1
1973	401·7	531·2	580·4	511·4	376·5	352·8	410·2	291·1	10·1
1974	677·0	797·9	1349·8	1029·0	513·7	504·7	504·7	296·6	5·1
1975	256·0	590·2	445·9	482·0	359·6	374·7	374·7	232·2	4·2
1976	n.a.	265·8	201·6	221·1	212·8	211·9	211·9	193·5	4·0
1977	n.a.	64·9	99·8	86·0	86·2	92·0	92·0	133(est.)	4·9

Sources:

(1) Banco Central, *Boletín*, June 1977 and January 1978, p. 42.

(2) Banco Central, *Boletín*, July 1977, pp. 10, 12, and January 1978, p. 53. Black market rates presumably not included.

(3), (4), (5) and (6) Ricardo ffrench-Davis (1973) p. 246; CEPAL (1977) p. 193, supplemented from Banco Central, *Boletín*, January 1978, pp. 50–1.

(7) Corrections to eliminate underestimations in official statistics, from Foxley *et al.* (1976) p. 29, and J. Ramos (1975) pp. 113–14.

(8) and (9) Banco Central, *Boletín*, January 1978, p. 66.

anathemising all collectivism. Nearly all the literature on contemporary Chile engages in the polemics raised by this transformation: can it be justified, or who is to blame, or how can it be reversed?[1]

In this chapter a much more limited and modest theme is discussed. It begins by briefly considering why the Popular Unity (UP) government's strategy for handling inflation failed, well before the socialist government itself was overthrown. Most of the paper concentrates on the period since the military coup of September 1973, and discusses why the process of price stabilisation took so long and demanded such sacrifices. At the end some tentative assessment is made of the durability of the current phase of apparent economic 'normalcy'. The seven-year period has been divided into the following five phases:

(i)   *October 1970 – mid 1972*: Popular Unity's strategy
(ii) *Mid 1972 – September 1973*: Loss of control
(iii) *September 1973 – April 1975*: Dictatorship, but not stabilisation
(iv) *April 1975 – mid 1976*: Shock treatment
(v)   *Mid 1976 – end 1977*: Semi-stabilisation.

(i) OCTOBER 1970–MID-1972

Substantial rates of inflation having been endemic in Chile for many decades, the interpretative literature is correspondingly large.[2] Some of it is relatively complacent, regarding moderate inflation as the lesser of evils and stressing how well the Chilean economy had adapted. Although careful not to commit himself explicitly to this view, Hirschman, for example, suggested that sometimes 'through the device of inflation society gains precious time for resolving social tensions that otherwise might reach the breaking point straight away.'[3]

At the time of the 1970 presidential election, although the rate of inflation had risen to 36 per cent, none of the three competing candidates was disposed to proclaim counter-inflation as a top priority of his economic policy; on the contrary, all three promised to reactivate an economy which was operating below full capacity. Interestingly, it was Allende who devoted most space in his programme to the issue of inflation and who put forward the most specific proposals for coping with it. Probably the other two candidates were waiting to see the results of the electoral contest before deciding how far to tolerate increased inflation as the price for obtaining more 'precious time for resolving social tensions'. Tomic, the new Christian Democrat candidate, put the greatest stress on accelerating growth, but the outgoing President, Eduardo Frei, took a pessimistic line on the accumulated problems of economic management:

> The country is destined to tackle the inflation either by consensus, which is the democratic approach, or by coercion; but an inflationary process like that which Chile has been experiencing over recent decades will lead inevitably to a grave social and economic crisis. The problem is more than merely technical. From the technical point of view the procedures for containing inflation are well known . . . But what happens here is that the patient calls the doctor and then doesn't want to take the medicine. The problem is mainly political . . . Everyone wants the sacrifices to be made by others than themselves . . . Every year I presented laws which would have enabled us to control inflation, and every year they were rejected. Then the very people who had rejected these laws and fomented conflicts were the ones who said the government was to blame for inflation. It is a game with sinister overtones.[4]

Needless to say, between 1970 and 1973 Frei's party adopted exactly the strategy he criticised in his opponents, once the Christian Democrats had exchanged places with Popular Unity, vacating the executive branch but predominating in Congress.[5]

For about the first eighteen months of Allende's presidency the initiative rested largely with the Marxist coalition. We therefore need to understand the UP's approach to inflation control. The electoral programme of Popular Unity gives a frank and concise account of the economic strategy adopted during this period. It promised a rational and co-ordinated system of economic planning based on a greatly enlarged state sector. The priorities would be (i) to resolve the immediate economic problems of the masses; (ii) to guarantee adequately paid employment for every Chilean of working age; (iii) to liberate Chile from its subordination to foreign capital; (iv) to ensure rapid and decentralised economic growth; and (v) to promote and diversify exports while putting a stop to the 'scandalous' policy of currency devaluations. The sixth point, on inflation, read as follows:

(vi) To take all the measures required for monetary stability. The struggle against inflation depends essentially on the structural changes we propose. It must also include measures which adjust the means of payment to the real needs of the market, which control and redistribute the supply of credit, and which prevent usurious interest rates. Also measures which rationalise commerce and distribution, which stabilise prices, and which prevent a structure of demand slanted towards high income groups from stimulating inflation.

At the beginning of 1972 the Planning Office published its assessment of Chile's economic performance in the first year of the Allende government. As a result of highly expansionary government policies the GDP had risen 8·5 per cent (with total consumption up 13 per cent) and the rate of open unemployment in Greater Santiago had fallen from 8·3 per cent in December 1970 to 3·8 per cent in December 1971. The share of national income received by wage and salary earners had risen from 53·7 per cent in 1970 to 59 per cent in 1971, an increase of particularly impressive proportions considering the fast rate of economic growth. The average real wage rose by about 25 per cent in 1971 (see Table 3.7 below). Despite a correspondingly dramatic increase in consumer demand, measured retail price inflation was down from 33 per cent to 20 per cent (see Table 3.1). This was achieved mainly by means of price controls (backed by the threat of nationalisation), and the adoption of a multiple exchange rate system, under which many favoured categories of imports were supplied at fixed and artificially favourable exchange rates. Another factor was the reduction of interest rates: for example, bank interest charges were cut from 20 per cent to 15 per cent and various forms of selective credit were provided on even more generous terms. All this was made possible by a reckless expansion of the money supply: 'In 1971 the Central Bank rate of money creation [to the private and banking sectors] came to 173%. This was attributable to domestic credit, mainly supplied to the Treasury, municipalities and public enterprises.'[6] According to one informant, this 1971 expansion of the money supply was more than double the rate initially anticipated by the pro-government officials in the Central Bank. However, the UP's planners still publicly entertained the hope that their programme of transformation from a market-oriented towards a state-controlled economy could prevent this huge expansion of liquidity from generating a massive inflation:

> Without a change in the structural conditions that prevailed in the past, it is true that this increase in the money supply would have produced catastrophic effects; however, in the context of the changes described herein, the process is very different. Firstly, the weakening of monopoly power and the existence of idle capacity has meant that the productive apparatus responded to higher demand with increases in output rather than in prices. Second, increased state control of monetary and credit mechanisms, formerly dominated by monopolistic groups, has meant a reallocation of credit from speculative to productive purposes. Third, there has been a major change in methods of transacting business, with a drastic reduction in deferred payments, so that more note issue is required. Lastly, the decline in inflationary expectations has led to a greater preference for liquidity. All these factors have contributed to a sharp drop in the velocity of circulation of money, from the unusually high levels previously found in Chile.[7]

The authors of this consoling report must have been uneasily aware of its shortcomings. In fact the public's preference for cash rather than bank deposits reflected distrust of the latter rather than confidence in the former. Property-owners not only withdrew their funds from the banks but disposed of their real estate at bargain basement prices, because so many were raising cash as a preparation for personal and capital flight. Although the Central Bank pegged the exchange rate for merchandise transactions, it was reluctant to provide foreign exchange at subsidised rates to the government's departing opponents, so that within nine months the price of dollars for foreign travel or study abroad was raised to 2·5 times the basic rate, with even higher rates to come. However the officially quoted spread of exchange rates greatly understated the true position. Calculations published by the Central Bank in 1977 indicate that the official exchange rate was probably substantially overvalued before Allende took office. Cyclically high world copper prices in the late 1960s no doubt facilitated this, but when copper prices fell in 1971 and 1972 the overvaluation was not reduced. On the contrary the figures confirm that the degree of overvaluation of the official rate was substantially increased in 1971, and again in 1972, only to swing very fiercely in the opposite direction from 1973 to 1975.[8] One indicator of the degree of distortion is that by the beginning of 1972 the black market rate for dollars stood at 4 times the official tourist rate (and by 1973 this widened to a multiple of about ten-fold). In Allende's first year it was estimated that about 300,000 Argentinians visited Chile to dispose of the escudos purchased from Chileans who had gone into exile. Clearly, in this context the low velocity of circulation was a temporary phenomenon, for wealthy Chileans would only hoard cash until they were ready to leave, and those remaining behind as customers (poor Chileans and foreign tourists) would run down their escudo balances once the supply of consumer goods at artificially restrained prices was exhausted.

Viewed in this light the apparent successes of the first year were not sustainable, for they were achieved by exhausting the country's foreign exchange reserves (from $378 million in September 1970 to $32 million in December 1971) and running down industry's cyclically high level of inventories. Moderate defenders of the UP would say that Allende's avowed aim was to establish not a totally state-regulated economy, but a mixed economy with a substantial non-monopolistic market sector. Under the UP's nationalisation policies the mixed and private sectors were still expected to provide almost three-quarters of total enterprise production and over three-quarters of industrial employment.[9] But the apparently more modest alternative of co-existence between public and private sectors also proved impossible once the abundance of 1971 turned to acute shortages in 1972, especially since decision-makers on both sides were persuaded that the economic contest between the two sectors was an extension of the national political struggle, a struggle increasingly viewed as a holy war. It came as no surprise to monetarist-minded economists when the 173 per cent increase in the money supply of 1971 was followed a year later by a 163 per cent rise in the consumer price index, nor were more moderate critics of the government (such as those who wrote in *Panorama Económico*) caught unawares.[10] In the administration itself, however, the magnitude of the coming price explosion was not recognised until rather late and then the situation was explained largely in political terms – as the product of bourgeois opposition and structural problems in sectors where a revolutionary transformation of the production process was under way. According to this perspective either the executive was not responsible for the inflation or there was little it could do to counteract it, until the transition to socialism had been completed. In reality a clearer diagnosis of the factors aggravating the inflation would have enabled the government to scale down its impact somewhat, without necessarily betraying its other objectives. However, it was not realistic for administration economists to believe that the 1971 fall in the velocity of circulation of money could be sustained or that the socialised sector of production and distribution could be effectively insulated from turbulence in the market sector. But by the time this conclusion became inescapable, the executive branch of government had virtually lost control over the management of the economy.

In this context the issue of international harassment and economic sabotage must be briefly mentioned. Before Allende had even been confirmed in office, we know that President Nixon instructed CIA Director Helms (in a secret meeting attended by Kissinger and Mitchell) to 'make the economy scream'.[11] This instruction was given before Allende had taken a single step affecting either Chile's democratic institutions or the implementation of any sort of economic policy or the renegotiation of Chile's relationship with the USA. Since the aggression came first from the White House, any judgement of Allende's policies once in office must take into account the fact that his supreme priority had to be the mobilisation of political support at home as a defence against unsolicited international hostility. There remains a wide area of disagreement over how wisely the Popular Unity government handled its international economic policy and how much of its domestic difficulties were due to what Allende himself denounced as the 'invisible blockade'. Table 3.2 summarises the record on credit-provision of the US government agencies and of the Washington-based supposedly multilateral financial agencies. Beyond doubt, these agencies acted together and used the allocation of credit as a weapon to punish Chile for electing a Marxist government and then to reward her for resorting to an anti-Marxist dictatorship. Nevertheless it has been plausibly argued that the term 'invisible blockade' greatly exaggerates the extent to which Allende's economic policies were constrained by a politically motivated credit squeeze.[12] American economic harassment certainly harmed the economy, although it was to some extent offset by the expansion of trade and credit relations with other parts of the world, particularly the social democracies. Such harassment may have contributed to a *fuite en avance* by the UP's economic policy-makers, but it does not provide the major explanation of Chile's dramatically worsened experience with inflation. The principal causes of that must be sought in internal politics.

TABLE 3.2   Official lending to Chile from Washington agencies (US$m)

	1968–70	*1971–3*	*1974–6*
US government agencies *a*	236	44	433
World Bank/BID	136	30	304

Note: *a*AID, PL480, Eximbank, Commodity Credit Corp. and Housing Investment Guaranty.

Allende's coalition was both fragile and embattled. Unless it could achieve a rapid expansion of support, and thereafter maintain an impressive show of strength, it would be crushed by its enemies and riven by internal factionalism. Therefore the option of orthodox and prudent economic management did not exist for the UP's economists, in addition to which they disbelieved in it. From this perspective the 'responsible' course was to demonstrate to the Chilean people the benefits of a transformation of economic structure and thereby to build up strength (*cumular fuerzas*) for the inevitable conflict with the market-oriented opposition. So long as it faced implacable resistance from the majority in Congress, the UP was obliged to forgo some of the major traditional instruments of economic management, and make do with those levers directly controlled by the executive: the exchange rate, public sector pricing, wage setting, and the allocation of credit. On their own these instruments were insufficient to regulate the economy for more than a brief period. In due course they would have to be co-ordinated with the economic powers reserved to Congress, either by means of compromise or through a seizure of power. If the aim was to achieve an eventual compromise, as Allende and the Communist Party probably intended, then short-term popularity should not be bought at too high a price in long-range economic consequences. On the other hand, as Economy Minister Vuskovic and the left of the coalition constantly stressed, if the government was too cautious in mobilising mass support at any cost, it would be too weak either to defend the social conquests of the administration or to carry through any 'transition to socialism'. Given the objectives they had set themselves, the UP's broad economic strategy was a very risky and ultimately unsuccessful effort to deal with an extremely dangerous predicament. There were serious misjudgements and inconsistencies, no doubt, but the UP's dilemmas were real and deep, and the results of its policies are not proof of simple incompetence or disregard for consequences.

To sympathisers with their aims this argument may justify the government's broad economic strategy, whereas those who deplore the ends. will also disapprove of the means adopted. The main explanation for the inflation lies in the fact that Chilean society was deeply, and rather evenly, divided on this fundamental question of long-term aims. One cannot pretend that the Chilean left's understanding of economic reality was entirely adequate to the tasks of government. Nevertheless the fundamental cause of the inflation rested not with these incidental factors, but with the underlying political context. For those who persist in the judgement of irresponsibility, it should be recalled that for the same reasons that the Marxists were unwilling to be flexible about exchange rate and public sector pricing policies and to limit public sector expenditure, their opponents (who controlled the majority in Congress) were unwilling to provide legislation curbing the black market or raising tax revenue.[13] It was political necessity, as they perceived it, rather than ignorance of the economic consequences or simple irresponsibility that led even highly experienced Christian Democrats to take this course.

(ii) JUNE 1972 – SEPTEMBER 1973

July 1972 saw the departure of Vuskovic from the Ministry of Economics, a 90 per cent devaluation, and even bigger increases in the official prices of some subsidised necessities, including foodstuffs. Strains within the UP became more acute as Allende and the CP attempted to impose some restraint, while opposition hostility acquired a new virulence with the so-called bosses' strike which led, in September, to the inclusion of leading military men in the cabinet. The official distribution system attempted to meet basic consumption needs through a programme of rationing that was mainly used by UP supporters, whilst the opposition encouraged and extended a network of black market operations which passed unpunished by the judiciary and were indeed described as a civic duty by those determined to subvert the government's economic strategies. In retrospect, June 1972 may be taken as a turning point, after which the opposition offensive gained such strength that coherent economic management became impossible. But too much importance should not be attached to the month. In fact the underlying economic situation had already deteriorated to an extreme degree before the government attempted to respond. This section will deal in turn with the two basic (and related) disequilibria for which economic stabilisation policies are conventionally required: balance-of-payments adjustment and the public sector deficit.

On the external account we have already discussed the so-called 'invisible blockade': politically-motivated action to cut off some major official credit lines to Chile. By 1972 these conflicts had escalated further, for Allende had signed into law a copper nationalisation bill which naturally halted the outflow of profits to the American copper companies and, by means of an 'excess profits deduction' clause, virtually ruled out compensation payments for the takeover. The expropriated enterprises responded by legal harassment through the international courts, laying claim to shipments of Chilean copper. With less publicity a great many other foreign enterprises operating in Chile also took precautionary or harassing measures, with adverse effects on the balance of payments. Once the foreign exchange reserves were exhausted,[14] these developments increasingly damaged the level of domestic production. However, these deliberate acts of retaliation accounted for no more than a small proportion of the balance-of-payments deterioration in evidence by 1972–3, especially if offsetting factors are considered.[15]

Obviously Chile did not participate in the great expansion of euro-currency lending to Latin America referred to in the Introduction. But she was affected at least as much as neighbouring republics by the strong cyclical movements in the world economy described at the same time. To what extent was her deteriorating balance of payments under Allende a reflection of these international developments, and to what extent a product of internal

TABLE 3.3   Chile: Foreign trade sector 1970–7 (US$m)

	1970	1971	1972	1973	1974	1975	1976	1977
World price of copper (cents per lb.)	64·1	49·3	48·6	80·8	93·3	55·9	63·5	59·5
Chilean copper production (ooo tonnes)	692	708	717	735	902	828	1005	1056
Returned value of copper exports	840	702	658	1026	1654	890	1247	1187
Returned value of non-traditional exports	n.a.	91	66	71	202	365	471	613
Returned value all merchandise exports	1249	962	836	1248	2153	1552	2083	2190
Registered imports to the public sector	319	515	872	1161	1371	685	752	700
Registered imports to the private sector	629	651	537	521	1042	653	932	1560
All registered merchandise imports	948	1166	1410	1681	2413	1338	1684	2260
Of which Fuel imports	58	89	86	81	273	257	392	446
Balance on current account (goods and services)	−91	−209	−410	−300	−126	−588	+141	−511

Source: Banco Central, *Boletín*, February 1978, pp. 355, 371, 378.

policies? Table 3.3 shows that the free market dollar price of copper fell about 20 per cent between 1970 and 1971, reflecting the international recession, and remained at that low level for Allende's first two years. On the import side, international market prices for a weighted average of Chile's agricultural imports rose 41 per cent in 1972, reflecting poor world harvests. Thus, taking 1970 as 100, the terms of trade between copper exports and food imports fell to nearly 50 in 1972.[16] This way of presenting the figures highlights to the maximum the damage attributable to international market trends, which were certainly adverse. But the acute foreign payments difficulties of 1972–3 cannot be blamed too heavily on world market forces. A shift in the terms of trade was to be expected after 1970, and a cushion had been provided in the form of the foreign exchange reserves. Apart from the reserves, the standard policy response would have been to increase the incentives to export and the disincentives against imports. Chilean policy was, of course, the reverse. In particular, overvalued exchange rates exports caused many imports to be subsidised. More important than this effect, however, was the fact that the steep climb in real income levels gave rise to greatly increased domestic consumption, some of it export-diverting and much of it import-enhancing. This was particularly noticeable for foodstuffs, since income redistribution raised demand, whilst land reform affected supply. From 80 per cent self-sufficiency in agricultural products in 1965–70, Chile moved to only 74 per cent reliance on domestic supplies in 1971 and only 67 per cent in 1972.[17] World prices soared at precisely the moment when national policies had made Chile most vulnerable to them. The nature of the resulting balance-of-payments disequilibrium is summarised in Tables 3.3 and 3.4: the current account deficit rose from 1·3 per cent of GDP in 1970 to 3·2 per cent in 1972, although investment in imported machinery fell from 4·9 per cent to 2·6 per cent over the same period. The scarcity of essential imported inputs became a famine, with grave social effects.

No doubt there would have been a balance-of-payments problem in 1972 whichever party had been in office. However, it was the excessive demand created by the UP's domestic policies that made the external disequilibrium so acute, and that made the scarcity of imported inputs such a spur to hyper-inflation. In its last year the administration proved unwilling or unable to restrain the excess demand its earlier policies had created.[18] Despite

TABLE 3.4 Savings and investment (percentage of GDP)

	1970	1971	1972	1973	1974	1975	1976	1977
Savings								
(i) By central government	(−0.2)	−0.4	−4.8	−4.3	5.7			
(ii) By private sector	6.1	3.7	5.6	8.0	−3.9			
(iii) Depreciation	8.5	8.9	8.1	8.6	9.7			
(iv) Domestic savings (sum of above)	14.3	12.1	8.9	12.2	11.6			
(v) Current account deficit	1.3	2.0	3.2	2.8	2.6			
Investment								
(i) In imported machinery	4.9	4.1	2.6	4.5	4.8	n.a.		
(ii) Gross fixed capital formation	13.7	13.0	11.8	13.4	14.1	10.7	9.8	10.6

Sources: Calculated from Banco Central, *Boletín*, June 1977, p. 966; investment figures for 1975–7 calculated from Banco Central, *Boletín*, January 1978, p. 204 (provisional).

the fast growth experienced in 1971, the policy of cheap and abundant credit, wage rises and price controls meant that spending on consumption and inventories rose from 85·6 per cent to 88 per cent of GDP in that year (see Table 3.5). In 1972 the process was carried further, with the result that the pressure of consumption demand pushed the ratio to 91 per cent of GDP, and even in 1973 it remained at an abnormally high 89 per cent.[19] Thus virtually throughout the Allende government the basic cause of inflation was the continuing pressure of excessive aggregate demand, a pressure that could not be choked off by the usual market adjustment through accelerating inflation, because money incomes were allowed to accelerate in line with the price level.

TABLE 3.5   The pressure of consumption demand, 1970–5
(percentage of GDP)

	1970	1971	1972	1973	1974	1975
Private consumption	70·8	71·9	74·9	74·9	67·5	68·6
Inventories	1·9	1·1	0·3	1·6	3·1	
Total consumption and inventories	85·6	88·0	91·0	88·9	86·8	85·0

Sources: Calculated from Banco Central, *Boletín*, June 1977, and supplemented by CEPAL (1977) p. 168.

The politics of wage and price determination in 1972 and 1973 is a complex subject which would bring us back to the vexed issue of how to apportion responsibility for the economic débâcle (Table 3.7 below gives data on the real incomes of that proportion of the population living from wages and salaries). There are genuine grounds for arguing that the UP and the CUT (Central Unica de Trabajadores) attempted to exercise a certain degree of wage restraint while they still had the initiative, but that by the approach of the April/May 1972 trade union elections, Christian Democrat and far-left attempts to outbid the administration on the wages front undermined an otherwise defensible incomes policy.[20] After the middle of 1972, with price controls crumbling, the exchange rate slipping out of control and the opposition stepping up the virulence of its attacks, no realistic incomes policy remained politically feasible. Competition between parties within the UP added to the wage pressure, with the Secretary-General of MAPU, for example, announcing on 25 August 1972 that, although state pensions and the minimum wage were being raised from 1 October by 100 per cent and all workers were to receive a massive across-the-board increase to compensate for inflation, this was not good enough for his party. There should also be a flat rate monthly bonus for all workers, almost double the level proposed by the government.

> We are fully aware that to confer this benefit, as we propose, will involve a great strain on the national Treasury. But we believe it is necessary, and that the increased deficit caused by this indispensable increase will have to be covered by a compulsory contribution levied in taxation on the higher income groups.[21]

In practice uncontrollable pay rises, fomented by the political parties who were competing for the allegiance of wage and salary earners and financed by Central Bank note issue (domestic credit supply rose 82 per cent during 1971, 156 per cent during 1972, and 461 per cent during 1973), were now matched by uncontrollable price rises, encouraged by the political representatives of the small employers and the self-employed. In the absence of any other form of restraint on the nominal level of incomes, only an accelerating rise in the price level could restore the inevitable identity between total demand and total supply in real terms.

When real incomes and consumption rise so much faster than *per capita* GDP the remaining sectors of the economy must contract, and by 1973, with *per capita* GDP slipping back to 1970 levels, the conflict over resources was bound to become much more intense. Tables 3.4 and 3.5 show how the squeeze was distributed. In addition to the drastic rundown of inventories, fixed investment also shrank to only a slender margin over depreciation. Between 1970 and 1972 the entire fall in investment was accounted for by the fall in machinery imports. Domestic savings fell much more sharply than investment, however, and within the savings account the deficit was concentrated entirely on the government sector. In fact private sector savings appear to have actually *risen*, despite the accelerating inflation. This was not due to enterprise savings, which were initially squeezed by price controls. The admittedly unreliable figures suggest that personal savings rose dramatically as a consequence of the high levels of real personal incomes and the growing unavailability of consumption goods. Of necessity, therefore, the residual sectors bearing the deficit corresponding to the excess of income over domestic output were the balance of payments and the public sector. The current account deficit rose to 3 per cent of GDP, financed by external public borrowing. Public enterprises lagged even further behind the rest of the economy in the price adjustments they could make to keep up with inflation. From a situation of near balance in 1970 the central government was dis-saving more than 4 per cent of GDP during the Allende years (Table 3.4), while its expenditures rose above 30 per cent of GDP. Income from copper virtually ceased, while subsidies to the public enterprise sector grew very large (Table 3.6).

Research by R. Zahler, in Foxley *et al.* (1976), disaggregates the public sector accounts, revealing that the largest deficits were incurred by those enterprises already incorporated into the public sector before 1970, and that it was the increase of current expenditure, unmatched by sales revenue, that was mainly responsible. For the social property sector (APS) as a whole, expenditure exceeded income by 32·8 per cent in 1972, and by about 44 per cent in 1973. Foxley *et al.* estimate that APS borrowing from the government rose from 13 per cent of the total money supply in December 1970 to 60 per cent in March 1973: 'During 1973 about 90% of the increase in the money supply went to finance the public sector deficit, a flow of funds mainly directed to the nationalised industries.'[22] The harsh economic reality of September 1973 was that unless some form of strong government action was taken very quickly to close this financial deficit (it is possible to imagine various methods, some leading to a recovery of the private sector, others not), total monetary collapse would ensue.

In conclusion, therefore, the root cause of the inflation, and of the acuteness of the balance-of-payments crisis, was the excessive pressure of aggregate demand that was maintained throughout the UP's period of government. The initial cause of this was the UP's conscious decision to reactivate the economy by sharply raising the wage level while curbing price rises. Initially output responded well to the increases in demand (Table 3.7 below gives the index of industrial production) but by 1972 inflation and the tense political climate were creating acute bottlenecks. When the limits of reactivation had been surpassed and the international

TABLE 3.6 Chile: Consolidated government finances 1970–7 (percentage of GDP)

	1970	1971	1972	1973	1974	1975	1976	1977
Government revenue								
From copper	5·0	0·7	0·4	0·3	2·3	2·2	4·1	3·5
From direct taxes	4·8	5·8	4·2	5·0	5·5	6·5	5·4	5·5
From indirect taxes	10·8	11·5	11·0	10·3	11·1	13·4	14·4	15·7
All revenue	24·2	20·2	17·9	19·2	21·3	23·2	24·5	25·3
Government expenditure								
Transfers to public enterprises	—	—	—	(1·5)	7·1	4·4	—	—
Debt service	3·6	3·3	1·1	1·4	4·4	5·1	6·5	5·0
Capital expenditure	—	—	—	—	11·8	8·1	—	—
All expenditure	27·0	31·0	30·7	42·7	31·7	26·2	27·2	27·9
Government deficit								
As % of expenditure	10·3	34·7	41·9	55·1	32·6	11·6	10·0	9·4
Deficit % of GDP	2·8	10·8	12·9	23·6	10·3	3·1	2·7	2·6

Source: Banco Central, *Boletín*, January 1978, pp. 64–5; CEPAL (1977), pp. 199–202.

economic environment had turned adverse, real output began to fall. At this point, however, the UP was unwilling or unable to restrain the pressure for nominal wage increases sufficient to keep ahead of the rise in the price level. The private sector and opposition politicians also took advantage of the weakening of the government's authority to step up the pressure of demands to maintain the real personal income levels of their clientèle, regardless of inflation. Only the public sector was unable to keep pace with the adjustments achieved elsewhere, and its losses (essentially those of the APS) were financed by the Central Bank allowing the money supply to rise 1790 per cent between December 1970 and August 1973. In consequence, public willingness to hold national currency was reduced to a nadir, and the allocation of resources through market mechanisms was replaced by a much more naked form of distributional struggle.

(iii) SEPTEMBER 1973–APRIL 1975

Before 11 September 1973 the pressures for consumption were irresistible, neither state officials nor others in authority possessing the power to retain or divert resources into accumulation. From the moment of the coup all this changed radically: the labour force was disorganised and deprived of all direct influence over economic decision-making. Power shifted to the apex of bureaucracies, both public and private. Public policy was put at the service of private accumulation; collective consumption needs were relegated to the lowest of priorities. By the eve of the coup the government was virtually unable to control spending, raise taxes, contract foreign loans, punish economic crimes and subversive strikes, or sack a single public employee. After 11 September all formal obstacles to the exercise of executive authority were erased. Congress remained closed, the courts became unconditional servants of the dictatorship, the doors to international financial assistance were thrown open, and job security was effectively withdrawn from all public sector employees.[23] The new principles of economic policy were the antithesis of the old.[24] State interventionism and collectivism now became regarded as the evils that had sapped the strength of the Chilean nation. Henceforth *laissez-faire* and individualism were to be at the core of official ideology, according to which self-reliant individuals proving themselves in a competitive market would soon unleash the creative energies necessary for national reconstruction. The political oppression and social injustice which has accompanied the implantation of this regime have been widely discussed (in particular, a posthumous article by Letelier (1976) reached a large audience). Less attention has been paid to the aspect most relevant to this chapter: the remarkable fact that despite the new power structure and ideology, and the ruthlessly deflationary policies pursued since early 1975, progress in curbing the rate of price inflation has been very long delayed. In January 1974 official spokesmen were predicting that prices would rise by 80 per cent that year, if there was expansion, or as little as 50 per cent if there was recession.[25] In fact Table 3.1 above shows that inflation was even higher in 1974 than in 1973, and did not fall back to below 100 per cent until 1977.

Both theory and the experience of similarly placed governments in other countries suggest that a sudden and complete cessation of inflation might have been accomplished by the new regime had it so chosen. After all, this was a government strong enough to grant wage increases or not as it chose, and to dismiss personnel at will. It also benefited from sharply rising production of both copper and of food, coupled with an unprecedented upsurge of export prices. The circumstances were in many ways less favourable in Bolivia in December 1956, when a sudden return to free convertibility with the dollar at an undervalued fixed parity turned a 365 per cent inflation rate (January/December 1956) into a 15 per cent fall in consumer prices the following year, after which parity with the US currency and price stability were maintained for fourteen years.[26] It must be admitted that this Bolivian stabilisation programme had contained some severe costs. Employment in import-consuming industries and the public sector had been drastically contracted, the state had abruptly relinquished many of its developmental functions, the political influence and economic power of the trade unions had been sharply curtailed, and a period of several years of recession had ensued before a new more private sector-oriented type of expansion could get under way. The Bolivian government had found these costs of stabilisation painful to accept, but at least the benefits of exchange rate parity and relative price stability had been genuinely and promptly achieved. Many of the consequences of stabilisation reluctantly accepted by Bolivia's civilian-led and popular-based regime were positively desired by the government that seized power in Chile in 1973. Of those features listed above, the sole one unwelcome to the junta was the prospect of several years of recession. However, whereas the price of tin (Bolivia's staple export) collapsed in 1957, the price of copper soared to record heights in the first year after the Chilean coup, making it possible for the recessive effects of drastic stabilisation to be mitigated.

In practice, of course, the junta did not attempt a Bolivian-style stabilisation. Probably the possibility was not seriously examined and, if it had been, the difficulties might well have appeared insurmountable. It was common in the 1950s for inflation-wracked countries to return to free convertibility at the dollar parity (Mexico did so in 1954, Bolivia in 1956, and as a general principle this was a favoured IMF prescription). But even when the idea was most fashionable, it was not taken up by Chilean policy-makers: the Klein-Saks stabilisation programme of November 1955 had opted instead for a unified but flexible exchange rate (precisely the system adopted by Pinochet in 1974). By 1973 the dollar exchange system had lost much of its international appeal, and the idea of pegging one's currency to the dollar would have looked particularly odd in the autumn of 1973, just when the world economy was shocked by OPEC's decision to quadruple oil prices. At this time, paradoxically, Chilean policy-makers would probably have rejected a sudden return to a fixed parity, by arguing that gradualism would be less disruptive. If the official figures given in Table 3.6 are correct and the public sector deficit had risen by 1973 to 23·6 per cent of GDP, then a sudden return to budget balance (the essential condition for exchange rate stability imposed under the Bolivian stabilisation) would have required an even more sudden contraction of the Chilean government's economic role than was in fact accomplished in 1974. However, the Chilean dictatorship would probably have been swayed by another, more basic, objection. The net foreign exchange reserves of the Chilean banking system were in deficit to the tune of $231 million at the end of 1973. To repeat the Bolivian stabilisation strategy would have required free reserves equivalent to not much less than $500 million.[27] It seems likely that Chile could have halted the inflation in its tracks only if external resources to the tune of at least $1 billion had been loaned for a stabilisation fund. Perhaps more would have been needed to cover, say, a year of government deficits before adjustment was complete (USAID contributed about 40 per cent of the Bolivian government's revenues at the time of the 1956 stabilisation). Whether or not the Chilean junta could have obtained such support in return for a Bolivian-style stabilisation package will remain conjectural. There is, however, a fundamental political reason why it would have been reluctant to try: the sovereignty of the Chilean state would have been placed in pawn to foreign powers, as indeed occurred in the Bolivian case.

The political dynamics of this period are not easy to reconstruct, but they are essential for explaining the economic policies actually adopted. Although a minority of Christian Democrats had stood out against the dictatorship, the majority endorsed it, and influential figures apparently harboured the illusion that they might outmanoeuvre the more reactionary elements of the victorious coalition. At least initially the overthrow of Allende had considerable lower-middle-class, and even lower-class, support and small property-owners and the self-employed certainly played a more prominent and a more valiant role in resisting socialism than the large landowners, bankers and industrialists who were destined to reap the main benefits of the conservative dictatorship. Certain themes were therefore stressed in the initial phase of consolidation of the regime that were to seem incongruous at a later date. Initially, for example, it was emphasised that the poor had been involuntarily misled by Marxist demagogy and had already paid a very high economic price for their mistakes. The government should therefore guarantee them a minimum income level and make the eradication of extreme poverty one of its priority goals. These statements are probably best understood as a reflection of a mainly Christian Democrat aspiration to win over the mass base that had formally belonged to the UP, and to use it as a counterbalance to the *revanchiste* inclinations of their more right-wing allies. Such aspirations soon proved illusory, of course, as the repressive methods used with reluctant Christian Democrat approval against Marxist-led organisations were duly extended to all varieties of trade unionists and to all forms of popular and democratic organisation. In due course even bankers and bishops too closely associated with the democratic past felt the force of the new dictatorship. But for almost a year this reality was masked for some by the generous redistribution of opportunities and by the appearance of national regeneration and economic recovery. The economic interests that were to emerge as predominant in the new regime needed time to reconstruct themselves and to ensure their grip on all the levers of power. In the meantime it was not politically expedient to impose too much austerity on the subordinate groups in the governing alliance. Nor did it seem very necessary to do so from the economic point of view, whilst major lines of output were recovering (see Table 3.7 and the copper production figures in Table 3.3) and a 70 per cent rise in export revenue permitted a doubling of imports by the private sector without as yet calling for a reduction in public sector imports (Table 3.3). One other condition was vital for the consolidation of a reactionary dictatorship – the Chilean state must not fall into a relationship of dependence on official aid-givers, for that might jeopardise the eventual scope for internal repression.[28] The Chilean junta has therefore been prepared to shoulder a very heavy burden of official debt servicing (see Table 3.8) in order to preserve its freedom from dependence on foreign aid. Private capital has been eagerly wooed, of course, but the higher economic cost of such resources is offset, in the eyes of the government and its backers, by the absence of political conditions.

Hence, what Chile in fact experienced during 1974 was a very determined consolidation of the dictatorship, combined with a relatively patchy and uncertain approach to the task of economic stabilisation. A remarkable windfall on international account was put to poor use (an October 1974 World Bank report, for example, observed that high copper prices had created an atmosphere contrary to planning or the rational control of expenditure), and on the internal front the rewarding of supporters and punishing of opponents (for which sovereignty was so indispensable) took precedence over soundly based economic recovery. Control of wages and the reduction of public sector employment were the twin instruments used with great vigour to tackle inflation – instruments which had the merit of hurting mainly the interests of those social groups displaced from power. As far as the beneficiaries of the coup were concerned, this was not a time of hardship. For example, in April 1974 import controls were abolished on about 2400 different products; and in May Chilean tourism to Europe and the USA was stimulated by an authorisation to purchase foreign exchange to a maximum of $40 per day. In August the government agreed to pay $253 million on compen-

TABLE 3.7   Indices of volume of production and real wages[a] (1969 = 100)

	1970	1971	1972	1973	1974	1975	1976	1977
Volume of industrial production (1969 = 100)								
(a) Consumer durables	115·6	141·2	128·3	111·2	123·9	88·1	75·9	82·5
(b) Non-durables	104·5	117·8	116·6	110·0	104·3	84·6	96·2	101·6
(c) Intermediate inputs for industry	100·6	111·1	115·5	113·8	132·9	113·1	130·5	139·0
All industrial production	103·5	114·7	117·6	109·9	111·1	85·0	95·4	104·2
Real wages (end 1969 = 100)								
(a) Mining	120·5	131·0	120·0	61·1	73·5	74·0	96·7	n.a.
(b) Manufacturing	104·3	138·8	131·1	115·5	93·8	89·9	108·8	n.a.
(c) *Instituciones fiscales*	94·8	110·3	102·7	106·6	106·6	95·3	113·5	n.a.
(d) *Obreros*	108·2	136·0	130·7	98·8	84·2	81·3	98·5	n.a.
(e) *Empleados*	104·3	127·8	113·5	87·1	89·5	81·9	96·6	n.a.
Average real wage	106·2	132·6	121·8	92·7	86·9	81·5	97·5	n.a.
GDP	103·6	111·6	111·5	107·5	111·8	97·1	101·0	109 (est.)
GDP *per capita*	101·6	107·5	105·4	99·9	102·0	87·0	88·7	94 (est.)

Sources: Banco Central, *Boletín*, February 1978, p. 396, for SOFOFA's industrial production index and for monthly indices of wages and salaries. I have calculated real wages using January/January wage indices divided by December/December consumer price indices, corrected as in column 7 of Table 3.1. GDP from Banco Central, *Boletín*, December 1976.

Note: [a] However, estimates of real wages are highly controversial and subject to a great margin of uncertainty because of the problems of correcting for inflation. Ramos, op. cit., p. 101, estimated the average real wage also using 1969 = 100. His method produced a substantially lower figure for average real wages in 1973–5. Yet Rufatt and Lagos (1975) estimated much bigger falls in real wages than those reported by Ramos. Ramos (1977) criticised them for politically motivated exaggeration. The figures in Table 3.7 are therefore offered very tentatively, their main merit being to provide a consistent and disaggregated series. The last row, showing real per capita GDP, is also subject to debate. An alternative series, showing GDP about 4 per cent lower than in Table 3.7 every year since 1972, can be extracted from the Banco Central, *Boletín*, February 1978, p. 60.

sation to Anaconda for the supposedly unjust terms of the 1971 copper nationalisation.[29] The armed forces, naturally enough, also received their rewards. Military expenditure rose from $222 million in 1973 (itself a record) to $433 million in 1974, or from 3·1 per cent to 5·3 per cent of GNP, and military employment rose from 75,000 persons in 1973 to 90,000 in 1974, and 110,000 in 1975.[30] These figures are hard to reconcile with the image of an austere regime solely dedicated to the restoration of economic equilibrium, a profitable environment for private enterprise and a minimal role for the state. Then, just as abruptly as it had shot up, the price of copper collapsed, and the junta was forced to impose deflation on a massive scale. By the time the policy of 'shock treatment' was announced, in April 1975, the junta had made poor use of its initial opportunities to re-establish economic equilibrium. As a result, inflation was no lower in 1975 than it had been in 1973, but the government's reputation in the world was far worse, and all prospects of negotiated international adjustment assistance had been wasted. The burden of 'shock treatment' was therefore imposed entirely on the Chilean people.

Certain aspects of economic developments in 1974 require further comment, namely the external sector and the policy on wages. Table 3.3 above shows that dollar export revenues virtually tripled between 1972 and 1974. However imports rose by 75 per cent and less than one-quarter of the increase was occasioned by the rise in oil prices. The current account therefore remained in substantial deficit (2·6 per cent of GDP, compared with 3·2 per cent in 1972). In March 1974 the Paris Club group of creditors agreed without much fuss to roll over 95 per cent of the repayments outstanding for 1974 and 1975, so that the debt service ratio, which had fallen from 31 per cent of exports in 1970 to 13 per cent in 1972, remained at only 13 per cent in 1974 (Table 3.8). However the external debt rose by one-quarter during that year. One reason for the rise in imports can be deduced from Table 3.5: inventory accumulation rose from 0·3 per cent of GDP in 1972 to 3·1 per cent in 1974, and Table 3.5 above shows that gross fixed capital formation and depreciation also rose. The decapitalisation of the economy was being tentatively reversed. Of greater significance is the trend in private consumption and savings revealed in the same two tables. Private consumption fell from 75 per cent to 67·5 per cent of GDP and it was only possible to maintain even *this* level because of a most dramatic turn-around in the savings account. Private sector savings swung from a surplus of 8 per cent to a deficit of almost 4 per cent of GDP.

TABLE 3.8   Debt servicing of Chile (US$m)

	1970	1971	1972	1973	1974	1975	1976	1977
Exports of goods and services	1255	1133	978	1429	2382	1727	2340	2539 (est.)
Interest payments	123	101	36	52	119	223	320	338
Amortisation	264	293	92	70	186	380	681	880
All debt servicing as % of exports	30·8	34·8	13·1	8·5	12·8	34·9	42·8	48·0

Source: Banco Central, *Boletín*, October 1977, p. 1632.

The source of this abrupt disappearance of excess consumption demand can be traced directly to the fall in real wages shown in Table 3.7. Comparing the indices on average real wages and average GDP per head, the former rose far out of line with the latter in 1971 and 1972. During 1973, however, real wages fell 24 per cent on 1972 and a further 6 per cent during 1974. It can also be seen that real wages in mining fell most dramatically during 1973 (virtually halving) while in manufacturing employment the fall was more gradual, and those who managed to retain their posts in *instituciones fiscales* belatedly achieved a small rise in average earnings in 1973 – a rise that was maintained in 1974. The means by which these falls in average wages were achieved was simple: a readjustment of wages scheduled for 1 October 1973 was postponed for three months, during which prices were freed from controls. On 1 January 1974 the government resumed the policy of periodic wage adjustments to compensate for inflation, but without allowing full adjustment for the price rises of the last quarter of 1973, which had not been fully captured by the official price index.[31]

Why did inflation continue at such a virulent rate throughout 1974, despite the drastic fall in real wages and consumption demand? Joseph Ramos has offered the following interpretation:

The fall in real wages made little contribution to the mitigation of inflation, but it has been the principal cause of the recession of 1974, and, together with the fall in the price of copper, explains the industrial collapse of 1975. In my opinion the fundamental error of the stabilisation policy dates from the last quarter of 1973, when prices were freed, and shot up far above the levels anticipated by the government, and implicitly taken into account by the wage readjustment of 1 January 1974. Moreover prices rose faster than cost pressures . . . It was the inflationary expectations of industrialists and traders that has undermined the stabilisation programme since the end of 1973. This was not necessarily due to abuse of power, but rather that in the absence of points of reference or guidelines, producers and traders fixed their prices at levels that would equilibrate supply and demand, not immediately but in three months' time, when they would have to buy their inputs for the next cycle of purchase and sales.

This interpretation puts a great deal of emphasis on the existence of very high inflationary expectations, and the exacerbation of this factor by the government's doctrinaire insistence on the abolition of all price controls, just at the point when realistic and flexible guidelines would have been most useful in enabling a stable set of price expectations to coalesce. It may provide some useful insights about the state of price-setters' opinions, especially during the first year after the fall of Allende, when many of the major parameters of the economic and social situation remained somewhat undefined and the market sector of the economy was still traumatised by its recent experiences of wildly distorted and unstable relative prices. During that period of stockbuilding and re-equipping it is more than likely that many entrepreneurs felt it safer temporarily to accumulate inventories rather than to trade. But in due course, if credit is being restrained and real wages are depressed, such entrepreneurs will face cash-flow constraints on their over-pricing. On its own, the explanation of 'inflationary expectations' can only account for a temporary price surge, which should be followed by intensified competition and price cutting. However in the Chilean case we have to explain a period of continuing 'overshoot' of retail prices, beyond the level that the market will bear, lasting for three or even four years. The highly concentrated structure of Chilean industry would not on its own prevent price competition for so long. Table 3.1 above highlights some of the cost-push pressures that were also powerfully at work. The official exchange rate depreciated almost eight-fold during the course of 1974, after a 5·3-fold devaluation in 1973. The prices of imported wholesale goods rose even faster, by no less than 13·5-fold in a single year, reflecting in particular the four-fold rise in the dollar price of oil. Thus in 1974 the costs of such essential inputs rose much faster than the final prices charged by Chilean producers for their goods, and other costs also rose exceptionally fast. Public sector enterprises, faced with a sudden drastic cutback in the subsidies they were receiving from the state, pushed up their prices as far as their often captive markets could bear, and the government's tax collection (in particular the burden of indirect taxation) also rose steeply in real terms (see Table 3.6 above). As domestic credit expansion was curbed,[32] M_1 in the hands of the private sector fell abruptly from 10 per cent to 5 per cent of GNP in a single year (Table 3.1) and real interest rates became severely positive after a long period of cheap credit. All told, it is not difficult to understand why retail prices rose five-fold in 1974, nor why, even so, the private sector was still so inflation-prone when deep repression struck the following year.

(iv) APRIL 1975 – JUNE 1976

The true extent of Chile's external economic vulnerability suddenly became clear in late 1974. Table 3.3 shows the violent impact of the world recession on copper export earnings – almost halved in value in 1975 as a consequence of the price fall and lower output. It is true that non-traditional exports, spurred by devaluation and strenuous government promotional policies, continued their secular growth through the recession, but this was far from sufficient to offset the copper cycle. Under severe IMF pressure a very fierce austerity programme was therefore introduced.[33] It halved the value of public sector imports in a single year, and also cut back heavily on private sector imports, although in the longer term the latter were to recover, unlike the former.

The political significance of this shift in economic policy was that it ended the ambiguities of the broad anti-Marxist front period. Public sector employees, Christian Democrats, and the petty-bourgeosie were no longer to be conciliated for their past services. A re-established economic and social élite was now secure enough to push ahead with its long-term objectives and to disregard the internal social consequences. Far from seeking to appease their internationl critics and thereby to gain access to official aid sources that might have political and human rights conditions attached, they chose to tailor their policies to the requirements of the world's private capital markets, which would enable the dictatorship to preserve national autonomy, albeit at the cost of deepening the domestic recession still further (see Table 3.8).

As a symbol of the new mood, in April 1975 Jorge Cauas replaced Fernando Leniz as Minister of Economics. Table 3.6 above shows the main consequences of the 'shock treatment' then applied. In 1975 GDP fell almost 15 per cent compared with 1974. Even so the government raised its revenue, as a share of the reduced total, from 21·3 per cent to 23·1 per cent. Changes in the tax system and intensification of anti-evasion measures pushed up the take both from direct and from indirect taxation, and government income from copper was maintained despite the price collapse. However, most of the effects were felt on the expenditure account: with subsidies to public enterprises cut by one-third, and capital spending down from 11·8 per cent to 8·1 per cent of GDP. By the second half of 1975 government transfers to CORFO were only one-quarter of the level a year earlier; and the Ministries of Housing and Public Works were spending at only 30 per cent of their previous year's levels.[34] With both the foreign sector and the government sector producing strongly contractionary effects on the economy, there were no mitigating effects from the side of consumption. Indeed its share of GDP actually fell further in 1975. A change in the system of wage adjustment adopted in September 1975 was designed to cut real wages further – with results that can be seen in Table 3.7. However, it was not the employed population that made the heaviest sacrifices in this phase of the stabilisation policy: rather it was the unemployed, who rose from 9·7 per cent of the labour force in December 1974 to 18·7 per cent in December 1975.

As Rosemary Thorp argues in her chapter on Peru, the economic structure of such countries is so lacking in flexibility that it takes a very large reduction in the level of activity, with long-term damage to both the human and the physical capital endowments, to secure a significant degree of short-term adjustment. In the Chilean case two types of adjustment were superimposed on each other, and forced through with brutal determination. One adjustment was to squeeze out the internal inflationary forces inherited from 1973 and exacerbated in 1974; the other was to restore an external equilibrium undermined by the world recession of 1975. The only remedy left for either maladjustment was severe demand restraint, made doubly severe when both problems were tackled at once. Nevertheless, by the end of 1975 the planners congratulated themselves that all this sacrifice had reduced that year's balance-of-payments deficit (initially feared to reach $600 million) to only $270 million. By a strange coincidence, this saving just about equals the amount the same government had cheerfully awarded to Anaconda and ITT a year before.[35]

1975 was the third year in succession in which currency devaluation proceeded at a much faster rate than internal price inflation, while money supply was fiercely reined back (see Table 3.1). With domestic demand so severely contracted, the exchange rate now heavily undervalued (the peso was one-third cheaper in comparative purchasing power terms in January 1976 than in July 1974), domestic credit only available on the most stringent terms, and fiscal pressure heavier than ever, cost-push pressures remained severe, and inflationary expectations were unabated. The public sector no longer generated increases in the money supply; these were very largely attributable to foreign exchange transactions. The scale of the resulting recession is indicated by the fact that both import supply and investment fell by about 30 per cent. These depressive effects in turn meant idle capacity and increased unit costs of production, which added to the internal inflationary pressures and reduced the rate of private sector savings. Therefore, after a year of 'shock treatment', not only was the economy prostrate but the rate of inflation was still running at over 200 per cent.

(v) JUNE 1976–DECEMBER 1977

There are some economies in which, once this stage of depression had been reached, the mechanisms of recovery would be powerful, spontaneous and quick-acting. Chile has not been such a case. Over the past six years the rate of aggregate investment has been barely sufficient to maintain the 1970 level of capital stock – a situation which has worsened considerably since 1975 (Table 3.4) – and almost as much productive employment has been destroyed as has been created. Since the labour force has continued to grow at a substantial pace, the underlying prospects for employment remain grim (Table 3.9). Furthermore, many new entrants into the labour force are the product of a severely diminished educational system, while a substantial proportion of Chile's expensive human capital has been lost: for example, the Association of Engineers found in 1976 that at least 25·7 per cent of Chile's professional engineers were living abroad. Whereas, during the 1960s, about 5 per cent of Chile's medical personnel emigrated each year, during the mid-1970s the rate had risen to 12·5 per cent. The costs of the 'shock treatment' in terms of decapitalisation are therefore as substantial as the more publicised and immediate 'social' effects. As for the short-term cyclical forces making for an upturn, at the close of our period (1977), these had still not acted powerfully enough to produce a full recovery. Warning signs of the deficiencies of the recent improvement include the astronomical real cost of domestic credit, and the continuing vulnerability of the balance of payments. For these reasons I have adopted the label 'semi-stabilisation'.

It is true that in 1977 the rate of inflation was finally brought back into two digits, that the squeeze on credit at last began to ease, and that real wages and consumer demand were finally allowed to rise again, producing a higher level of capacity utilisation and a significant decline in unemployment. Nevertheless the character of this reactivation was quite unusual. The 'shock treatment' had, of course, driven most productive enterprises to the limits of solvency. In 1975–6 not only did they freeze their investment plans and postpone provision for depreciation, but in many cases they also ran down their working capital and went deeply into debt to the recently denationalised domestic banks. Neither domestic capitalists nor foreign-owned enterprise earned easy profits in the first three years after the fall of Allende.[36] In a normal recovery, as domestic demand recovered, these enterprises would once again begin generating profits which they could use first to replenish working capital, then to reduce their indebtedness, and eventually to finance investment.[37] However, in the recent Chilean recovery this has hardly been possible, at least for enterprises dependent on the home market. There was also a

TABLE 3.9 Employment and unemployment in Chile, 1970–7 (000s)

	1970	1971	1972	1973	1974	1975	1976	1977
Greater Santiago (December figures)								
Unemployed	86·8	40·9	39·3	58·9	119·2	239·0	179·2	180·9
Unemployment rate	8·3%	3·8%	3·6%	5·6%	9·7%	18·7%	13·6%	13·2%
Employed in manufacturing	254·7	295·2	290·8	250·5	262·2	225·7	254·2	
Employed in construction	45·4	62·9	45·5	63·1	64·8	42·2	42·2	
Employed in commerce	160·5	154·6	163·2	169·0	184·1	159·8	210·6	
Employed population	1051·6	1079·1	1101·3	1043·0	1105·3	1103·7	1195·8	
National (annual figures)								
Unemployed	180	115	96	152	298	482	466	368 (est.)
Unemployment rate	6·1%	3·8%	3·1%	4·8%	9·2%	14·5%	13·7%	10·5% (est.)
Employed population	2770	2906	2998	3016	2945	2840	2939	3123 (est.)
Labour force	2950	3021	3094	3168	3244	3321	3405	3490

Source: Banco Central, *Boletín*, January 1978, p. 44.

tremendous scarcity of domestic credit. Emerging from a period of
unprecedented recession *and* unprecedented inflation, it was almost impossible for voluntary savings to be internally generated,
and even harder to persuade those who did hold financial reserves
to channel them to Chile's overstretched domestic enterprises.
The reactivation of 1977 meant an increase in enterprise demand
for credits, but little diminution in the reluctance of savers to lend
to enterprises. Even at the end of our period most capital-market
transactions remained extremely short-term, with domestic de-
positors only willing to commit their funds for up to ninety days at
a time and gross spreads charged by intermediaries remained
very large (2 per cent a month). In the view of McKinnon (1978),

> Because depositors are in fact earning a positive real return, it
> appears that at least part of the inflation tax is being levied on
> borrowers through the very high real rates of interest they must
> pay: perhaps still as high as 35−40% real per year. Certain
> kinds of working capital, which is very important at the margin,
> can be financed at such rates. But entirely new projects would
> seem virtually prohibited [p. 15].

A small group of highly monopolistic financial groups have
therefore become the sole domestic source of finance available to
much of the Chilean private sector. By the end of 1977, despite the
reactivation, most of Chile's productive enterprises remained
very heavily indebted, with little success as yet in generating their
own resources for recuperation and renewal. Of course it is true
that a sustained recovery in demand and further falls in the rate of
inflation would eventually restore profitability and growth to the
private enterprise sector. There are some signs that this may be
occurring in 1978 (although real interest rates remain extremely
high, reflecting the social scarcity of domestic savings), but in the
period under review the recovery was still largely awaited, hence
the label 'semi-stabilisation'. In 1976 and 1977 the major banking
conglomerates came to exercise an unprecedented degree of
monopoly power and appeared to profit at the expense of the rest
of the economy. But it is far from certain that these apparent
banking profits were what they seemed to be (many enterprises
within the conglomerates are kept from bankruptcy only by
inter-conglomerate transfers), or could have been made available
to finance productive investment.

In principle, when domestic savings are so scarce and expensive, orthodox economists would expect private foreign savings, attracted by the high interest rates, to flow in and accelerate the recovery. Indeed there were important short-term capital inflows during the first year of 'semi-stabilisation', perhaps attracted by the interest differential or perhaps by the prospect of a reversal of the peso's initial severe undervaluation.[38] However, the Chilean political and economic environment has probably only attracted very costly short-term speculative inflows rather than reliable and lasting transfers of foreign savings.[39] Both McKinnon (1978) and ffrench-Davis (1978) express concern that the large private capital inflows of 1976 and 1977 caused by high interest rates may have led to the overvaluation of the exchange rate, and may therefore prove volatile and destabilising when real interest rates fall, or expectations develop that the parity is likely to be adjusted downwards. This view provides one reason why the existing modest stabilisation achievements may be regarded as precarious.

The second reason is that the mild recovery in domestic demand has sucked in imports at an accelerating rate, while the growth prospects of Chilean exports remain in some doubt (Table 3.3). This could be serious for an economy servicing such a high burden of external debt and relying on what may prove to be short-term speculative inflows to bolster its slender margin of foreign exchange reserves.[40] There is little expectation that either the volume or the price of Chile's copper exports will rise much before the end of the decade, and other exports that have recently performed so well must now contend with a much more unfavourable exchange rate and the apparently continuing sluggishness of world trade. However, it is the restructured economy's appetite for imports that raises the biggest questions about the recovery. Some of the import requirements are not the product of the junta's economic policies. For example, domestic petroleum production has continued to fall, and increased imports of fuel and spare parts were inevitable once the internal recession eased. However a great many other elements in the import bill have been greatly stimulated by the junta's sweeping trade liberalisation policies, which have proceeded at breakneck pace since 1974, almost regardless of the economic cycle. The average duty payable on imports other than motor vehicles was reduced from 94 per cent in December 1973 to 67 per cent in June 1974, 44 per cent in August 1975, and 18 per cent in August 1977. A further fall to about 10 per cent is now envisaged. Also, in October 1976 Chile withdrew from the Andean Pact. Part of the theory justifying these measures is that under the pressure of competition from the best and cheapest products the world market can supply, Chilean producers will be obliged to raise their efficiency and not add to inflation by pressing for excessive mark-ups. The incidental political advantages of supplying a small class of wealthy Chilean consumers with cheap imports cannot have passed unperceived.[41] It is claimed that Chilean enterprises also benefit because they can choose their inputs from a broader range of suppliers and can therefore compete more effectively on export markets. But the suspicion remains that such indiscriminate tariff reductions may be promoting imports that the Chilean economy can barely afford, far more than they contribute to the stimulation of exports. On this view the balance of payments remains vulnerable and the stabilisation precarious, even assuming continued suppression of those social groups that the economic model excludes.

CONCLUSION

The decisive test of the junta's trade liberalisation policies must, of course, come from the future performance of the Chilean economy. It will be very remarkable if the results live up to the expectations of many of the policy's supporters. Chilean monetarists have argued that thirty years ago the country's income levels were no lower than those of Japan or Spain, countries which supposedly pursued free market development strategies while Chile did not. Now that she has at last adopted the correct approach, the argument goes, she can expect to repeat the growth performance of the most dynamic economies. Some opponents of the policy go to the opposite extreme, predicting the annihilation of much of the country's industrial base and its reversion to the status of a peripheral or semi-colonial supplier of raw materials. As with many other aspects of Chilean affairs, the dispute can become highly ideological on both sides, more an expression of loyalty than an evaluation of reality. There are, however, some relevant considerations that must, in due course, force their attention on the contending parties. The figures on real GDP *per capita*, are an example. Between 1945 and 1970 the real income of the average Chilean rose by about 50 per cent, an annual rate of rather less than 2 per cent. From 1970 to 1975 it fell by 14 per cent, an annual rate approaching 3 per cent (Table 3.7), bringing the annual average for the thirty years 1945–75 to well below 1 per cent. Making the very optimistic assumption that the investment rate quickly recovers to such an extent that Chilean real GDP *per capita* doubles between 1975 and 1990 (implying an annual average growth rate of the economy as a whole over 7 per cent, the rate forecast in ODEPLAN's hopeful guidelines for 1978–83) the real income of the average Chilean would only have risen at a rate of 2·5 per cent a year from 1970 to 1990 – hardly faster than the rate recorded from 1945 to 1970. In other words, after the damage caused by the violent policy swings of the past seven years, there is a great deal of leeway to be made up.

Another point resisted by both critics and supporters of the junta is that it is false to claim that the present mixture of economic policies is the uniquely accredited pathway to capitalist development. Marxist critics sometimes endorse the idea that capitalist economic policies must take the doctrinaire form practised by the junta. In reality, of course, the theories of Milton Friedman have only recently acquired a mass audience among the policy-makers of the advanced capitalist world, and even now they are far from commanding a consensus of professional opinion. Take, for example, the trade liberalisation policies which junta economists tend to regard as the centrepiece of their long-term strategy, opening the home market to international competition, stimulating efficiency and optimising the allocation of resources. Hardly the Japanese strategy of development, one might note in passing, but also regarded with some scepticism even by impeccably orthodox economists at the US National Bureau of Economic Research. Here is the verdict of their recent country study on Chile before 1970, one of ten case studies examining the historical record of trade liberalisation experiments in less developed countries:

> General equilibrium analysis ... suggests that the impact of devaluation on the balance of payments and on employment is much less positive than has been suggested by partial equilibrium-analyses ... An evaluation of the success or failure of such policies ... may depend crucially upon what time period is relevant ... If the empirical measures derived from the Chilean experience are appropriate indicators, substantial effort may have been misplaced in the considerable recent literature on

alternative protection and resource-cost estimates . . . the point is not that overvaluation plus exchange control is without costs, but that there are substantial costs as well as possible benefits to moving away from the type of payments régime which has been dominant in Chile for the past four decades.[42]

Within the economics profession criticism of the 'Chicago Boys' tends to explain their policies as the product of misguided and doctrinaire applications of a particularly ambitious and rigid school of economic theory. But, as I have attempted to demonstrate in this chapter, Chilean economic policy-making cannot be realistically interpreted in abstraction from the political forces at work. Those who concentrate on the internal logic of the arguments used by the junta's economic advisers often neglect to explain why it was that these technocrats were given so much power to persist in the application of their ideas, and fail to examine the political constraints which channelled or perhaps even modified the practical content of their theories.[43] One of the major consequences of a ruthless application of the doctrine of comparative advantage to the Chilean economy is to contract drastically substantial portions of the industrial sector, particularly those large enterprises supplying the domestic market where the organised working class was strongest. The figures on manufacturing employment in Greater Santiago (Table 3.9) show how dramatic the effects have been (almost one-quarter of 1971 jobs have been eliminated by 1975), and doubtless national statistics would reveal a similar trend as industrial centres in the provinces were forced to contract. Disaggregating the rise in Santiago unemployment as the recession deepened we find only 4·5 per cent of *empleados* were unemployed in 1974, rising to 7·4 per cent in 1975; but for *obreros* the rate rose to 10·8 per cent in 1974 and 20·6 per cent in 1975 (and for construction workers from 13·0 per cent to 31·6 per cent).[44] It may be that some degree of de-industrialisation was unavoidable by 1973 but can the abruptness and severity of the contraction be attributed simply to the doctrinaire zeal of certain powerful economic policy-makers? The political scientist or historian looking at the figures on manufacturing employment would be bound to recall that it was the industrial cordon around Greater Santiago that provided the main bastion of organised resistance to the military takeover of 1973. Initially it was by physical force that those centres of opposition were subjugated. The economic policy of the junta can therefore be viewed as a continuation by non-military means of an onslaught against working-class collectivism initially carried out by generals rather than economists. Admittedly this was a reaction to left-wing economists who had used economic policy to boost working-class collectivism artificially in the first place. At any rate, viewed from the perspective of a political analyst the technical rationality of the economic doctrines seems unlikely to be their most crucial attraction to the dictatorship. Rather it is the practical effectiveness of this economic policy as a means of punishing opposition and rewarding adherents, that determines how forcefully it is applied. Even though there may be other, more reliable, paths to the re-establishment of capitalist accumulation, the forces supporting the dictatorship would not favour them at the expense of their own security and monopoly of power. This perspective, of course, yields a different standard of judgement for evaluating the character and success of the stabilisation programme from the conventional criteria.

It is not only the effects on the domestic correlation of forces that should make political observers sceptical of orthodox explanations of the junta's economic strategy. A major key to the violent shifts in Chile's recent economic policy is her distinctive international position. One plausible interpretation of the rationale behind Allende's economic policy was that he was creating the political preconditions that might suck in a large volume of Soviet resources; after his December 1972 visit to the Soviet Union, however, he returned empty-handed. A small, capital-hungry economy, distant from the world's political and economic centres of gravity, was therefore available for internal reconstruction in accordance with the support it could elicit from outside. Having failed to suck in Soviet resources, the Chilean state has been reconstructed to meet the specifications supposedly desired by private banks and transnational corporations. Reliance has recently been placed on attracting in *private* funds, rather than the type of public borrowing from the West that characterised the Christian Democrat government, less for reasons of economic doctrine than because the military see dependence on official credit sources as a security risk. The political strength of the Chicago Boys rests on their claim to understand what internal policies will lure in the requisite volume of resources from the private capital markets of the world. Unfortunately for them, so far the internal benefits have come slowly and have been painfully costly to secure. Indeed the international corporations have somewhat resembled the Soviet bloc in their slowness to turn goodwill into major capital inflows. Although by April 1978 the junta had issued permits for foreign investments totalling $1·6 billion, this was nearly all for the development or expansion of copper mines, very long-term projects of slow gestation that will only go ahead if prospects for the world copper price look favourable and the Chilean regime remains secure. It is the misfortune of Chile's international position that there is a disproportion between the capital commitments she requires urgently for recovery and the leverage she can exert, above all at a time of generalised recession. Perhaps it is the marginality of her international position that has obliged her to make such extreme efforts on the internal front over the past seven years.

Those seven years of Chilean economic history make gloomy reading. It should be possible for a society so rich in talent and resourcefulness to manage its affairs more successfully and to avoid mistakes that have proved so costly. That much may be agreed by a broad spectrum of Chilean opinions, especially since the country has such a long tradition of quite skilful and well-balanced policy-making. It remains to be seen whether the dictatorship can consolidate its internal front and escape its international isolation and economic vulnerability. Certainly success has been slow in coming, and time is running short. The only alternative internal arrangement it seems possible to envisage would be a return to conventional democracy – no easy task after the deep divisions of the recent past. Since a restored Chilean democracy could not attract much private foreign capital, or generate a large internal surplus, its economic viability would presumably depend upon receiving another transfusion of official aid – a mini-Marshall Plan or perhaps a gesture of atonement by the US government. Lack of confidence in such an alternative does as much to sustain the present regime as any positive confidence in the junta's economic achievements and prospects.

NOTES

1   The extensive literature on these questions generally overlooks the issues of economic management. Three exceptions are Nove (1976), de Vylder (1974), and Whitehead (1974).

2   Albert O. Hirschman's celebrated essay 'Inflation in Chile', Hirschman (1963), covers the period 1878–1962 and stresses the historical and political

context. The recent period is analysed more systematically by Ricardo ffrench-Davis (1973). Also of interest here is Sierra (1969), who compared the three stabilisation attempts made between 1955 and 1967.

3   Hirschman (1963) p. 222.

4   Quoted in *Ercilla* (Santiago), 26 August–1 September 1970.

5   Reviewing Congressional responses to Allende's budget proposals, de Vylder (1974) concludes: 'No political force in Chile could – or wanted to – halt the wage rise, and the attitude adopted by the opposition-controlled parliament rendered increased taxation of the wealthy impossible' (p. 100).

6   ODEPLAN (1972) p. 38.

7   ODEPLAN (1972) p. 12. From 1965 to 70 the year-end money stock held by the private sector (the reciprocal of the velocity of circulation) remained stable at around 10 per cent of GDP. It rose to 16·8 per cent in 1971. The ODEPLAN report sought comfort in the demonstration that only Paraguay, out of twenty-four countries compared, showed a ratio of less than 10 per cent in the late 1960s. For the USA the figure was around 25 per cent, for Argentina 20 per cent, etc. (pp. 40–1). However, since 1972 there has been a spectacular flight from cash, as can be seen from the last column of Table 3.1.

8   It is highly debatable at which point in the cycle the official rate was correctly valued. The Central Bank took the October 1973 rate as 100 and calculated the following index, under which the nominal rate of exchange has been corrected both for internal and international inflation:

1970	*1971*	*1972*	*1973*	*1974*	*1975*	*1976*
64·2	59·3	55·2	73·2	114·7	155·8	138·9

Source: Banco Central, *Boletín*, July 1977, p. 1012. However, McKinnon (1978) publishes an alternative series, which uses a more accurate estimation of Chilean internal inflation. On this view, with 1968/69 = 100, we have:

1970	*1971*	*1972*	*1973*	*1974*	*1975*	*1976*
101·4	95·0	93·6	77·0	104·9	115·2	102·7

9   The results achieved by 1973 corresponded quite closely to the original plan. Foxley *et al.* (1976) estimate that the share of industrial output generated by the social property sector rose from 11 per cent in 1970 to 32 per cent in 1973 and its share of industrial employment rose from 9 per cent to 24 per cent. Table 3.3 shows the public sector's growing share of total imports.

10 Officially, retail prices rose only 40 per cent in the twelve months to June 1972, but thereafter inflation rocketed out of control. By September 1972 the annual increase was 114 per cent, by December 163 per cent, by March 1973 183 per cent and by June 1973 283 per cent. Nove (1976) confirms the view that the policies pursued in 1971 made inevitable much of the economic dislocation of 1972.

11 White House meeting, 15 September 1970. The handwritten note by Helms reads:

> One-in-ten chance perhaps, but save Chile.
> Not concerned risks involved.

No involvement of Embassy.
Ten million dollars available, more if necessary.
Full-time job – best men we have.
Make the economy scream.

Source: *US Senate Hearings* (1976), p. 14.

12 Sigmund (1974).

13 Government spokesmen estimated that between January 1972 and August 1973 Congress only authorised new taxes sufficient to finance 20 per cent of the new social expenditure it approved. Left and right both recognised the need for increased taxation, but were unable to agree on the distribution of the burden. Nevertheless Chilean tax revenues were surprisingly inflation-proof (see Table 3.6).

14 By September 1973 commercial suppliers of imports were obliged to wait six months or more for payment. The 'invisible blockade' was partly commercial in motivation.

15 In spring 1972, for example, the Paris Club of Chile's main creditor nations granted a 70 per cent moratorium on payments due that year, with six years' grace for the balance. The overall outcome of that year's negotiations was that of the $400 million due for payment as interest and amortisation only about one-quarter was paid, and in the first nine months of 1973 virtually no debt service payments were made. (See Table 3.8 for debt service payments.)

16 de Vylder (1974) p. 207.

17 Ibid., p. 206.

18 A representative example of the internal resistance such a policy shift would have entailed can be found in the policy documents of one of the six coalition parties, MAPU. In December 1971 the party's fourth plenum was told by its leaders that 'in revolutionary politics the budget has a very different significance from that known under bourgeois governments ... We cannot refuse to sustain and expand the health, education, and housing programmes, and the necessary productive investments, that the bourgeoisie is unable to accomplish. Therefore an initially unbalanced budget cannot drive us to adopt a policy of cutbacks, seeking budget balance on the basis of abandoning our political objectives' (Jaime Gazmuri, quoted in MAPU Documentos, 1972, pp. 46−7).

19 The source is ODEPLAN's national income statistics (see Table 3.5).

20 While expressing caution on the coverage of the data, Foxley *et al.* (1976) provide substantial evidence that it was the private sector (seeking to avoid conflicts that might lead to nationalisation) which took the lead in raising real wages in 1971, whilst the public sector, and especially the newly nationalised enterprises, exercised considerable restraint (pp. 28−30). On the other hand, although the administration initially attempted to restrain the level of real wages per worker, from the outset it encouraged a great increase in the level of employment in the public sector so that, even if the initial incomes policy line had held, the total wage pressure implied by UP policies would have been very high (ibid., pp. 31−5). In the social property sector employment rose 12·2 per cent in 1971, 7·1 per cent in 1972, and 7·3 per cent in 1978.

21　MAPU Documentos (1972) pp. 296–8.

22　Foxley *et al.* (1976) p. 41.

23　In October 1973 the number in public employment in the Greater Santiago region had fallen as follows, compared with two months earlier: public administration, down 19,100 (24·4 per cent), education down 16,000 (23·7 per cent), health 14,300 (31·5 per cent).

24　See, for example, Valenzuela (1976) and Whitehead (1976). The US Senate Selection Committee on Intelligence has disclosed that 'CIA collaborators' helped plan the economic measures enacted immediately after the coup. Committee witnesses maintain that some of the 'Chicago Boys' received CIA funds for such research efforts as a 300-page economic blueprint that was given to the military leaders before the coup. Fernando Leniz, a former chairman of the *Mercurio*, became the junta's first civilian Minister of Economics in December 1973.

25　'Balance para el primer trimestre', *Ercilla* (Santiago, 2–8 January 1974), p. 23.

26　See the exhaustive account by the American adviser who designed this stabilisation package, George Jackson Eder (1968), cost of living index, p. 590.

27　The Bolivian Central Bank was lent US$25 million for stabilisation purposes and as a reserve against the country's entire net circulation and deposits. Eder explained to President Siles that '$25 million gave adequate security as, even if everyone lost confidence and tried to buy dollars, there were not enough bolivianos available to buy $25 million' at the new exchange rate (ibid., p. 640). At the end-1973 tourist exchange rate, Chile's total stock of privately held credit was not enough to buy $500 million.

28　As early as 1974 the US Congress began placing restrictions on official American assistance to the dictatorship, and by mid-1976 the Ford Administration was increasingly ineffective in its attempts to circumvent these restrictions. See Salzburg and Young (1977). However, compare Table 3.2. The Carter administration has since accentuated US economic and diplomatic pressures against the Pinochet regime, although not to the same degree as Allende suffered.

29　Even ITT, nationalised after revelations of its political subversion in Chile, and consequently refused indemnification by the Overseas Private Investment Corporation, received from the junta a present of $125 million.

30　US Disarmament Agency (1976).

31　The real wage figures do not provide a full measure of the decline in labour costs during 1973 and 1974. Table 3.9 shows that there was also a sharp fall in the number employed, particularly in the manufacturing sector, while Table 3.7 shows that the volume of industrial production rose.

32　And its composition was shifted dramatically into interest-bearing quasi-money, company reserves, and foreign currency deposits.

33　The IMF's role in enforcing the 'shock treatment' of 1975 has recently been confirmed in an interview with a leading junta economist, Sergio de Castro, who said: 'after the price of copper went down . . . we projected a deficit in the balance of payments of $1·2 billion. In conversations with the IMF we were told we could not have a bigger deficit than $50 million because we would not get financial support for more than that. After a lot of haggling we came to an agreed deficit of $240 million. The only way to do that was to cut down very drastically.' *Euromoney* (London) July 1978, p. 5.

34 CEPAL (1977) p. 167.

35 In his comparative study of the stabilisation policies of 1955−8, 1959−62 and 1965−7 Sierra (1969) concluded that 'In the latter two cases the greatest contribution to the deceleration of the rhythm of inflation was undoubtedly made by the external sector' (p. 143). In 1974−7, however, the initial contribution from the external sector in the form of renewed credits was partly nullified by the various agreements to compensate for nationalisation. Later, the decision to meet official debt service obligations in full, rather than accept renegotiations qualified by human rights conditions, again reduced the contribution available from the external sector. The junta has made much of the $510 million-worth of direct private foreign investment projects approved by the end of 1976. However, only $211 million of this had actually been contracted for, and only $45 million of such investment had actually arrived: mainly manufacturing firms 'catching up' on the backlog of investment neglected in 1971−3.

36 Only impressionistic evidence on the profitability of Chilean-owned enterprises has been available. However, the US Department of Commerce publishes annual statistics on total direct US investment in Chile, from which the following picture emerges:

	1969	1970	1971	1972	1973	1974	1975	1976
Earnings ($m)	162	46	−10	−4	6	16	0	22
Book value	904	797	734	670	632	622	293	238
Implied rate of return (%)	17·9	5·8	−1·4	−0·6	0·9	2·6	0	9·2

Naturally these figures are open to qualification, but the broad picture is probably correct. (Calculated from *Survey of Current Business*, August 1977, and earlier issues.)

37 To accelerate these processes the government lowered the rate of tax levied on profits from a crushing 62·2 per cent in 1975 to 52·6 per cent in 1976 and below 50 per cent in 1977.

38 See the figures in Note 8. Despite the extreme orthodoxy of their monetarism, Chile's economic managers have not relinquished control over the exchange rate to the free play of market forces. The rate was unified in 1974, and then devalued two or three times a month by administrative *fiat* from the Banco Central (using a formula related to comparative purchasing power parities). Since mid-1976 the adjustments have been made daily, according to a schedule announced two months in advance.

39 The US Department of Commerce gives the following information on total capital expenditure in Chile by all majority-owned affiliates of US corporations (actual $million to 1976, planned for 1977 and 1978):

1971	1972	1973	1974	1975	1976	1977	1978
4	2	2	5	16	11	17	17

Source: *Survey of Current Business*, September 1975 and September 1977.

40   From 1 January 1978 private Chilean Banks have been authorised to borrow abroad up to one-quarter of their capital and reserves. The reliance on private foreign debt appears, therefore, to be increasing while public debt is being repaid.

41   Imports of consumer goods other than foodstuffs rose from $100 million in 1976 to $342 million (15·5 per cent of all imports) in 1977. Many of the imported items – radios, television, toys, textiles – had previously been supplied by domestic producers.

42   Behrman (1976) pp. 36–7. This study ends in September 1973. For a severe critique of the trade liberalisation extremism practised thereafter, by a Chicago-trained economist of acknowledged ability, see 'La Política de Comercio Exterior en 1974/7' Richard Ffrench-Davis, in *Mensaje*, Santiago, January–February 1978.

43   It should also be noted that figures such as Cauas and Harberger only became so extremisst in their prescriptions a year or two before their acquired power.

44   CEPAL (1977) p. 18.

REFERENCES

Behrman, Jere R. (1976), *Foreign Trade Regimes and Economic Development: VIII: Chile*, National Bureau of Economic Research, Columbia University Press, New York.
Chossudovsky, M. (1975), 'Hacia el Nuevo Modelo Económica Chilena: Inflación y Redistribución del Ingreso', *Trimestre Económico*, no. 166, vol. XLII, no. 2, Mexico City.
Comisión Económica para America Latina (CEPAL) (1977), *Estudio Economico de 1975*, UN, New York.
De Vylder, Stefan (1974), *Allende's Chile: The Rise and Fall of the Unidad Popular*, Cambridge University Press, Cambridge.
Eder, George Jackson (1968), *Inflation and Development in Latin America: A Case History of Inflation and Stabilisation in Bolivia*, University of Michigan Press, Ann Arbor.
Ffrench-Davis, Ricardo (1973), *Políticas Económicas en Chile 1952–70*, Nueva Universidad, Santiago.
Foxley, Alejandro, *et al.* (1976), *Redistribución del Patrimonio y Erradicación de la Pobreza*, CIEPLAN, Santiago.
Hirschman, Albert O. (1963), 'Inflation in Chile', Chapter 3 of *Journeys Towards Progress*, Twentieth Century Fund, New York.
Letelier, O. (1976), 'The Chicago Boys in Chile', *New Statesman*, vol. 92, no. 2382, 12 November 1976, London.
MAPU Documentos (1972), *El Segundo Año del Gobierno Popular*, MAPU, Santiago.
McKinnon, Ronald I. (1978), 'Financial Intermediation, the Foreign Exchanges and Monetary Control in Chile', paper delivered to Ford Foundation seminar on Developing Countries and the International Financial System, Central Bank of Barbados, Bridgetown, Barbados, 11–14 January 1978.

Nove, Alec (1976), 'The Political Economy of the Allende Régime', in P. O'Brien (ed.), *Allende's Chile*, Praeger, Washington.

ODEPLAN (1972), *Informe Económico Anual 1971*, ODEPLAN, Santiago.

Ramos, Joseph (1975), 'El Costo Social: Hechos y Interpretaciones', *Estudios de Economía*, no. 6, University of Chile, Santiago.

Ramos, J. (1977). 'A Comment to "Military Government and Real Wages in Chile"', *Latin American Research Review*, vol. XII, no. 1, Chapel Hill, North Carolina.

Rufatt, O., and Lagos, R. (1975), 'Military Government and Real Wages in Chile', *Latin American Research Review*, vol. X, no. 2, Chapel Hill, North Carolina. (Also their defence in LARR, vol. XII, no. 1.)

Salzberg. John, and Young, Donald D. (1977), 'The Parliamentary Role in Implementing International Human Rights: A US Example', *Texas International Law Journal*, vol. XII, nos 2 and 3, University of Texas School of Law, Texas.

Sierra, Enrique (1969), *Tres Ensayos de Estabilización en Chile*, Universitaria, Santiago.

Sigmund, Paul E. (1974), 'The "Invisible Blockade" and the Fall of Allende', *Foreign Affairs*, January 1974, New York.

US Arms Control and Disarmament Agency (1976), *World Military Expenditures and Arms Transfers 1966–75*, Government Printing Office, Washington.

US Senate (1975), *Senate Hearings on Intelligence Activities: VII: Covert Action*, Government Printing Office, Washington.

Valenzuela, Carlos J. (1976), 'El Nuevo Patrón de Acumulación y sus Precondiciones: El Caso Chileno: 1973–6', *Comercio Exterior*, vol. XXVI, no. 9, Banco Nacional de Comercio Exterior, Mexico City.

Whitehead, Laurence (1974), *The Lesson of Chile*, Fabian Research Paper no. 317, Fabian Society, London.

Whitehead, Laurence (1976), 'The Chilean Dictatorship', *The World Today*, vol. XXXII, no. 10, Royal Institute of International Affairs, London.

4 The Stabilisation Crisis in Peru 1975–8

ROSEMARY THORP

The interest – and the difficulty – of the Peruvian case resides in the fact that it exemplifies in an extreme form the conditions under which even the most short-term targets of orthodox stabilisation policy appear impossible of achievement.[1] Since the emergence of acute macroeconomic disequilibrium in 1975, the authorities, under increasing pressure from the international financial community, have struggled to implement orthodox programmes, only to fail time and again to achieve any success even with regard to the balance of payments. At the time of writing yet another attempt has been made (June 1978) of which the outcome is still uncertain – though the analysis of this paper does not leave much room for optimism, without an improvement in external conditions. Failing this, pressures seem likely to grow for a 'Pinochet' solution as the only means of dealing with popular resistance to further austerity.

Thus, although it is the long-run consequences of orthodox policies that remain the most important aspect, these are not the aspects which Peru can as yet illuminate. The particular value of this case study is that it enables us to delineate rather clearly the conditions under which orthodox policy appears unable to achieve even limited first-order goals. At the same time it is also clear that such policies may also appear in the circumstances to be the only option, given the structure of the international system, the effect of the international recession on base metal prices, and the country's internal situation. The crisis this is provoking not only for Peru but also for the international financial community lies behind a recent description of Peru as 'the IMF's Vietnam'.[2]

The first section of the paper explains the background to recent policies by describing the growing structural disequilibrium which has emerged since the 1950s. This was compounded by international events in the early 1970s, leading to the acute disequilibrium of the last three years. In the second section we analyse the impact of the policy response to this disequilibrium, up to July 1977, when the orthodox policy response itself ran into a crisis of political inviability. The third section attempts to illuminate recent developments by comparing them with previous attempts, showing how various features of the evolution of the economy have narrowed the impact of stabilisation measures, so reducing both their efficiency and their political feasibility. In the fourth section these points are drawn together to explain the crisis in stabilisation policy since mid-1977 and to comment briefly on attempts to find an alternative.

I THE GROWING CRISIS

It is essential to realise how far the problems of 1975–7 were superimposed on a growing structural crisis. This is crucial to our analysis here not only because it vitally affects the handling of the situation, but also because it colours the entire discussion of the increasing difficulty of stabilisation: that difficulty stems before all else from the fact that in forty years Peru has not faced a problem of such severity.

Since 1948, the year when a conservative military dictator took over, ending a brief and incoherent period of interventionist economic policies, Peru had been almost a textbook example of commitment to *laissez-faire*, export-led growth. The forces which operated elsewhere in Latin America to push the continent to more inward-looking development strategies, in Peru were felt only in a weak form, with the result that by 1948 Peru had a relatively small public sector, a long tradition of little intervention in the economy and a welcoming attitude to foreign investment. The reasons for such a situation lie in the country's rich resource endowment, its long periods of steady export expansion, and the manner in which the traditional groups had been able to further their own interest in close alliance with foreign capital and without the need for a highly developed state.[3]

But in the course of the next twenty years strains began to develop, despite rapid growth of exports and of the economy as a whole (see Table 4.1). The key symptoms are revealed in Tables 4.2 and 4.3, showing trends in export supply and in investment which in the light of previous rates of growth made some kind of adjustment crisis inevitable. These phenomena were related both as cause and effect to a third aspect: a growing disillusion with traditional policies, partly with their overall performance but more with their distributional aspects. With political and social

TABLE 4.1   Peruvian GNP and exports, 1950−70 (1963 prices[a])

	GNP	GNP per capita; annual average growth rates	Exports
1950−5	6·0	3·9	7·9
1955−60	4·3	1·6	10·4
1960−5	6·6	3·5	4·9
1965−70	4·2	1·0	3·1
1970−5	6·4	3·2	−4·0
1976−7	0·8	−2·5	7·7

Source: Banco central, *Cuentas Nacionales del Peru*; *Memoria*, 1977.
Note: [a] 1971−7 based on 1970 prices.

TABLE 4.2   Quantum index of exports, 1960−77

1960	76	1970	109
1964	100	1971	100
1965	97	1972	106
1966	96	1973	83
1967	100	1974	80
1968	112	1975	76
1969	101	1976	72
		1977	90

Source: Thorp and Bertram (1978); Banco Central, *Memoria*.

TABLE 4.3   Investment as a percentage of GDP, 1955−76

	Private	Public
1955−8	17·5	4·8
1959−63	15·3	3·3
1964−8	10·8	4·6
1969−73	7·9	4·8
1974−6	6·5	8·8

Source: FitzGerald (1979).

changes as the economy grew in breadth, and with increasing awareness of the implications of foreign penetration, there was a growth both in nationalism and in a sense that the propertied class ('oligarchy') had betrayed its responsibilities. This was to culminate in pressures for radical ownership reforms after 1968; in the meantime it interacted with other factors to aggravate the structural crisis – for example, by precipitating a withholding of investment on the part of the multinationals in the mining sector during the early 1960s, despite good international prices, in the hope of pressuring the government into a return to their former generosity.[4]

Unfortunately, these mining projects were more crucial to the continued functioning of the model than was realised in Peru at the time; the gestation period in a major mining project is several years, and export proceeds were rising rapidly as a result of investments in the 1950s. This concealed the fact that, as Table 4.2 shows, Peru was soon to be facing an extraordinary stagnation of export supply – a situation unique in her economic history, since it was for once not a problem of external markets, as it had been for guano, and for all products in the 1930s. In part it was the product of natural resource constraints, as in fishing (though aggravated by poor resource management). Oil likewise faced a constraint of nature: despite great hopes and large investments by the multinationals, little was found. Sugar and cotton faced the limit of cultivated land – though here the nature of the constraint is complex, since there were major irrigation projects to be carried out which could relieve the constraint, but which required a more dynamic and developmental state than was the product of this type of model.

In a real sense, therefore, neglect of the export sector did lie behind the export crisis – but with export revenue still rising strongly in the 1960s, as past investments in copper came to fruition and as fishmeal approached its peak, it would have required a far-sighted government to realise the urgency of the impending problem.

The problems in the export sector in turn explain the decline in the investment coefficient, though this is related also to the growth of rural unrest and the discontent with the distributional aspects of the model we have mentioned. This made it obvious that some form of land reform was inevitable and further discouraged investment in agriculture. Such problems were behind a shift in the focus of policy towards industrialisation: by the early 1960s Peru was embarked on a wave of import-substitution, with massive incentives, much-increased protection and heavy participation by the multinationals. This was not enough to compensate for the decline in investment elsewhere, the net result being the steady fall in the coefficient shown in Table 4.3. It also in no way compensated for the declining dynamism of traditional exports; in fact it aggravated the problem owing to the high import content of the new industries[5] and the cost of imported technology, while it was very far from providing a source of foreign exchange.

Under President Belaúnde (1963–8) there was an expansion of public spending, in response to social and political changes, partly in an attempt to balance the declining dynamism of the private sector. As Table 4.3 shows, the increase was not enough to outweigh the decline in private investment. Even so, it was not adequately financed; resistance to tax reform pushed the government into borrowing abroad, with effects on the foreign exchange content of the investment programme.[6] The increasingly unfavourable repercussions on the balance of payments are shown in Table 4.4, while debt service as a percentage of exports rose from 6 in 1963 to 13 in 1968.[7] Also reflected in Table 4.4 is the tapering off of the inflows of private foreign capital by the mid-1960s, and the increasingly negative balance on capital transactions that resulted.[8] The worsening internal and external disequilibria were thus closely related, and were the short-term symptoms of a long-term problem.

The military government of General Velasco which took over in 1968 was temporarily rescued from short-term problems by the world boom in commodities: Table 4.5 shows the upturn in Peruvian terms of trade. The internal disequilibrium was alleviated by domestic recession, by the effects of the tax reform Belaúnde had achieved, too late for his own rescue, and by the time-lag involved in reorganising the public sector and launching new projects. Freedom from problems of short-term economic management facilitated major ownership reforms which were meant, by their effect on the generation and control of the economic surplus, to set the economy on a new course. But unfortunately – if not tragically – false assumptions and misguided resource allocation led to an outcome which was oddly like that under the preceding government: a massive increase in state spending without an adequate financial base.

TABLE 4.4   The balance of payments under three governments, 1950–68 ($m, annual averages)

| | Odría | Prado | | Belaúnde | | |
	1950–5	1956–8	1959–62	1963–5	1966–7	1968
Exports	244	314	458	641	765	840
Imports	−234	−363	−382	−565	−811	−673
Visible trade balance	10	− 49	76	76	− 45	167
Net services and transfers	− 20	− 38	− 35	− 69	− 72	− 56
Profits and interest	− 20	− 36	− 57	− 75	−130	−138
Current account balance	− 30	−122	− 15	− 68	−246	− 28
Long-term capital:						
Public	11	8	− 1	83	106	81
Private	15	79	22	21	11	− 26
Basic balance	− 3	−34	6	36	−129	27
Short-term capital	3	22	−14	−14	37	12
Monetary movements and errors	0	12	−20	−22	92	− 39

Source: Banco Central, *Cuentas Nacionales*, various issues.

TABLE 4.5   Terms of trade 1960–75 (1960 = 100)

1960	100	1970	154
1965	95	1971	136
1966	107	1972	121
1967	101	1973	178
1968	123	1974	193
1969	138	1975	142

Source: Banco Central, *Boletin* and *Memoria*, 1976.

The assumptions can be reduced to four. First, it was believed that there was great latent potential in the Peruvian private sector which would respond to the nationalistic reforms with a surge of investment. Second, nationalisation was presumed to give access not merely to potential but to actual surplus. Third, a continued role for foreign investment on new terms was thought to be quite compatible with the government's plans. All these assumptions had implications for a fourth underlying premise: that in various rather unclear ways the reforms would have significant and fairly rapid dividends in terms of the various disequilibria affecting the economy.

It will be obvious that the government was soon to be disillusioned on all fronts. First, the Peruvian private sector – not noticeable for its dynamism, anyway, after years as the junior partner of foreign capital – had its confidence badly shaken by the Industrial Community legislation and by the generally increased level of intervention in the economy.[9] An 'investment strike' followed, with considerable capital flight, despite the almost total protection available, very high profitability,[10] and easy credit conditions after restraint in the first year or so of the regime.

Second, the facile expectation that nationalisation of a profitable foreign firm would give ready access to surplus proved false: enterprises often proved on takeover to have been run down, if not decapitalised, and to be actually in need of an input of funds.[11]

Third, it proved, not surprisingly, to be decidedly difficult to persuade foreign firms to invest on the scale required by the planners. What were to prove disastrous delays occurred, especially in mining, as deals were negotiated with very great difficulty, and eventually at the cost of some shift in the government's position.

As to the fourth assumption, there is no evidence, for example, that nationalisation did much to improve the balance-of-payments impact of the sectors in question. Presumably there was some reduction of profit outflow with nationalisation – but in contrast to Chile, the Peruvians were willing to pay compensation and outflows on account of technology and capital goods continued unabated.[12]

At the same time it has to be admitted – even by those most sympathetic to the goals of the Velasco regime – that there was considerable misallocation of limited resources (of which the increase in defence spending was only the most conspicuous) and a total failure to develop adequate budgeting and control techniques to monitor the spending of the mushrooming public agencies and even of the ministries themselves.

The result of all these factors was that while on the one hand the government was forced to do more than it had originally intended, given the failure of the private sector, on the other hand the resources available to finance that increased role were less than anticipated. The problem became worse as the modern sector labour force, its expectations aroused by government propaganda surrounding the creation of labour communities, began to press for a larger share of the cake, thereby cutting still further into state enterprise profits (given that fear of accelerating inflation placed a restraint on price increases). Real wage and salary figures are shown in Table 4.6.[13]

TABLE 4.6   Real wage and salary indices, Lima, 1968–76

	Wages	Salaries
1968	100	100
1969	103	114
1970	101	115
1971	112	122
1972	122	126
1973	133	133
1974	126	122
1975	126	122
1976	106	95

Source: Organization of American States (OAS), *Study on Remunerations in Peru,* 1977, cited in Stallings (1978) p. 52.

One obvious possibility was tax reform. But the military were unprepared to bite either into profits or the living standards of the middle classes.[14] Their unwillingness was made more feasible by the coincidence of acute financial need with surplus world liquidity and the peak of the search of the international banks for customers.[15] Between 1972 and 1974 Peru was able to borrow abroad, and to refinance its growing debt with an ease that *ex post* appears suicidal, but at the time reflected apparently solid expectations as to petroleum wealth. This permitted the continuation of a massive boom in imports, both on the part of public and private sectors, and including a very rapid increase in imports of military equipment. As Table 4.7 shows, the result was a rise in debt service as a percentage of exports from 16 per cent in 1970 to 34 per cent in 1975, while the overall public sector deficit rose from 2 per cent of GDP in 1969 to 10 per cent by 1975. The critical situation which evolved in the external balance is shown in Table 4.8.

The implicit logic of the strategy followed since 1968 was that,

TABLE 4.7 External public debt of Peru, 1968–76[a] (US$m.)

	1968	1969	1970	1971	1972	1973	1974	1975[b]	1976[b]
Gross inflow	186	221	190	184	285	574	990	1046	1348
Servicing	129	134	167	213	219	347	343	474	511
Net inflow	99	132	69	28	121	309	740	762	1077
Outstanding debt	737	875	945	997	1121	1430	2170	3050	4127
Debt service as percentage of exports	15	16	16	24	23	33	22	34	32

Source: 1968–74: FitzGerald (1976) p. 71; 1975–6: IMF (1977). The 1976 figures are preliminary estimates.
Notes: [a] Debt of more than one year. By 1977 total debt including short-term was estimated by the Central Bank to be some $8·5 billion.
[b] 1975–6: includes a small figure for loans repayable in local currency. The figure comparable to $3050 million in 1975 for total debt outstanding in 1974 is $2288 million.

TABLE 4.8 Peruvian balance of payments 1969–76 (US$m.)

	1969	1970	1971	1972	1973	1974	1975	1976
Exports	880	1034	889	945	1112	1503	1290	1360
Imports	-659	-700	-730	-812	-1033	-1909	-2390	-2100
Visible trade balance	221	334	159	133	79	-406	-1100	-740
Financial services								
Public	-37	-31	-48	-51	-66	-104	-231[b]	
Private[a]	-147	-117	-78	-70	-115	-114		-450
Non financial services and transfers	-37	-2	-67	-44	-90	-183	-206[b]	
Current account balance	0	184	-34	-32	-192	-907	-1537	-1192
Long-term capital								
Public	124	101	15	116	314	693	793	480
Private[a]	20	-77	-43	-2	70	202	342	196
Basic balance	144	208	-62	82	192	88	-402	-516
Short-term capital	-56	21	-80	24	-125	244	-173[c]	-351
Monetary movements, errors and omissions	-88	-229	142	-106	-67	-332	-575[c]	-867
Export quantum index, 1968=100	90	97	89	95	74	75	66	76
Commodity terms of trade, 1968=100	112	125	110	98	144	156	115	n.a.

Source: Thorp and Bertram (1978); Banco Central, *Cuentas Nacionales*.

Notes: [a] Undistributed profits of foreign firms are here treated as outflows on current account and inflows on capital account, in accordance with present Peruvian practice.

[b] Services and transfers are aggregated in the Banco Central *Memoria*. They have been disaggregated here using the relative shares shown by Reynolds (1977).

[c] Errors and omissions are included with short-term capital in this year.

with greater command over the economic surplus, investments could be made which would reduce the vulnerability of the economy, by increasing export supply, by increasing value added in the export sector, by expansion of domestic food supplies and by import substitution at the level of intermediate imports, as well as by hardening the terms on which foreign capital entered and by moving into exports of manufactures. Unfortunately, not only did the financial aspects of the plan prove to be based on fatally mistaken assumptions, as we have explained above, but also the gestation period of crucial investments proved lengthy,[16] and at times the net foreign exchange effect less dramatic than was hoped.[17] The financial constraint plus the political importance of urban food prices also led to a disastrous policy on the internal terms of trade.

By 1974 the looming external disequilibrium was also accompanied by increasing signs of internal disequilibrium. As Table 4.9 shows, up to and including 1973 the increased spending by the government was barely enough to compensate for the continued sluggishness of private investment. There was no great concern about inflation: as Table 4.10 shows, the cost of living rose at a modest 6 or 7 per cent through those years. By 1974, however, prices began to accelerate (rising 17 per cent in the year) as public sector spending rose, private sector spending at last recovered (Table 4.9) and import prices rose sharply (some 30 per cent).

TABLE 4.9   Gross Domestic Product by expenditure 1971–6 (indices, 1970 prices, 1971 = 100)

	1968[a]	1970[a]	1972	1973	1974	1975	1976
Private consumption	84	96	104	117	128	132	135
Public consumption	85	94	109	113	118	134	134
Gross fixed investment	73	82	107	113	147	177	164
Public	41	72	109	128	201	225	213
Private	84	85	106	103	114	147	134
Exports	104	105	109	89	84	81	82
Minus imports	97	100	100	109	144	162	136
Gross Domestic Product	82	94	106	112	120	124	128

Source: Banco Central, *Memorias* and *Cuentas Nacionales*.
Note: [a] Based on 1963 prices.

TABLE 4.10   Percentage change in consumer prices 1967–77

1968	+19·1
1969	+6·3
1970	+5·0
1971	+6·8
1972	+7·2
1973	+9·5
1974	+16·9
1975	+23·6
1976	+33·5
1977	33·0[a]

Source: Banco Central, *Memorias*.
Note: [a] Widely acknowledged to be an underestimate. Inflation in the first few months of 1978 is estimated at an annual rate of 60 per cent.

I STABILISATION POLICIES, JUNE 1975–JUNE 1977

This section first outlines briefly the chronology of the measures taken, before discussing their *modus operandi* in an economy like Peru's.

The policies

In June 1975 came the first serious signs that the Government was planning a shift in policies in the face of falling reserves, the huge balance-of-payments deficit and accelerating internal inflation. In that month the controlled prices of food and petroleum were raised. But this did not avert a change of presidency in August, when Morales Bermudez, Velasco's Minister of Finance, took over from him, as it became apparent that the severity of the economic crisis necessitated a new broom: a 'second stage' in which mistakes could be blamed on the Velasco era and a new direction sought. There followed a moderate devaluation in September, but still the main solution was yet more borrowing from abroad. Budget cuts and tax increases were announced in January 1976, with further price increases: as Table 4.11 shows, however, the measures were barely enough to do more than stabilise the overall government deficit at −9 per cent of GDP. By mid-1976 urgent debt repayment problems, plus net international reserves at an all-time low of −$553 million,[18] brought Peru to negotiate directly with the major private banks: in a unique decision, the banks agreed to roll over the debt *without* the 'seal' of an IMF Standby Agreement, provided Peru co-operated in a programme which was generally assessed afterwards as having been almost as stringent as the Fund's would have been.[19] The measures involved a shift towards greater fiscal and monetary restraint, devaluation, more favourable treatment of foreign investment, and a firm reversal of the anti-private sector trend of certain of Velasco's policies. There followed more increases in controlled prices, including a doubling of the price of petrol, and a further modest devaluation, and the fishing fleet was sold back to private enterprise. This was thought to herald more such moves, though in fact nothing more was done. Table 4.14 below reveals though how little was in fact done in the area of fiscal restraint. Expenditure continued to rise in real terms, the only impact on the deficit coming from the increase in public enterprise prices (chiefly the increase in petrol prices). But credit to the private sector was cut, on top of the fall in liquidity produced by the drain in reserves.

By early 1977, inflation was running more rapidly than ever, at over 40 per cent (see Table 4.9 and footnote [a]), industrial output was falling,[20] real wages had fallen over 40 per cent since their peak in 1973 (Table 4.6), and under-employment had reached over 50 per cent.[21] The balance of payments was still unfavourable and gross reserves were due to be totally exhausted by the end of July. The private banks had found their role of 'policeman' too uncomfortable.[22] This time they insisted that a standby agreement be signed with the IMF. The negotiations with the IMF produced demands by the Fund mission for targets in terms of public spending, money supply and external debt which were unacceptable to the Central Bank,[23] let alone to the country as a whole. Private sector representations as to the effect of a continued squeeze brought a new Minister of Economy from the private sector: Piazza introduced measures representing a severe dose of deflation but by his attempt to deflect pressure slightly from the private industrial sector, by increasing food and petrol prices and by attacking military spending, major riots were provoked in a number of provincial cities and the military were pushed into demanding his resignation. With this, and with the first general strike in twenty years, in July 1977, the stabilisation policy appeared to dissolve into incoherence, price increases were rescinded, negotiations with the Fund were broken off and the

Central Bank team resigned. Events since then are described in the final section of the paper.

The modus operandi of 'orthodox' stabilisation

To clarify the reasons for the crisis of July 1977, it may be helpful to consider how this type of measure operates in an economy like Peru's.

Basically, the analysis behind the policy is extremely simple. To summarise the Fund's own version, excessive expansion of public sector spending, without adequate tax measures, and a passive monetary policy, had led by 1975 to

> demand pressures which were manifested in an acceleration in the rate of inflation to 24 per cent from an average annual rate of 10 per cent in 1971–4, and in a widening of the current account deficit of the balance of payments to 11·5 per cent of GDP from close to equilibrium in the 1971–2 period. The deterioration of the current account further reflected the progressive increase in domestic costs of production relative to those abroad, nurtured by an extensive system of protection to industry, including import prohibitions, licensing, and tariffs.[24]

The basic tools to deal with the disequilibrium lay therefore in contraction of demand and adjustment of relative prices; hopefully, it would also be possible to reduce the excessive protection provided to the industrial sector, though this was recognised as difficult in the immediate future.

Taking first the external gap, the inadequacy of the analysis will be evident already from the discussion in Section I. The policies prescribed rely on contraction of demand and on relative prices to reduce imports and, hopefully, to stimulate exports. Further, with the maintenance of a realistic exchange rate, 'sound' financial policies and reduced use of controls, there would be less incentive to capital flight. We would argue that even as short-term expedients, these policies would be extremely costly and slow to work in an economy of this sort.

The first problem is that the tool of relative prices will yield almost nothing in the short run in an economy such as this. In any case, 50 per cent of imports are for the state; the remainder comprise inputs and capital goods which for the most part cannot be substituted in the short run. Anyway, as we shall see, the effect of the numerous different measures of relative price adjustment is generally to provoke such strong cost-push inflation that the stimulus to import substitution is rapidly eroded. Table 4.10 shows the increase in the internal price level. Export sales are typically extremely insensitive to the exchange rate in the short-run in Peru: we have already seen that the problem with existing export lines was not lack of competitiveness but a very fundamental supply constraint which would not be broken by price stimuli in the short-term. Non-traditional lines formed a minute proportion of the total, and in a time of world recession it was hardly to be expected that they could quickly rescue the situation.[25]

Further, while capital flight was admittedly given strong incentives in earlier years by the controlled exchange rate, it also occurs in response to many other variables: in particular the atmosphere of credit squeeze, depression, riots and political instability of mid-1977 could hardly be relied on to hold funds in the country, whatever the exchange rate policy.

Thus the burden of such a policy falls on one instrument: the contraction of demand. But here a number of factors combine to make this an inefficient and costly instrument.

First, as we have already seen, there were many underlying unfavourale trends accounting for the balance-of-payments problem, which were entirely omitted from the analysis of excess demand and price distortions, and which were quite unaffected by the measures taken. These include factors such as the growth in debt repayments, the expansion of defence commitments, the increasingly unfavourable impact of foreign investment, and, most importantly, the long-run export supply problem.

Second, the reduction of internal demand could make no contribution even in the short-term to the solution of the export supply problem, since the internal consumption of exportables is low: only in the case of sugar is a significant proportion of output allocated to the internal market – and by 1975 the international sugar price was falling sharply.

Thus the measures operated on one variable – imports – against ongoing unfavourable trends in many other variables. But, above all within the area of imports, contraction of demand forms an inefficient and costly tool. This arises from the structure of imports, which is shown in Table 4.11. A major difficulty in this

TABLE 4.11   The composition of imports, 1974

Food[a]	12
Fuel	12
Non-food consumer goods	6
Raw materials and inputs for agriculture	5
Raw materials and inputs for industry, excluding food processing[b]	29
Capital goods, including military equipment[c]	36

Source: Banco Central, *Memoria*, p. 182.
Notes: [a] This includes final and intermediate goods, and is based on IMF (1977) p. 40.
[b] The weight of food processing was estimated from the data for 1974 given in Table 4.8.
[c] See the discussion in the text.

table arises over defence imports; no figures on these are available, but they are hidden in 'various' and in 'capital equipment'. A minimum estimate for 1975 appears to have been 20 per cent of total imports. If we accept this figure, then we find that if we take food and fuel as sacrosanct, and defence as outside the discussion, we have already accounted for 44 per cent of imports. The initial decision of the Peruvians was, commendably enough, to attempt to keep the major state investment projects going: given all these constraints, this left inputs to bear the burden of economies. But here we encounter a further phenomenon: the concentration of such inputs in a few industrial sectors. Table 4.12 gives a break-

TABLE 4.12   Imports by selected industrial branches as percentage of total industrial imports, 1974

Industrial sector:	
Food products	23
Of which milk products	(6)
wheat products	(12)
Chemical products	17
Vehicles	23
Of which CKD kits[a]	(21)
Total	63

Source: Ministerio de Industria, unpublished data.
Note: [a] i.e. unassembled kits.

down of industrial inputs for 1974: it shows that 60 per cent are accounted for by three sectors, which together comprise a mere 20 per cent of industrial value added. Thus to economise on imports only by cutting overall demand requires an enormous sacrifice in terms of output, employment and welfare.

The third point has already been mentioned; and overlaps with the above: 50 per cent of imports in any case lie totally outside the impact of these mechanisms, since they are imported by state enterprises. In this respect the figures for the two years preceding stabilisation are rather dramatic, as we see in Table 4.13. (The rising price of oil imports admittedly accounts for some, but by no means all, of the rise in public sector imports in 1974.) Perhaps more starkly than any other, this table reveals the developing crisis in the public sector in terms of lack of control mechanisms over spending, and shows that it was here that the central effort was required. It will be seen that in the first year of stabilisation public sector imports fell 20 per cent as imports for certain investment projects passed their peak, while the internal recession was certainly successful in reducing imports in 1976, but as the above analysis makes clear this required a large fall in investment and economic activity. Investment in real terms fell by 17 per cent in 1977 and GDP *per capita* by 3 per cent.[26] Industrial output slowed down in 1976, as Figure 1 below shows, and fell in early 1977 (see Note 20). Against the other trends in the balance of payments, however, even a fall of $347 million in imports in the course of the year could not halt the loss of reserves. Net international reserves were $116 million at the end of 1975, −$553 million in June 1976 and −$752 million by the end of the year.[27]

TABLE 4.13   Private and public sector imports (US$)

	Total	Private sector	Public sector
1975 shares	100	41	59
1974	+84%	52%	+127%
1975	+25%	+6%	+43%
1976	−14%	−6%	−19%

Source: Boloña (1978).

All this is not to suggest, of course, that there was an alternative short-term policy readily available but rejected by the Fund and the Peruvian authorities. It is unfortunately clear that policies such as import controls and careful selective cuts or taxation of particular sectors require considerable sophistication and experience, and could not be lightly embarked on in a moment of extreme crisis. As the Introduction stresses, this reflects the weak development of the non-orthodox alternative.

Turning to the internal gap, the intention of the measures was to impose cuts in demand via restrictions on both public and private sectors. It follows from the IMF diagnosis of the causes of the crisis that they consider that the brunt should be borne by cuts in public expenditure. But Table 4.14 reveals how different the

TABLE 4.14 Public sector revenue and expenditure 1974–6 (percentage of GDP)

	1974	1975	1st half 1976	2nd half 1976
Central government				
Current expenditure	13·9	16·5	14·9	16·5
Wages and salaries	5·3	5·9	5·7	5·3
Military outlays	3·5	4·6	4·4	5·5
Investment	4·5	5·1	4·0	5·5
Total expenditure	18·4	21·6	18·9	21·9
Revenue	15·2	16·0	14·4	14·2
State enterprises				
Current expenditure	12·7	15·4	17·9	15·8
Investment	4·7	5·3	5·3	4·7
Revenue	13·1	14·5	17·3	20·2
Total public sector				
Current expenditure	28·7	33·6	34·0	33·7
Investment	9·1	9·5	8·7	9·8
Revenue	31·6	32·7	33·2	35·8
Overall deficit	−6·2	−10·4	−9·4	−7·7

Source: IMF (1977).

performance turned out to be: even following such an apparently serious programme as that of June 1976, there appears to have been no economy in current central public spending. Part of this clearly results from the lack of will to cut military spending, and part from the difficulty of reducing the wage and salary component without resorting to actual dismissals. But within current spending there remains a significant 5 per cent of GDP which continued to rise in 1976, reflecting the underlying political problem which had led to a failure to develop control techniques. Public investment usually bears the brunt of those economies which cannot be achieved in current spending: it is arguably to the credit of the Peruvian authorities that they delayed resorting to the abandonment of ongoing development projects – though unfortunately it appears that certain projects were so ill-conceived that abandonment could well have come much sooner.[28]

The overall impact of public sector spending was certainly a deceleration in real terms in 1976 compared with 1975: this can be seen in Table 4.9 above, where constant price estimates reveal that, taking the year as a whole, expenditure was held at 1975 levels. This was enough to contribute significantly to the depression of demand – but not enough to make much impact on the public sector deficit, given what was happening on the revenue side. Here we observe a feedback effect occurring; with the depression and the fall in imports, revenue as a percentage of GDP actually declines with stabilisation, despite sales tax increases. Income tax, for example, was 4·9 per cent of GDP in 1974, and only 2·8 per cent in 1976. The only success is via increases in public utility prices, but these represent a direct cost-push impact for the private sector. Thus the economy is depressed but the deficit is still huge, implying within the model a need for yet more deflation with yet more negative feedback effects.[29]

In the absence of techniques and the political will necessary to curb public expenditure, and with revenue falling rather than rising, there remain only two areas where the programme may be implemented with more success. The first is wages and salaries: Table 4.6 above shows that in 1976 the fall in real wages was 16 per cent and in real salaries 22 per cent (recent estimates suggest a larger fall in 1977). The second is credit to the private sector. As Table 4.15 shows, the contraction of credit was extremely sharp, though public sector financing was hardly reduced. Such credit restrictions no doubt were borne unevenly by different elements in the private sector: although we do not have data for this specific case, it is widely accepted that larger borrowers, and borrowers with access to international sources, suffer less than small firms in such a credit squeeze. Meanwhile the banking sector gains; the high profitability of banking in Peru recently has been documented.[30]

But neither falling private sector wages nor credit restrictions helped the fiscal gap; in fact the growing economic depression to which they contributed tended to worsen the gap, by the effect on tax revenue, as we have mentioned, and through a declining proportion of voluntary private financing of the public sector: while sales of public bonds to the private sector had risen in 1970–4 they failed to rise thereafter.[31] (This was probably in part a reaction to increasingly negative real interest rates as inflation accelerated.)

In summary, then, the programme accelerated inflation in the short-run by the cost-push effects of the relative price adjustments. But while it caused depression it made almost no impact on the fiscal deficit. The depression was enough (eventually) to reduce imports, but since no element of the programme counteracted the stagnation in export volume and value and the growing debt burden, the reserves continued to fall. The uneven impact of the measures was closely related to their growing lack of political feasibility, as became evident in July 1977.

The difficulties and destructive effects of attempted stabilisation were something new in Peru. Peru had in fact been widely regarded in the early 1960s as a showcase of successful stabilisation following the programme of 1959. It will enable us to clarify the nature of the difficulties faced in 1975–8 if we attempt to delineate the changes that occurred in the intervening years in the political and economic structure. It will be our contention that the *modus operandi* of such policies has significantly changed with the years. At the same time, we shall argue, past experiences conditioned policy expectations and attitudes – expectations which did not fully allow for the changed conditions. A historical perspective will also serve to emphasise how far attitudes towards deflation become bound up with wider questions, in particular the entire question of commitment to a 'new' model orientated to development spending and to a wider spreading of the benefits from growth. The next section compares and contrasts the three most recent experiences of stabilisation, with these aims in mind.

III A COMPARATIVE ANALYSIS

It will be the argument of this section that this phenomenon of the concentrated impact of orthodox measures upon a relatively small part of the economy has become worse with time, while in parallel, and more importantly, a number of factors have gone to make the crisis itself more serious with time. This is a matter

TABLE 4.15 Comparative data on the three stabilisation programmes, 1958–76

	1957–60	*1966–8*	*1973–6*
Credit contraction (money and quasi-money as % GDP)	−8%	−17%	−22%
Money supply of internal origin	−7%	+3%	−22%
Public spending % GDP	−2·7 points	−1·7 points	+1·8 points
Tax revenue % GDP	+1·1 points	+0·2 points	−2·2 points
Public sector deficit	1958	1968	1975
% GDP	−2	−3	−10
Cost of living average annual % change	1956–59 7·7		
	1960–3 6·8		
	1965–8 13·6		
	1969–72 6·3		
	1974–6 24·7		
	1977 33·0[a]		

	Balance of payments	
	Current a/c balance as % of exports	*Basic balance as % of exports*
1957	−43	−11
1958	−42	−9
1959	−11	−2
1960	+2	+6
1966	−29	−9
1967	−38	−25
1968	−5	+3
1969	−0	+16
1973	−17	17
1974	−54	6
1975	−119	−31
1976	−88	−38

Source: Banco Central, *Cuentas Nacionales*; *Boletín*; *Memoria*; IMF (1977).
Note: [a] Widely acknowledged to be an underestimate.

partly of the increasing degree of structural crisis already outlined in Section I, and partly of a number of factors which increasingly allow the system to run on to an ever deeper point of crisis before a halt is called.

Table 4.15 and Figure 4.1 present comparative data on the three major instances of stabilisation policies in recent years: 1959, with Beltrán as Prime Minister; 1967–8, at the end of the Belaúnde epoch, and the period already discussed, 1975–7.

In 1959, a programme was implemented in mid-year by Pedro Beltrán, with strong backing by and pressure from the IMF. Beltrán is the stereotype of a conservative, *laissez-faire* economist, and he implemented a severely orthodox programme of fiscal and monetary restraint, plus devaluation and other relative price adjustments. Since we have discussed this programme in detail elsewhere,[32] a brief summary must suffice. The key element in the 'success' of the programme was the recovery of exports at precisely the same moment, for long-run reasons rather than the Beltrán policy. (Not that the devaluation was not necessary: it was. But the expansion of supply in copper, iron ore and fish meal would have occurred anyway.) A much more minor element in the programme was Beltrán's success in imposing wage restraint.

With the recovery in exports, the vicious circles we have emphasised above could be completely avoided. There was a fall in public expenditure – concentrated on investment – but because of the rise in exports the level of activity did not fall. This plus the rise in profits tax with the entry into production of the Toquepala copper mine meant that tax revenue *rose*, and the goals of the programme could be accomplished with relative ease.

With the recovery of the balance of payments, the main goal was immediately accomplished (the rate of internal inflation was not the main preoccupation, and was not affected by the programme).

With Belaúnde we have an altogether more complicated period of policy-making to study. We have explained above the pressures on his government leading to increased spending: the total resistance by APRA to an adequate increase in taxation led to increased borrowing from abroad and to inflationary internal borrowing.[33] By 1967, with exports slackening, the situation was reaching crisis point. The Central Bank apparently hoped that an appeal to the IMF for credit would bring effective external

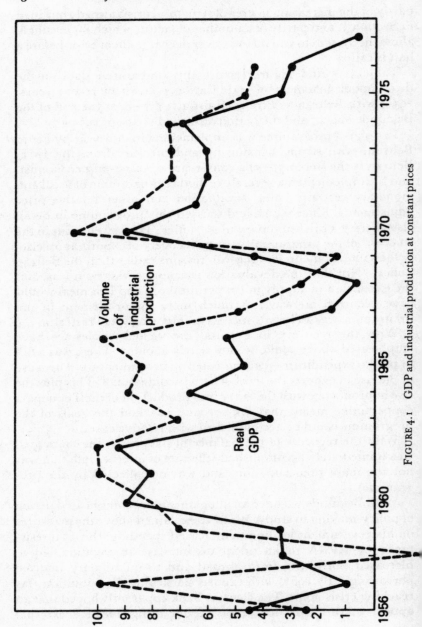

FIGURE 4.1   GDP and industrial production at constant prices

pressure for tax reform; however, Peru was at this point still within its first *tranche*[34] and the Fund mission came and went without playing the role hoped for it.[35] So the ensuing efforts at stabilisation were made without Fund pressure, and never amounted to a full 'orthodox' programme. In 1967 the measures comprised devaluation and very little else. In early 1968 a number of rather unorthodox measures were introduced – such as controls on local borrowing by foreign firms and import controls.[36] There was an increase in the price of petroleum but this was not applied to the Sierra. Rather weak attempts were made at credit restriction and control of expenditure – the latter, in particular, appears to have been totally ineffectual.[37]

Finally in mid-1968 the APRA realised that by provoking financial chaos it might also be provoking the military intervention which would prevent the election on which it had pinned its hopes. The government was granted emergency powers and rushed through a major tax reform, but too late to avert the coup, which occurred in October 1968.[38] In the following months the Military were able to practise conservative virtue in an economy which had already passed through the necessary relative price adjustments, and accomplished an impressive tax reform.

The chief point to notice, then, is the staggered nature of the programme (though programme is a misnomer). It seems that the cost-push effects of the devaluation were relatively modest. This, we would assume, is because this was not one of a large number of simultaneous adjustments. We would suggest that a non-linear relationship holds between the number and size of relative price changes and the stimulus to the wage-price and other adjustments; thus simultaneous adjustments on a number of fronts run a more than proportionate risk of provoking chain reactions. Apparently, what was also important was the wage restraint practised by the APRA-dominated unions.[39]

Turning now to the comparative aspects of the programmes, Table 4.15 immediately makes evident the shift in the weight of the measures, from the fiscal to the monetary side. In the first, contraction of the money supply coefficient was a mere 8 per cent; in the second the contraction was entirely the result of the loss of reserves, as money of internal origin expanded. In the third, both external forces and internal policies worked powerfully to secure a major contraction – a fall of 22 per cent in the coefficient. The public spending coefficient, on the other hand, fell heavily in the first – with the cuts lying all in investment – less heavily in the second, and actually rose in the third. The 'feedback' effects on tax revenue were only really felt in the third, as will be clear from our description.

What also emerges is the increasing burden carried by wage and salary earners; what cannot be presented so easily in comparable statistics is the growing burden carried in terms of unemployment and under-employment.

Perhaps even more vividly, however, the table makes clear the basic reason for the growing burden: the increasing severity of the crisis. This is reflected in the size of the fiscal disequilibrium, in the balance-of-payments deficit, and in the acceleration of inflation. As suggested earlier, the increasing gravity of the situation was related fundamentally to the underlying long-run trends – but was also a product of a number of factors which allowed it to run on to an ever-deeper point of crisis before action was taken. These factors are related to underlying changes in the socio-political and economic structure, with industrialisation and the growth of a middle class and of organised popular classes with some sense of social rights. This meant, for example, a change in attitudes on devaluation. In the 1950s, with traditional exporting groups dominant, exchange rate changes came relatively frequently; the adjustments were small and not overly disturbing.[40] By the 1960s, with the growth of a middle class enjoying imported consumer durables, or domestically produced consumer goods with a high import content, and with the related growth of industrial groups, the whole balance of interests had shifted. This is shown up in the size of the disequilibrium: in the 1959 programme the devaluation was 20 per cent while in 1967 it was 45 per cent – with a far larger devaluation occurring in the course of the following year, bringing the final figure to over 150 per cent.[41] This becomes a totally different matter in terms of the cost-push repercussions.

A further product of the same shifts in structure was a change in the political backing for orthodoxy. In the 1950s it is clear that openly orthodox measures could produce a political consolidation on the right which was important for their implementation.[42] By the 1960s the political spectrum was far more complex, which is reflected in Belaúnde's mix of orthodox and unorthodox measures; he appeared to lack a base for a clear shift in policies either to the right or to the left. Again, the same situation is reflected in the hesitant application of stabilisation policies in 1975, meaning that the 1976 measures had to be far harsher than would originally have been necessary – and so leading to political crisis.

Underlying the questions of attitudes, and relevant to explaining how the crisis was allowed to become so great, is also the fact that these earlier programmes were apparently relatively successful. How far and in what way this influenced the perceptions of policy-makers is a question for further research: we suggest that it may have been important in two very different ways. First, those favouring deflation derived confidence in the likely success of orthodox measures from past experiences, a confidence which neglected the changed conditions. Second, those giving priority to development spending may in their turn have derived confidence from a sense that crises had been survived in the past with apparent ease and without drastic deflation.

The second perspective ignored the seriousness of the new crisis; the first ignored not only the nature of past experiences but also the changed *modus operandi* of the measures, in particular their increasingly concentrated impact given the new pressures, interests and changes in economic structure. This was to lead to more destructive results and to more political resistance than had been encountered before.

In part the problems faced by such policies were the result – paradoxically it may seem – of the growing role of the state. With the growth of pressures for state spending and the gradual emergence of a 'developmental' state, more and more areas became 'priority' areas, forcing the pressure more and more on to the private sector. This we see dramatically in Tables 4.14 and 4.15; in the final programme state spending actually rose as a percentage of GDP. While the textbook world of economics might appear to imply that, with more areas directly under state control, the administration of restrictions could be simpler and more efficient, the actuality is easily explained in terms of political economy, as more and more groups secured direct means of protecting their own interests, and removed themselves from the 'automatic' impact of the measures.

The second factor increasing the concentration effect was the shifting structure of imports. In part it was the consequence of the import-substitution process, which increased the weight of essential items in the import bill. And in part it was the result of the neglect of traditional agriculture, which maintained and even increased the weight of food imports in the total.

It also seems probable that the factor we have emphasised above – the concentration of imported inputs in a few sectors – has increased with time, again because of the *modus operandi* of the industrialisation process.[43]

A further element is the increase in industrial concentration, both within sectors and in terms of the links between sectors.[44] It can reasonably be assumed[45] that this has meant that as the burden has fallen increasingly on credit restriction to the private sector, so, too, increasingly the more powerful have been able to protect themselves – again, concentrating the impact on a smaller area.

IV THE CURRENT SITUATION

In the light of the above discussion, the difficulties faced by the policy by July 1977 are only too easily understood. The measures faced a crisis of resistance at three key points: the private sector, particularly industry, was desperate for credit, foreign exchange, and for some revival of demand to improve its sales; the labour force had reached a point of reaction to falling real incomes almost unheard of in Peru;[46] and various elements of the Military were determined not to cut back defence and other forms of state spending, which they felt were essential to national security. As described above, these elements of resistance led to the loss of two finance ministers in fifty days and the breakdown of negotiations with the Fund.

Events since then reveal the lack of options faced by a relatively small dependent economy once it reaches such a point of crisis. The only conceivable alternative, short of a Cuban-style switch of alliances, to accommodation to external pressures was a moratorium on the external debt and a vigorous and sophisticated policy of selective controls. In practice, the size of the debt burden was such that only a complete moratorium would be of any assistance: this was – realistically – assumed to mean that as a consequence not only would inflows of private and public capital be suspended, but that most supplies of imports would be cut off, as well as all possible sanctions imposed on the export front. An economy as vulnerable as the Peruvian, as dependent both on imports and on external supplies of capital, was hardly a good candidate for the resulting complications. A non-orthodox policy of intervention and control, without moratorium, would not have had the necessary room for manoeuvre given the lack of experience and the non-existence of the necessary institutional machinery.

In fact it was very clear that no positive alternative policy really existed, despite attempts by the Instituto Nacional de Planificación to put forward a *'Plan de Reactivación'*. The government bought time – expensively – by arranging 'swap' agreements with a number of Latin American countries and by ruling that all import credits must be for 180 days instead of the previous minimum of 90 days. A mission then went to the USA to attempt to negotiate with the chief creditors without the blessing of the Fund, the incentive being the renewed commitment to elections in 1980, with a Constitutional Assembly to be elected in 1978, and a promise to reduce defence spending. The election pledge was also an attempt internally to offer circuses where bread was lacking. Not surprisingly, the reaction of the international banks and other creditors was to say that they had no confidence in existing policies and that Peru must work out a settlement with the IMF before refinancing would be forthcoming.

By October 1977 a new agreement was reached with the IMF, though it was not signed until December. The Peruvians won acceptance of the need to freeze subsidies and petrol prices; but they had to agree to a sharp deflation of public spending. The exchange rate system was reformed, with a new system of controlled depreciation introduced.

According to the agreement, the central government's current deficit was to swing from −3·4 per cent of GDP in 1977, to +2 per cent in 1978. If we look back to our analysis of Table 4.14 the degree of improbability here will be seen to be very great. Tax measures introduced included increased charges on passports, an increase from 2 per cent to 4 per cent in the tax on fees for the self-employed, a once-only increase of one-third of the tax on firms' assets – hardly enough to counterbalance, let alone outweigh, the continuing effect of the depression on tax regimes. This left expenditure to bear the brunt of the cuts; unless the Military were genuinely prepared to cut defence spending, it was obvious that the agreement must be broken. The renegotiation of the debt with international banks was postponed to February 1978.

By that date, it was abundantly clear that the agreement had not been kept. Prolonged negotiations with the IMF eventually broke down in March 1978, with the economy surviving from day to day on last-minute arrangements to roll over part of the debt. Meanwhile there was a slight improvement evident in the external balance by the end of 1977, as copper sales rose by enough to outweigh the falling world price, coffee benefited from good prices and the volume of iron ore exports rose.[47] The depression generated a very slight fall in imports.

Nevertheless, this slight improvement was still not enough to stop reserves falling: by May the country was apparently only able to avoid outright default on overdue payments by persuading Occidental Petroleum to make an advance deposit of $23 million.[48] At this point the Government achieved an agreement with the IMF and the US Treasury on tax reforms and elimination of subsidies, which it was hoped would be enough to persuade the private banks to roll over some $250 million of the debt, even though the price rises would be delayed until after the elections for a Constitutional Assembly on 6 June.[49] Meanwhile Chase Manhattan began to press more strongly for a special decree-law guaranteeing that the proceeds of the sales from the copper mine should go exclusively to the servicing and repayment of the $500 million package of loans financing Cuajone (and carrying on government guarantee)[50] a measure strongly resisted in Peru. A cabinet shake-up produced a new Minister of Economy, who decided that the austerity measures must come at once. Accordingly price rises of 50–60 per cent in foodstuffs and transport were introduced in late May, and the elections were postponed for two weeks, in a new atmosphere of repression, with universities and schools closed and widespread arrests and deportations.[51] At the time of writing it appears that this has at least secured the hoped-for roll-over of the debt and a tiny breathing space. Whether this can be made use of, and how, remains to be seen.

V CONCLUSION

If we attempt to situate Peru among Latin American experiences of stabilisation policy, it is noticeable how far until the late 1960s the country opted for the application of conservative policies of a relatively unsophisticated type. In general there was far less willingness to experiment with innovatory policies, over imports,

regulation of foreign capital, manipulation of domestic investment, than in Brazil or Mexico, say, or even countries of a smaller
size, such as Colombia. This is one reason why the Velasco
experiment attracted so much attention.

This in part reflects a history of lack of such policies which is
self-reinforcing; there is a definite 'learning-process' which operates in this area, and Peru has never embarked very seriously
upon it. This has the undoubted consequence that in the short
term such policies either do not appear to be an option, or else are
seriously mishandled.

While export-led growth was working smoothly, as in the
1950s, this never appeared to matter, for in a real sense the
international system looked after its own. Flows of investment
secured an expansion of exports which safeguarded the system,
and orthodox policies could 'work' precisely because they were
never placed under serious strain. But with the advent of the
strains within the model which we have discussed here, the
safeguards worked less surely – so much so that we suggested at
the start of this chapter that the value of this case study from a
comparative perspective was precisely to illuminate the conditions under which even the short-term goals of stabilisation
appear nearly impossible to achieve. The study has shown how,
with time, the room for manoeuvre both in political and economic
terms has become far narrower while the costliness and inefficien-
cy of the measures have increased.

It is time now to reverse the process and ask what is the value of
the other case studies for Peru. Some might conclude from the
above that the solution was a still firmer implementation of
stabilisation, even though it undoubtedly implies distasteful but
necessary measures of repression. But the importance of the cases
here discussed which have followed this route is to raise serious
doubts as to the longer-term success of such measures, in the sense
of creating a viable system of accumulation supported by an
adequate political framework. Meanwhile, the study of Argentina
suggests eloquently how drastic stabilisation may create an institutional response in the form of more adequate defence
mechanisms, which worsen the inflationary problem in the long-
run. This effect has not yet arrived in the case of Peru, but it can be
predicted to lie ahead, if the lesson is not learned.

In view of these considerations, we would argue strongly for an
alternative conclusion: if orthodoxy is no solution, yet the pres-

sures of the international system appear to force it on a country once it reaches this point of crisis, then the Peruvian people will be forced to pay a very high price for the unsuccessful attempts of their leaders to tackle the country's underlying problems. Whether international opinion can be persuaded to cushion the shock in this case remains to be seen. But in general such generosity should not be relied on. Therefore the broader lesson is the importance of avoiding such vulnerability; the political and institutional base for more adequate and more sophisticated policies must be found and room for manoeuvre must be retained. The mistakes and the lack of coherence of the Velasco regime must not be allowed to discredit yet again – as in 1948 – the name of interventionist policies in general.[52]

NOTES

1   See the discussion in the Introduction.
2   *Le Monde.*
3   This summarises themes developed at length in Thorp and Bertram (1978).
4   A clear example of the dangers of half-breaking with one model, while no clear alternative has been developed.
5   See Abusada (1978) for instances of negative value added at world prices.
6   A point which has not yet been adequately documented, but is strongly suggested by, for example, Kuczynski's description of rushing through foreign tenders for building cargo boats in 1967, in order to secure the cash loan which was part of the contract (Kuczynski, 1977, pp. 100–1).
7   Instituto Nacional de Planificación (INP) (1977) p. 103.
8   See INP (1977) for a demonstration of the increasingly unfavourable impact on the balance of payments of foreign investment up to the present.
9   It seems also to be a common problem that domestic investors are more conscious of the 'attack on capitalism' aspect of measures against foreign capital, than of their protectionist aspect.
10 The 'Industrial Register' forbade imports of goods which could be produced locally, and was in practice administered in a very protectionist fashion. The high level of profitability is difficult to document quantitatively, but is clear in many qualitative sources.
11 This was true both of IPC and Cerro.
12 ITINTEC was the agency created by the General Law of Industries to further the development of local technology and to supervise foreign contracts. But it had very little impact, suffering from institutional factors as well as the long-term nature of the problem. As for imported content, state enterprises appear to buy preferentially abroad (FitzGerald (1976) p. 54). Certainly, state imports rose almost unbelievably, as we see later.
13 The pressure on consumption was no part of the private sector's investment problems, however. It is clear that profitability was extremely high; confidence was the problem.

14 See Webb (1977) Chapter 4 for an analysis of the tax policies of the Velasco regime.
15 See the discussion in the Introduction.
16 Partly because of the unexpected difficulties in organising external co-operation.
17 This was in part related to the financial aspect, which necessitated borrowing abroad for all major projects, reducing the favourable balance-of-payments effects.
18 i.e. reserves net of liabilities: Banco Central, *Memoria*, 1976, p. 200.
19 Though apparently the Central Bank president insists that the programme was Peru's own idea – see Stallings (1978).
20 The data came from an unpublished report of the Ministerio de Industria (1977). They suggest rather clearly the worsening income distribution: output in general was very depressed in the first months of 1977, but output of consumer durables and cars was still rising, while certain inferior products such as margarine experienced increased demand.
21 Ministry of Labour, as cited in *Actualidad Económica*, April 1978.
22 See Stallings (1978) for an extremely interesting account of the role of the private banks.
23 The argument between the Central Bank and the Fund was made public in *Equis* in several issues in March and April 1977.
24 IMF (1977) p. 1.
25 The official figure is 11·6 per cent of exports in 1973 – but a large part of this represented refined minerals. 'Manufactures' proper were 1·5 per cent of the total (GIECO, 1974).
26 Figures cited by the Minister of Economy in a speech, October 1977 (see *La Prensa*, 11 October 1977).
27 Banco Central, *Memoria*, 1977, p. 200.
28 The Majes project being a conspicuous example.
29 Including, for example, rising unit costs as output falls – see Fishlow (1973) for an estimate of this in the case of Brazil.
30 *Andean Report*, December 1977.
31 Data supplied by the Banco Central de Reserva.
32 Thorp (1967).
33 From the social security system. As Kuczynski (1977) p. 95 shows, the one inviolable rule was that there should not be borrowing from the Central Bank. The authorities therefore borrowed abroad and from social security: both measures were inflationary but *legal*.
34 Drawings equal to the first half of a country's drawing rights may be made with few or no conditions. Thereafter the conditions become increasingly severe.
35 Kuczynski (1977) p. 164.
36 Thorp and Bertram (1978) p. 294.
37 The 1967/68 budget could not be passed owing to APRA's refusal to allow tax reform; for many months the finances of ministries and public enterprises continued in a completely *ad hoc* and unco-ordinated fashion.
38 On the reasons for the coup, see Philip (1978).
39 Kuczynski (1977) argues this point (p. 185). Wage data in Peru are poor, but appear to confirm it.

40 Dragisic (1971) is very helpful on this.
41 The final instance was of course worsened by the world commodity price boom and the boom in lending, both of which also contributed powerfully to allowing the disequilibrium to run on.
42 Again, see Dragisic on this.
43 The sectors which dominate the import structure are food processing, automobiles and chemicals (between them accounting for 63 per cent of imported inputs). The two latter have increased their weight in the production structure, while other sectors have also experienced a fall in their import coefficient.
44 See the studies by the Ministerio de Industria (e.g. those of 1974 and 1977) and the work on ownership links by Anaya, F. (1975) and Torres, Z. (1976).
45 This would be worth exploring. Much work now exists measuring concentration, but its implications have not been fully developed.
46 In the form of the general strike of July 1977.
47 *Latin America Economic Report*, 14 April 1978.
48 *Latin America Economic Report*, 19 May 1978.
49 *Latin America Political Report*, 19 May 1978.
50 *Latin America Economic Report*, 26 May 1978.
51 *Financial Times*, 16 June 1978.
52 The way the mishandling of non-orthodox periods of policy is in itself a product of export-led growth, and the relations of Peru with the international system, is one of the themes developed in Thorp and Bertram (1978).

REFERENCES

Abusada, R. (1978), 'El Costo de Ahorro de Divisas Externas', *Economía*, vol. 1, no. 1, Universidad Católica, Lima.

Actualidad Económica, Lima, monthly.

Anaya Franco, E. (1975), *Imperialismo, Industrialización y Transferencia de Tecnologia en el Perú*, Editorial Horizonte, Lima.

Andean Report, Lima, weekly.

Banco Central, *Boletin*, Lima (monthly).

Banco Central, *Cuentas Nacionales del Perú*, Lima (annual).

Banco Central, *Memoria*, Lima (annual).

Boloña, C. (1978), 'Importaciones del Estado 1971–1976', *Apuntes*, año IV, no. 8, Lima.

Dragisic, J. (1971), 'Peruvian Stabilisation Policies, 1938–68', University of Wisconsin Ph.D. thesis.

Financial Times, London.

Fishlow, A. (1973), 'Some Reflections on Post-1964 Brazilian Economic Policy', in A. Stepan, (ed.), *Authoritarian Brazil: Origins, Policies and Future*, Yale University Press.

FitzGerald, E. V. K. (1975), *The State and Economic Development: Peru since 1968*, Cambridge University Press.

FitzGerald, E. V. K. (1979), *The Search for National Development: The Political Economy of Peru 1956–76*, Cambridge University Press, forthcoming 1979.

Grupo de Investigaciones Económicas (GIECO) (1974), *Evaluación de las Exportaciones no Tradicionales con destino a la subregión Andina*, Universidad Nacional de Ingerie, Lima.

Instituto Nacional de Planificacion (INP) (1977), El Caso de la Deuda Publica Peruana: 1965–1975, Las Empresas Transacionales y el Endeudamiento Externo, Lima, mimeo.

International Monetary Fund (IMF) (1977), *Peru – Recent Economic Developments*, Washington DC.

Kuczynski, P. P. (1977), *Peruvian Democracy under Economic Stress: the Belaúnde Years*, Princeton.

La Prensa, Lima (daily).

Latin America Economic Report, London (weekly).

Latin America Political Report, London (weekly).

Ministerio de Industria y Turismo (1974), 'Efectos de la Politica Industrial sobre la Inversión en el Sector', Lima, MS.

Philip, G. D. E. (1978), *The Rise and Fall of the Peruvian Military Radicals 1968–1976*, University of London, Institute of Latin American Studies, Monograph no. 9. Athlone Press.

Reynolds, C. (1977), 'Social Reform and Foreign Debt: the Peruvian Dilemma', memo to Wells Fargo Bank, mimeo.

Stallings, B. (1978), 'Peru and the U.S. Banks: Who Has the Upper Hand', University of Wisconsin, mimeo.

Thorp, R. (1967), 'Inflation and Orthodox Economic Policy in Peru', *Bulletin of the Oxford University Institute of Economics and Statistics*, vol. 29, August 1967.

Thorp, R. and Bertram, G. (1978), *Peru 1890–1977: Growth and Policy in an Open Economy*, Macmillan, 1978.

Torres, Z., J. A. (1976), *Protecciones Efectivas y Sustitucion de Importaciones en Perú*, CISEPA, documento de trabajo, no. 33, Universidad Católica, Lima.

Webb, R. C. (1977), *Government Policy and the Distribution of Income in Peru: 1963–1973*, Harvard University Press.

5 Stabilisation Policy in Uruguay since the 1950s

M. H. J. FINCH*

On three occasions in the last twenty years measures to restrain the rate of increase in the level of prices have apparently taken priority over other objectives in Uruguayan economic policy. Stabilisation programmes were adopted in 1959–60, 1968, and 1973–4. Each of these programmes may be analysed in respect of the explicit or implicit diagnosis made of the causes of the inflation, of the measures taken to reduce the rate of inflation, and of the effect of these measures on inflation, output, employment, the trade balance, etc. But the success or failure of these programmes is not judged here primarily as a technical achievement in making price stabilisation consistent with other policy aims.[1] Indeed, it is disputable whether in any of these three periods relative price stability has in fact assumed priority over other policy objectives. Rather, the starting point for the analysis in this chapter is that the inflationary process in Uruguay, and the reactions of policy-makers to it, are unintelligible except in the context of a profound and deepening economic and political decline which first became evident in the mid-1950s. The stabilisation periods correspond to distinct phases of the crisis, characterised by changes in the structure of the state, by shifting alliances within the capitalist class, by worsening symptoms of economic decline affecting the mass of the population, and by the emergence of new relationships with an evolving international economy. The three periods of stabilisation policy are a response, therefore, to specific sets of circumstances prevailing at moments of crisis within a long-run process of economic stagnation and political decay.

BACKGROUND

Uruguay has traditionally been regarded as somewhat exceptional among the nations of Latin America.[2] Although territorially the smallest of the South American republics, the high ratio of natural resources (mainly primitive pasture) to population enabled the country to achieve levels of *per capita* exports and income which were probably unequalled elsewhere in the region during the first half of the twentieth century. But in spite of the overwhelming proportion of exports accounted for until recently by rural production, the development of the Uruguayan economy and society has been basically urban in character. Immigrants in the late nineteenth and early twentieth centuries found neither available land nor employment in the rural sector, and either remained in Montevideo or moved on to Argentina. Even before the First World War the capital held 30 per cent of the population – the proportion in 1975 was 45 per cent of the total population of 2.8 million – while primary sector employment absorbed less than 30 per cent of the labour force. The large size and rapid growth of Montevideo, and the relative political weakness of the landowning class, permitted the development of a political ideology during the presidencies of José Batlle y Ordóñez (1903–7, 1911–5) which dominated the life of the nation almost without interruption until the military coup of 1973. The visible expressions (though not necessarily innovations) of *batllismo* were protectionism, an expanded public sector, labour legislation, and a well-developed and generous social security system. *Batllismo* both based itself on and contributed to an urban, predominantly middle-class social system, by devices which redistributed part of the surplus of the rural sector. The prosperity of the country, its political stability, constitutional innovation and legislative achievement, appeared by the mid-1950s to make Uruguay a model for the rest of Latin America.

The previous decade, following the end of the Second World War, had witnessed a vigorous growth process dominated by the strategy of import substitution. The stimulus to industrial growth which became apparent in some sectors in the second half of the 1930s, but was concealed mainly by adverse external factors during the war, produced an average annual rate of industrial growth of 6 per cent over the ten years.[3] Arable agriculture also expanded greatly during the period, under the stimulus of high guaranteed prices. The sense of increased national autonomy during this period was heightened by the purchase by the state of the most important British-owned public utility companies, especially the railways. By the mid-1950s, when the growth process gave way to an economic stagnation which was to persist over the following two decades, Uruguay enjoyed a *per capita* income of almost US$950 p.a., higher than that of any other Latin American country.[4]

The factors which stimulated the growth of import-substituting activities, especially in industry, and which brought the process to an abrupt end, may be briefly outlined. When the crisis of the inter-war period reached Uruguay, cutting export receipts by over 40 per cent between 1930 and 1932, the country already had one of the more highly industrialised economies in Latin America. Although the coup of 1933 installed in power political groups directly representing the landowners who produced the country's staple export commodities, in place of the urban-oriented *batllistas*, the withdrawal of support by Britain as a consequence of the Ottawa Agreements greatly weakened the regime. Moreover, it was unable to dislodge the important if small group of manufacturers; nor could it ignore the significance of existing industry for the economy of Montevideo. Protectionism thus continued during the 1930s, and the downward pressure on real wages, characteristic of the 1933 regime, began to be reversed at the end of the decade. The restoration of the *batllista* wing of the Colorado Party from 1942 onwards introduced a new phase of urban, interventionist and redistributive policy. The system of social security, already well advanced, was further elaborated. Wage bargaining was to be conducted in a new regime of wages councils (Consejos de Salarios) in which the state was represented alongside labour and capital. The state sector was itself extended.

The post-war decade of industrial expansion was achieved largely by the use of policy instruments operating on the external sector—trade and exchange controls and multiple exchange rates—which had evolved from measures employed to meet the crisis of the 1930s. There was no overall industrial policy, nor were there credit or technical institutions capable of guiding the industrialisation effort. The opposition which might have been expected from the landowning class to the new orientation, and especially the system of penalty and preferential exchange rates which appeared in developed form at the end of the 1940s, was limited both by the mobility of capital between the rural and urban sectors, and by the very rapid growth of export values in the immediate post-war and Korean War periods. The heavy foreign currency requirements of industry were met by the high level of export earnings at the beginning of the 1950s, and from reserves accumulated during the Second World War.

The limitations of Uruguay's post-war economic strategy were revealed in the second half of the 1950s. To some extent they reflected the inevitable disadvantages of small market size. Though the *batllista* tradition of redistributive policy endowed Uruguay with a relatively equal income distribution, the population of less than 2.5 million could not continue to support an industrialisation effort which was based exclusively on the domestic market. Indeed, while a number of 'dynamic' industries were established after the war, it is significant that three traditional industries—food processing, beverages and textiles—still accounted for almost half of the industrial product in 1955, as they had a decade earlier.[5]

While the nature of the market set long-term limits to the import substituting industrialisation model (ISI), the timing and severity of the crisis was determined by the collapse of the export sector. Production of beef and wool had been subject to long-run stagnation for several decades, as a result of the limited animal-carrying capacity of the land, and the failure to invest in land improvements or develop techniques producing an increased pasture yield. During the 1950s there was a sharp deterioration. From their peak value in 1952–4, export receipts fell steadily to a level 46 per cent lower by 1958–60. Though this decline was exaggerated by falling prices in the 1950s after the Korean War boom, in volume terms (1961 prices) exports were down over the same period by 30 per cent. The results for industry were disastrous. To the decline in domestic purchasing power was added the effect of a massive deterioration in the balance of payments on imports of new equipment, and that of a diminishing supply of raw materials to the food processing and textile sectors, which depended heavily on domestic sources.

STABILISATION BY THE BLANCOS, 1959–60[6]

The policy response to the exhaustion of the ISI strategy was delayed until the end of the 1950s. The ruling Colorado Party, representing an alliance of industrial capital and urban labour, was re-elected in 1954, and remained wholly commited to the growth of manufacturing. The alliance was increasingly difficult to sustain, however, and with growing opposition from the rural sector was defeated in the electoral victory of the Blanco Party in 1958 (with decisive support from the rural middle class, represented by the Liga Federal de Acción Ruralista).

The entry into office of the new government in March 1959 was followed within months by an IMF mission and the promulgation of a stabilisation programme, the Reforma Cambiaria y Monetaria, at the end of 1959. In the course of that year the rate of inflation had accelerated sharply to almost 40 per cent. The diagnosis made by the IMF of the inflation process attributed it primarily to losses sustained in the operations of the multiple exchange rate system, the excessive expansion of credit to the private sector, and the operating deficits of the state corporations. In addition to action to correct the latter two causes, the Fund recommended a unified and freely determined exchange rate, and the termination of the structure of trade and exchange controls.

The measures introduced by the Reforma Cambiaria were generally faithful to the source of its inspiration. Collectively they expressed the ideology of liberalism and free markets, in place of what had become an enormously complex system of trade and exchange controls. The objectives were to establish internal and external equilibrium by creating a free exchange market and single exchange rate, while dismantling controls and reversing the trend to bilateralism. These measures were accompanied by a restriction of the money supply,[7] and a substantial devaluation. To minimise the difficulties of the transitional period, export taxes, import surcharges and advance deposits against imports were introduced in what was intended to be a temporary regime. The levels of the taxes, surcharges and deposits were variable according to the nature of the commodity traded, such that an essential characteristic of the multiple exchange rate system was reproduced. A short while later, in September 1960, a par value for the peso was agreed with the IMF, the Uruguayan quota with the Fund was doubled to US$30 million, and the way was open for the inflow of dollar credits.

Stabilisation did not, as it did elsewhere in Latin America, interrupt the process of economic growth. GDP at constant factor cost in 1959 had contracted by 6·2 per cent compared with two years earlier, and this loss was regained by 1961. The explanation for the renewal of growth lies in the recovery of the livestock sector from a severe decline in the level of output during 1958–9. As a result, visible exports achieved in 1961 their highest level for five years in volume terms, as shown in Table 5.1 (though this was no more than the average level of 1945–55 and would not be reached again until the late 1960s). The revival of exports, and the removal of import controls, produced a surge in the level of commodity imports, resulting in an accumulated visible trade deficit for 1960–2 of US$120 million. In real terms the supply of commodity exports in 1960–1 was over 40 per cent greater than in 1958–9 (Table 5.2). The increase was particularly well-marked in the case of consumer durables and capital equipment, but the supply of raw materials also expanded. None the less, and in spite of the failure of stabilisation policy to reduce real wage levels, the resumption of growth did not end the stagnation of manufacturing industry. Livestock raising, agriculture and commerce were the only sectors to show important signs of growth.[8]

The recovery of exports from the disaster of 1959 was not due solely to the redistribution of income effected by the devaluation of the peso; in part it reflected the recovery of the rural sector from the very severe floods which had disrupted production that year. Nor did the new policy resolve the structural problems of the livestock sector. Revival was also linked with the fact that especially during the later 1950s a substantial part of exportable production was withheld from the market and sold illicitly across the border in Brazil, a practice made less attractive following devaluation. Even the intention to shift the internal terms of trade in favour of those producing for export was to be frustrated: against the general price index (1961 = 100), prices to producers of beef, wool and linseed (the principal export commodities) rose from an average of 92 in 1954–8 to 137 in 1960, only to fall to 89 in 1962 and 80 the following year.[9] The gains achieved by the rural sector were therefore only temporary. So, equally, was the increase in government revenue resulting from the higher yield of export taxes, which contributed to modest budget surpluses in 1959–60. By 1962 the budget deficit as a proportion of central government spending was 20 per cent. Following three successive years in which the rate of price increase had fallen, reaching 11 per cent in 1962, a new and more rapid phase of the inflationary process was under way.

An explanation of the Reforma Cambiaria and its eventual fate cannot be made without reference to the inherited political tradition of the country. It is clear, first of all, that by 1958 the strategy of ISI had run its course, and that the defeat of Luis Batlle's Colorado Party in elections that year represented the weakening of the alliance of industrial capital and urban labour in the face of rural discontent now expressed politically as well as economically. The incoming government of the Blanco Party had strong backing from the rural upper and middle classes. Taking office in the midst of an acute balance of payments crisis, and without a coherent programme of its own, it was inevitable that the new government should seek the assistance of the IMF. Indeed, the Colorados had previously done so, though without success. None the less the Blancos were not an exclusively 'rural' party, any more than the Colorados could afford to represent only urban interests. As multi-class parties, each sought the support of a wide spectrum of interests, and both had developed to a high degree the techniques and practices of clientelism. Certainly, the urban-oriented development of Uruguay, with an expanded state sector and a high level of welfare provision, was the achievement of the *batllista* Colorados. But these were assets forming part of the patrimony of both political parties, each having the right to nominate for public appointments and the capacity to manipulate the welfare state apparatus in the interests of an electoral clientèle. The Blancos, no less than the Colorados, were prepared to employ the devices of the *batllista* state (originating in conditions of economic growth) to sustain themselves in power. The degree of autonomy of the political system in relations with the dominant class at this period was enhanced by increasing popular demand for political mediation as the economic crisis deepened,[10] and by the failure of the rural sector to construct alliances with other factions or classes on the basis of which it could sustain its dominance. As a result of this *impasse*, the inflationary process developed new momentum in a phase marked particularly by the growth of foreign currency speculation and capital flight.

STABILISATION BY PACHECO, 1968

The interval between the first and second stabilisation periods was marked by continued stagnation and accelerating inflation. Assuming a rate of population increase of 1·2 per cent,[11] the level of

TABLE 5.1 GDP, industrial production, export and import indices in Uruguay, 1955–77

	Rate of growth of GDP at 1961 market prices %	Rate of growth of industrial production 1961 market prices %	Exports		Imports		Terms of trade (1961=100)
			Volume index (1961=100)	Price index (1961=100)	Volume index (1961=100)	Price index (1961=100)	
1955			90·3	116·7	112·5	101·2	115·3
1956	1·7	5·5	114·8	109·6	94·4	106·4	103·0
1957	1·0	1·7	67·4	116·4	111·2	109·2	106·6
1958	−3·6	−1·3	88·6	101·1	63·8	107·7	93·9
1959	−2·8	−4·2	63·3	98·0	82·6	102·4	95·7
1960	3·6	2·9	71·6	104·0	107·1	96·7	107·5
1961	3·0	−2·1	100	100	100	100	100
1962	−2·2	0·2	87·6	100·2	115·5	95·3	105·1
1963	−1·0	−0·9	93·3	101·3	84·8	99·4	101·9
1964	3·3	7·2	88·8	115·3	95·1	98·8	116·7
1965	1·3	−0·2	99·3	110·2	71·4	98·1	112·3
1966	3·4	1·9	94·8	112·3	82·1	96·6	116·3
1967	−3·2	−4·5	86·8	104·6	86·2	95·7	109·3
1968	1·6	4·2	108·5	94·5	76·9	98·5	95·9
1969	6·1	5·0	111·4	103·0	96·6	98·3	104·8
1970	4·7	4·9	124·8	106·7	100·5	100·5	106·2
1971	−1·0	−2·1	114·1	103·2	118·0	90·6	113·9
1972	−3·6	−1·2	93·0	125·9	114·9	88·6	142·1
1973	0·8	0·4	103·7	180·8	120·7	113·6	159·2
1974	3·1	3·5	121·7	179·4	102·4	228·9	78·4
1975	4·4	6·7	159·3	138·3	109·7	244·2	56·6
1976	2·6	4·0	228·3	141·6	122·2	231·3	61·2
1977	3·4	6·1					

Sources: Instituto de Economía, Uruguay: Estadísticas Básicas, Tables 25–6, 37, 64; Banco Central del Uruguay, Boletín Estadístico Mensual.

per capita income attained in 1961 was not reached again until 1970
(Table 5.2). The rate of inflation of the first stabilisation year,
1959, was exceeded in 1964 and continued to increase. Added to
the operating losses of the public sector, central government
current spending exceeded revenue in each year after 1964.[12] The
trade deficits sustained during the years of the first stabilisation,
on the other hand, were eliminated by the abandonment in May
1963 of the exchange rate fixed by the Reforma Cambiaria. The
new rate of 16·50 pesos to the dollar was further devalued at the
end of 1964, twice during 1965, and at the end of 1966. The fixed
rate before 1963 had secured a degree of price stability, but at the
cost of trade deficits, speculative pressure against the peso, and
heavy foreign borrowing. Devaluation virtually ended the drain
into foreign currency in 1963, but in the following three years
capital flight is estimated at not less than US$190 million, as
more rapid inflation stimulated renewed currency speculation.[1]
A further problem derived from the level of external indebtedness
which had increased markedly in the early 1960s. With approximately US$100 million in interest, and amortisation falling due
for payment in 1967, a further round of stabilisation was predict-
able.

After an initial period of reluctance by the newly elected
Colorado administration, an accommodation with the IMF was
sought late in 1967. The decision was precipitated (as it had been
in 1959) by successive periods of drought and flood during the
year, which reduced the volume of exportable production (Table
5.1). In line with the agreement with the IMF which was signed in
February 1968, the peso was devalued in November 1967 in the
official market from 99 to 200 to the dollar. Demand was restricted
by reduced central government expenditure (particularly
through the declining real value of transfer payments), which
contributed to the virtual elimination of the budget deficit, and
the expansion of the money supply was sharply curtailed. The
cost-push pressures generated by devaluation were severe, however, and by April 1968 the price level was already 34 per cent
above that of the previous December (though the monthly rate
was slackening). A further devaluation of 25 per cent was decreed
at the end of that month but, with wages and prices continuing to
advance,[14] a general wage and price freeze was decreed two
months later. The Consejos de Salarios were replaced by the

TABLE 5.2   Gross national income in Uruguay 1955, 1960–77 (thousands of new pesos, 1961 prices)

	Gross domestic expenditure					Exports	Imports	GDP	Terms of trade effect	Gross domestic income	Net income from abroad	Gross national income
	Private consumption	Government consumption	Gross fixed investment	Change in inventories	Total							
1955	12·821	1·763	3·135	19	17·738	1·914	2·814	16·838	320	17·158	−29	17·129
1960	12·934	1·794	2·488	336	17·552	2·008	2·758	16·802	−24	16·778	−41	16·737
1961	12·536	1·828	2·753	318	17·435	2·467	2·623	17·279	—	17·279	−70	17·209
1962	13·087	1·913	2·810	−71	17·739	2·118	2·975	16·882	188	17·070	−85	16·985
1963	12·691	1·889	2·327	133	17·040	2·211	2·283	16·968	77	17·045	−108	16·937
1964	13·444	1·962	2·049	61	17·516	2·296	2·498	17·314	320	17·634	−176	17·458
1965	12·383	2·113	1·951	41	16·488	2·939	1·906	17·521	31	17·552	−172	17·380
1966	13·228	2·301	1·919	167	17·615	2·606	2·113	18·108	444	18·552	−217	18·335
1967	12·747	2·294	2·165	89	17·295	2·432	2·362	17·365	177	17·542	−292	17·250
1968	12·560	2·485	2·010	−11	17·044	2·784	2·186	17·642	−76	17·566	−287	17·279
1969	13·587	2·488	2·568	−23	18·620	2·781	2·688	18·713	158	18·871	−323	18·548
1970	14·454	2·783	2·745	−12	19·970	2·928	3·304	19·994	87	19·681	−270	19·411
1971	14·611	2·595	2·871	176	20·253	2·718	3·567	19·404	316	19·719	−260	19·459
1972	14·559	2·249	2·341	209	19·358	2·526	3·171	18·713	710	19·423	−291	19·132
1973	14·594	2·711	2·017	441	19·763	2·554	3·448	18·869	1·218	20·087	−242	19·845
1974	14·333	2·892	2·134	206	19·565	3·123	3·232	19·456	−420	19·036	−203	18·833
1975	14·265	2·749	2·919	—	19·933	3·766	3·379	20·320	−1·194	19·126	−318	18·808
1976	13·571	2·867	3·191	−245	19·384	5·049	3·585	20·848	−1·510	19·338	−342	18·996
1977	13·535	3·099	3·800	−56	20·378	5·065	3·886	21·557	−1·337	20·220	−287	19·933

Source: Banco Central del Uruguay, *Producto e Ingreso Nacionales*, 1977, p. 7, and *Indicadores de la Actividad Económico-Financiera*, Dec 1978, p. 66.

Comisíon de Precios e Ingresos (COPRIN), which regulated tl
freeze. Control over wages was supplemented by a repressi
policy towards trade unions, including the arrest of leaders a
the prohibition of strikes and demonstrations. The power of tl
executive, already augmented by the constitutional reform
1966 which replaced the nine-member presidential committ
(Consejo Nacional de Gobierno) by a single president, w
further strengthened by the semi-permanent imposition of secu
ty measures. An additional change of significance was the filling
ministerial posts by *técnicos* and those representative of the priva
sector, and the exclusion to a large extent of traditional politic
groups. The stabilisation, introduced at a time when inflation hʒ
reached an annual rate of 177 per cent (June 1967–June 196ƨ
was remarkably successful in securing an abrupt fall in the rate
price increase. The strategy remained largely intact until its ov
contradictions, especially the increasingly overvalued exchanʒ
rate and the requirements of the election campaign of 1971, forcʜ
its relaxation and abandonment.

The wage freeze and subsequent control on wage-rate adjuɪ
ments – measures impossible at the beginning of the 1960s whʜ
batllista modes of government were still dominant – in the shoɪ
term produced a very severe fall in real wages (Table 5.3). Tl
confrontation between government and organised labour was n
significantly lessened by the recovery of wages in 1969– 70 to
level slightly above that of 1967. A politics of confrontation, aɪ
the concentration and extension of executive power, indicate th
the second stabilisation corresponded to a more advanced stage
the economic and political crisis. None the less, in two remarkab
respects the results of the 1968 policy resembled those of 1959,
that the decline of real wages was short-lived and the econon
emerged (though only briefly) from its long period of stagnatioɪ

The explanation of the performance of wages resides partly
the success of the stabilisation policy in holding price increases ʜ
the use of controls to about 20 per cent in 1969 and 1970 (Tab
5.3), and the real recovery made by output and exports. GDP :
real terms contracted by over 3 per cent in 1967, but grew slight
in 1968 and by over 5 per cent in each of the two succeeding yea
(Table 5.1), a recovery in which industry producing for tl
domestic market played a full part. Domestic growth was in tuɪ
sustained by a relaxation of credit restrictions in 1969, and
notable increase in the level of government expenditure whiʜ

TABLE 5.3 Annual change in prices, real wages and means of payment, rate of unemployment, 1955–77

	Rate of change in consumer price index, Montevideo		Index of real wages		Rate of change of M₁	Unemployment in Montevideo	
	Year average %	Year end %	Year average 1955–68: 1961=100 1968–77: 1968=100	Year end Av. 1968=100	year end	% of labour force	Labour force as % of population
1955	8·9	10·4	96·9		10·8		
1956	6·8	6·1	100·1		10·5		
1957	14·7	18·3	103·1		9·9		
1958	17·6	19·6	100·5		30·2		
1959	39·3	48·7	91·5		35·2		
1960	38·8	36·2	93·3		32·0		
1961	22·6	10·3	100·0		18·7		
1962	10·9	11·2	104·4		2·6		
1963	21·2	43·6	102·9		27·5	10·2	
1964	42·5	35·4	96·8		39·4		
1965	56·5	88·0	91·3		98·3	8·5	
1966	73·5	49·4	98·6		40·2	7·2	
1967	89·3	135·9	96·1		112·1		
1968	125·2	66·3	85·7/100·0		65·3	8·4	
1969	20·9	14·5	111·5		51·5		
1970	16·4	20·9	110·0		12·7		
1971	23·9	35·6	115·7		54·2		
1972	76·5	94·7	95·9	83·5	57·0	7·1	38·0
1973	97·0	77·5	94·3	90·2	75·6	7·7	37·5
1974	77·2	107·2	93·5	85·7	62·9	8·9	37·7
1975	81·4	67·1	85·2	83·0	52·2	8·1	38·6
1976	50·5	39·9	80·2	76·6	61·6	12·9ᵃ	42·1ᵃ
1977	58·2	57·3	70·7	71·0	40·2	11·8ᵃ	43·4

Sources: Instituto de Economía, Uruguay: *Estadísticas Básicas*; Banco Central del Uruguay, *Boletín Estadístico Mensual*; Dirección General de Estadística y Censos, *Encuesta de Hogares*.

Note: ᵃ Average of two half-years. Data for other years is a half-yearly figure.

was not matched by an increase in revenue. Wages policy, moreover, evidently sought to maintain purchasing power. But of more fundamental significance to the success of the policy was the coincidence of improving terms of trade – from 95·9 in 1968 to 106·2 in 1970 (1961 = 100) (Table 5.1) – with good climatic conditions in the rural sector which raised the volume of exports in 1969–70 24 per cent above the average level of the previous five years. As a result, export earnings were the highest recorded for fifteen years. The increased availability of imports, and the confidence created in the private sector by the refusal of the new administration to treat with organised labour and its success in confining the traditional political groups to the legislature, encouraged a revival in investment which was higher in real terms in 1969–70 than in any year since 1962 (Table 5.2). It appeared – briefly – that price stability would be matched by political and institutional stability on terms which would allow private capital to prosper.

Though relative price stability lasted into 1971, the dynamism of the economy ended after two years. In 1971 and 1972 GDP in real terms contracted and by 1972 the objective of price stability was also lost. The reasons for the failure of the model are to be found partly in its own limitations, and partly in the transitional character of Pacheco's government. As to the first, it is clear that inflationary pressures were not eliminated, but rather suppressed through the non-orthodox use of price controls. The level of demand remained high through continued expansion of the money supply and public sector deficits. In 1968 central government spending had been cut and the deficit almost eliminated, but spending then rose from 13·2 per cent of GDP in 1968 (the lowest in the decade) to 19·7 per cent in 1971 (the highest).[15] Externally, and in spite of continued improvement in the terms of trade, the trade balance moved deeply into deficit in the second half of 1971. The explanation lies both in the reduced supply of cattle for slaughter, as producers once more moved cattle illicitly to Brazil, and the lack of restriction on domestic beef consumption, which reduced the proportion of total slaughter exported from 46 per cent (1970) to 25 per cent (1971).[16] The consequent pressure on the peso revealed a further departure from orthodoxy, in the commitment of the government to maintain the value of the peso at the rate established in April 1968. This decision, which was responsible for the re-emergence during 1970 of currency speculation and the contraband traffic in cattle in 1971, reflected a contradiction in Pacheco's strategy. Having looked to private capital to support his arbitrary rule, backed by a politically impassive military and implemented by *técnicos*, while ignoring the political parties and confronting the trade unions, the tradition of constitutional government was none the less still strong enough to force Pacheco to operate within the framework of an electoral system. Hence stable exchange rates were maintained in order to minimise increases in the cost of living, but at the cost of currency speculation, increased foreign debts and the erosion of the real income gains by landowners and the export sector. Stabilisation was further jeopardised by increased public spending – interest-free loans to public employees, for example – during the months preceding the elections of November 1971. Though Pacheco's nominee, Bordaberry, was successful in those elections, the *pachequista* strategy was exhausted. Within a month of the new regime the peso was devalued from 250 to the dollar, and by the end of 1972 stood at over 700. The volume of exports slumped to its lowest level since 1967, and the contraction of GDP continued. Overshadowing the resumption of economic decline, however, was the intervention of the armed forces, which led directly to the military coup of 1973.

The significance of *pachequismo* was fundamentally that of an intermediate stage. Perhaps the most important change effected by the regime was to separate the political 'class' from the source of its sustenance, the monopoly of appointments to the public sector, thus confining it to the legislature in which it finally capitulated in mid-1973. Why was the crisis of the *batllista* political system so long deferred? It survived the first stabilisation period because the traditional techniques of political mediation were still viable and because social stability was still a desirable objective to the industrial capitalist class, not least because income redistribution helped to maintain its market. By the late 1960s these factors were ceasing to operate. The increasing degree of social unrest during the decade served to undermine the usefulness of *batllista* politics to the economic system. Moreover the state found it progressively more difficult to secure a share of the national income adequate to sustain its role as an agent of social cohesion. The inflationary implications of such a situation, while offering short-term gains to some sectors of the dominant class, none the less threatened the long-term stability of the capitalist class as a whole. Adverse climatic conditions in 1967, the acceleration of inflation to three-figure rates, and the sudden accession of Pacheco to power on the death of President Gestido, prompted the change in orientation.

Nevertheless, the 1968 regime contained a number of apparently paradoxical features, appropriate to its intermediate status. These relate both to the aims of the stabilisation policy itself, and to the economic strategy which it expressed. The exchange rate was maintained in the official market at the level set in mid-1968 in the face of mounting speculation against it, and price controls were maintained in an attempt to restrain inflationary pressures which other aspects of policy seemed to promote. These aspects were, first, the maintenance of domestic demand through a considerable expansion of the money supply in 1969 and – remarkably, given the hostility of the regime to organised labour – the quick recovery of real wage levels following the shock of the wage freeze. The rate of growth of output of manufacturing industry in 1969–70 has been noted already, and suggests that the underlying strategy was still to secure an alliance of industrial capital with the landowning and export sectors. The second 'traditional' aspect of the regime was the recovery in government spending which occurred. Though the ratio of central government expenditure to GDP was enormously inflated in 1971 by electoral considerations – itself an indication of the extent to which the political system retained its autonomy – the ratio in 1969 and 1970 was higher than in any of the three preceding years, while revenue failed to match the increase.

STABILISATION BY THE MILITARY REGIME, 1974

Background

Although the immediate cause of the military coup in 1973 was the army's successful campaign against the *Tupamaros* the previous year, the event was also precipitated by the recrudescence of electoral politics towards the end of Pacheco's term of office, and by the unprecedented mobilisation and unification of left-wing forces as the Frente Amplio. Following another year of economic decline in 1972 relieved only by the continued improvement in world beef prices, the prospect of a further period of social instability and the restructuring of the political system around more obviously class-based parties was not tolerable. Having enforced the acquiescence of Bordaberry in February 1973, military control or dissolution of the legislature, trade unions and university, followed later in the year.

The regime formally designates itself as *cívico-militar*. The civilian component is comprised of a titular president, a Consejo de Estado, and the heads of ministries. In practice, the only effective centre of civilian authority has been the group of *técnicos* in the Ministry of Finance and the Central Bank; and the only outstanding individual has been Végh Villegas as Minister of Finance between July 1974 and September 1976. The repression of conventional forms of political expression is almost complete. A presidential election to be contested by only one candidate is scheduled for 1981. The effective exercise of the political function occurs within a very small group of senior officers and those civilians whom they have selected to hold office. This group is apparently impenetrable to the representatives of at least some of the traditionally powerful fractions of the capitalist class, notably the landowners and domestic industrialists. Both the Asociación Rural and the Cámara de Industrias have failed in their attempts to exert a significant influence on policy, and indeed in 1975 the President of the Federación Rural was arrested for voicing criticism of the regime's economic policy. Moreover, Végh in speeches during 1974–5 went out of his way to criticise the conduct of pressure groups.[17] It seems therefore that the capacity of traditionally dominant groups to influence the political process, which was exercised quite directly during the early years of Pacheco, has now receded.

The economic strategy of the armed forces began to take shape late in 1973. Its main principles followed those set out in the *Plan Nacional de Desarrollo 1973–77*,[18] a document prepared by the conservative fraction of the Colorado Party which was victorious in the 1971 elections. The Plan was published in April 1973, two months after the publication of military communiqués which, in calling for a number of radical changes including land redistribution, implied the existence of an influential group of officers seeking structural reforms.[19] The communiqués as an indication of military intentions, were highly misleading. At the conclave of military and civilian leaders at San Miguel in August 1973 the proposals of the Plan were ratified, the central principle being 'the

objective of the Government to restore to the price system its
guiding function in the allocation of resources'.[20] For the armed
forces the reasons for the adoption of the Plan were probably
two-fold: first, it offered a reasonably coherent guide to policy in
an area in which they were entirely inexperienced; second, the
Plan embodied principles of economic liberalism, which offered
the best chance of consistency with what was apparently the only
ideology common to all the armed forces: anti-Marxism.

The Plan proposals centred on the greater use of the price
mechanism, in opposition to the interventionism of the ISI
period. The profitability of private investment was to receive
greater emphasis as an instrument for the fulfilment of the Plan's
objectives.[21] Income redistribution would essentially be left to
occur naturally as a result of the process of economic growth
itself.[22] State participation in the economy would contract, especially in directly productive activities. The degree of openness of
the economy was to increase, with export diversification and
growth, particularly the increased processing or manufacture of
national raw materials, the principal commercial objective. To
provide an appropriate body of fiscal exemptions and incentives,
a Law of Industrial Promotion was already under study, and at
San Miguel a proposal to establish a regime for the promotion of
foreign investments was approved. The Plan declared a rate of
inflation of 20 per cent or more to be incompatible with sustained
economic growth, and therefore envisaged a transition period
before this could be achieved, in 1974 or 1975. Wages and Central
Bank credit were identified as 'the two principal autonomous
inflationary factors in the Uruguayan economy', with which
short-run policy instruments should be competent to deal.[23]

In mid-1974 Végh Villegas was appointed by the armed forces
to superintend the implementation of the new economic model.
By then the economic position of the country had deteriorated still
further, as the impact of the oil price rise in late 1973 made itself
felt. The trade balance, carried into surplus in 1973 by the
massive increase in export prices, was sharply reversed by the
addition of US$100 million to the oil import bill (see Table 5.6
below). Although central government expenditure and the
budget deficit were both relatively low in 1973, and the level of
liquidity contracted sharply, in 1974 the effect of imported inflation was supplemented by a deficit in central government spending equal to 4·4 per cent of GDP. To the long-term task of

restructuring the economy along the lines laid down by the military was added that of reducing the large trade gap and the fiscal deficit.

Stabilisation measures

In spite of the priority attached in the Plan to the rapid reduction in the rate of inflation, it was evident in Végh's economic programme that neither the need to stabilise nor the deterioration in the world economy should be allowed to interfere with the overall economic strategy. Unlike the programme of 1968, with which Végh had also been associated, stabilisation in 1974 was not to be achieved by the shock treatment of a freeze and controls, but rather by a process of gradual adjustment. The principal reason given by Végh for the change in approach related to the large public sector deficit in 1974, necessitating further expansion of the money supply and therefore additional inflationary pressures.[24] There were certainly additional reasons, however. One was the adoption of the practice of mini-devaluations of the exchange rate in 1972, which obviated the need to protect export sector incomes through a drastic cut in the rate of inflation. Another was the intention to let markets function freely, which was plainly incompatible with the extensive exercise of price controls, particularly if, as with COPRIN after 1968, their use became integral to the stabilisation effort rather than a transitional measure.

Accordingly, the central weapons in the anti-inflation policy from 1974 onwards were restrictions on the rate of growth of the money supply and the containment and restructuring in favour of investment of public expenditure. In 1974 credit contracted sharply (Table 5.4), but central government spending and the size of the deficit both increased (see Table 5.5). Although approximately 96 per cent of items in the cost-of-living basket were subject to price control in the second half of 1974, it does not appear that control was used at this period as an instrument to suppress inflation. However, in April 1975 certain basic features of policy were suspended, constituting a pause in the gradualist approach (or alternatively a limited adoption of shock measures). With the rate of inflation over the previous twelve months reaching 100 per cent, the balance of payments fully exposed to the effects of the oil price rise, and difficulties encountered in negotiations in March with the IMF over a further standby credit, it was

TABLE 5.4 Domestic money supply 1971–7 (million new pesos, end December)

	Means of payment M_1	Annual growth M_1 (%)	M_1 at constant (1968) prices	M_1 plus time and foreign currency deposits M_2	Annual growth M_2 (%)	M_2 at constant (1968) prices	Ratio of foreign currency deposits to total time and FC deposits (%)	Ratio of M_2 to GDP
1971	120·1	54·2		176·6	51·5		15·9	24·0
1972	188·6	57·0		285·1	61·4		30·1	23·0
1973	331·2	75·6	45·8	505·8	77·4	74·4	22·5	19·6
1974	539·5	62·9	36·0	858·0	69·6	65·0	32·1	18·6
1975	821·4	52·2	32·8	1596·5	86·0	79·3	42·9	19·1
1976	1327·0	61·6	37·8	3280·1	105·5	126·6	56·2	26·2
1977	1860·1	40·2	33·8	4969·1	51·5	172·6	67·3	24·2[a]

Sources: Banco Central del Uruguay, *Boletín Estadístico Mensual*, and *Producto e Ingreso Nacionales*, 1977.

Note: [a] Estimate.

TABLE 5.5 Central government income and expenditure 1971–7 (million new pesos)

	Income	Expenditure current	Expenditure investment	Gross saving	Deficit	Deficit as % of expenditure	Deficit as % of GDP	Expenditure as % of GDP	% of deficit financed by Central Bank credit
	1	2	3	1-2	1-2-3	4	5	6	7
1971	103·1	142·8	1·9	-39·7	-41·6	28·8	5·7	19·7	87·5
1972	167·5	185·7	13·7	-18·2	-31·9	16·0	2·6	16·1	93·3
1973	370·2	372·2	34·3	-2·0	-36·3	8·9	1·4	16·0	57·4
1974	587·9	709·4	80·1	-121·5	-201·6	25·5	4·4	17·1	46·5
1975	985·5	1203·8	145·0	-218·3	-363·3	26·9	4·3	16·1	26·2
1976	1721·7	1808·0	239·4	-86·3	-325·7	15·9	2·6	15·8	53·1
1977	2937·6	2795·9	382·3	141·7	-240·5	7·6	1·1	16·0	

Source: Banco Central del Uruguay, *Boletín Estadístico Mensual*, and *Producto e Ingreso Nacionales*, 1977.

decided to hold wages, prices and the exchange rate at their existing levels. Agreement was reached with the IMF on the terms of the credit in May.

Though the effectiveness of the measures was quickly apparent, the reasons for the change in approach are in doubt. Végh did not conceal his limited aspirations for the new tactics:

> I do not believe in price control as a fundamental element in the fight against inflation . . . The backbone of the anti-inflationary strategy is monetary containment. It must be so since there is no effective way of combating inflation other than the slowing down of the rate of expansion of the quantity of money. Price control has a supporting role to play in the first phase of the process, so that monetary restriction does not achieve its results through excessive unemployment.[25]

The explanation is not wholly convincing, since the published estimate of unemployment for 1974 did not show an increase over the previous year, while the very high levels of unemployment in 1976–7 have not been taken to justify any modification of the economic strategy. In a later discussion Végh agreed that, having begun to implement appropriate monetary and fiscal measures, shock measures to reduce inflationary expectations were justified. It would moreover permit the consolidation of 'a structure of relative prices which was considered adequate and which harmonised the legitimate interests of the consumer with the necessary profitability of the productive sector'[26] – although the central government deficit showed virtually no improvement in 1975 (Table 5.5), and there were therefore further inflationary pressures in the pipeline. But an interval of relative stability had obvious attractions at this stage, since a number of factors impairing the functioning of the price mechanism – including subsidies to consumers, low house rents and low public utility tariffs – had been substantially rectified. At the end of September 1975 the sequence of mini-devaluations was resumed, and price and wage increases followed at the end of the year. The effect of the 'pause' was certainly to moderate the rate of price increase, and accelerate the decline in real wages. Inflation, at 67·1 per cent by December 1975, showed a marked decline compared with 1974.[27] Real wages averaged 87 during January–May 1975 (1968=100), fell to 77·3 in October, and recovered only to average 80·8 in the first five months of 1976.[28]

The increased degree of price stability was sustained into the first half of 1976, with the price index in June less than 9 per cent above that of December 1975. The inflationary process thereafter acquired a new momentum, with an increase of 66 per cent in the following twelve months. Price controls, most of which had been lifted in early 1976, were reimposed in March 1977 by Arismendi, who had succeeded Végh as Minister of Finance the previous October. While the fiscal performance showed a marked improvement over the previous two years, credit to the non-bank private sector in real terms grew by 30 per cent in 1976, compared with 10 per cent and 21 per cent in the previous two years.[29] An additional and novel factor contributing to monetary expansion in 1976 was the improvement in the external sector (Table 5.6), resulting in a substantial addition to the gold and foreign exchange reserves as shown in Table 5.7. Both of these expansionary factors operated in 1977, with real private sector credit up by 38 per cent and a further gain in the level of international reserves, but the annual rate of increase of M_2 was none the less the lowest in any year since 1971. At the beginning of 1978 it was clear that the inflationary process had not been brought fully under control, in the sense that sharp increases in the rate of price increase had enforced reversals of policy, giving stabilisation temporary priority over other objectives. On the other hand, the rate in the second half of 1977 was reduced to 22 per cent; and in addition it is open to doubt whether price stability is regarded as an important objective by the regime

TABLE 5.6   Summary balance of payments, 1971–6 (US$m)

	1971	1972	1973	1974	1975	1976
Visible exports	197	242	328	381	385	565
Visible imports	203	179	249	434	496	537
Visible trade balance	−6	63	79	−53	−111	28
Total net services and transfers	−57	−44	−42	−65	−92	−102
(net interest and profit)	(−22)	(−24)	(−25)	(−43)	(−71)	(−72)
Long-term capital	51	19	15	25	122	62
Basic balance	−12	38	52	−93	−81	−12
Short-term capital	51	7	15	123	37	100
Errors and omissions	−51	−20	−30	−82	−6	−10

Sources: IMF, *International Financial Statistics*; Banco Central del Uruguay, *Boletín Estadístico Mensual*.

in comparison with the long-term policy of restructuring the economy.

TABLE 5.7   Gold and foreign currency reserves and import ratio, 1971–7 (US$m)

	Total gold and currency reserves	*Total imports*	*1 ÷ 2 (%)*	*Total gold and currency reserves*	*3 ÷ 2 (%)*
	1	*2*		*3*	
1971	181	325	55·7	181	55·7
1972	203	305	66·6	201	65·9
1973	240	398	60·3	240	60·3
1974	232	634	36·6	.232	36·6
1975	218	717	30·4	392[a]	54·7
1976	315	785	40·1	496[a]	63·2
1977	413[b]			757[a]	

Sources: (1) and (2), IMF, *International Financial Statistics*; (3), Banco Central del Uruguay, *Boletín Estadístico Mensual*.

Notes: [a] From December 1975 the gold held by the official banks was revalued at US$90 per ounce troy.
[b] November.

Both stabilisation and restructuring in the context of a regime dedicated to the greater utilisation of the price mechanism and private incentives for resource allocation have required a programme of financial reforms. Among the more important of these have been measures to increase total tax revenue both to finance the budget deficit and to compensate for the declining yield of fiscal impositions on exports and imports as a result of trade liberalisation; and to restore financial incentives to savers and improve the allocation of credit. In the first category, the efficiency of tax collection was improved and a number of unproductive taxes suppressed. Also, taxes on personal income, inheritance and company dividends were eliminated. New developments have included the concentration of the tax base more heavily on a value-added tax and consumption of fuel, and the introduction of a tax on the potential yield of land (IMPROME). In the second category, interest rate ceilings were raised from late 1974 to permit positive real rates of return and end the necessity for credit rationing.[30] This, and the freeing of the financial exchange market, have been reflected in the rapid growth of time and foreign currency bank deposits. Treasury bonds bearing variable interest rates have been issued, and provision made for the private sector also to issue adjustable bonds in an attempt to stimulate the domestic capital market. The importance of interest rates as regulators of economic activity has been emphasised since the second half of 1976 in the use of open market operations to regulate the supply of credit.[31]

The restructuring model

The long-term economic strategy of the regime may be defined as an attempt to secure the closer integration of the Uruguayan economy with the world economy. By increasing the degree of openness of the economy the structure of domestic prices is to be brought more in line with international prices, thus reversing the policy of protection for non-traded goods of the ISI period. The implication of this strategy for economic growth is that the growth process is to be led by the export of commodities in which Uruguay has relatively low costs of production. To secure the necessary increase in investment the supply of domestic and foreign savings is to be increased, and by depressing consumption while reducing the level of protection the market should allocate the funds to the traded goods sector. The role of the price mechanism for resource allocation is, as we have seen, an article of faith for the regime. To that extent the inspiration of the model is economic liberalism. None the less, there are a number of fundamental interferences with the market mechanism, some a stubborn legacy in 1978 of earlier interventionism, others introduced since 1974 as instruments of the restructuring, such that there is room for doubt whether liberalisation is an adequate description for the changes in the management of the economy since the coup. This doubt translates into further uncertainty about the unity and coherence within the regime of civilian and military aspirations for the economic and social development of the country.

Summarising the effects of the restructuring programme, GDP at constant prices grew continuously in the five years 1973–7 at an annual average rate of 2·9 per cent. (Table 5.1 above.) While the rate of growth was low, this was the first five-year period of sustained growth since the early 1950s. Gross fixed investment increased as a proportion of GDP from 10·7 per cent in 1973 to 15·3 per cent in 1976 and probably over 16 per cent in 1977.

Government consumption expenditure has shown little consistent variation in real terms; but private consumption has been hit very severely, declining from 77·3 per cent of GDP in 1973 to 64·4 per cent in 1976. While it has been policy to encourage voluntary savings, the principal explanation for the fall in real consumption must be found in the quite dramatic cut in real wages. Between the election year 1971 and 1977 the fall was 40 per cent, with the greatest declines in 1972 and 1977 (Table 5.3). In spite of falling consumption, manufacturing output grew by an average 5 per cent annually over the four years 1974–7. Quite clearly it was the external market which stimulated the major part of this growth. By 1976, when the visible trade deficit produced by the oil crisis had been closed, the ratio of total trade to GDP had reached 38 per cent, compared with 25 per cent during 1970–2.

It is evident from the abbreviated data in the previous paragraph that there have been significant shifts in the structure of the Uruguayan economy since 1973. The fall in real consumption and the expansion of exports are particularly noteworthy. Neither of these effects is attributable to 'liberal' policy, nor will their achievement necessarily facilitate the conversion of the economy away from interventionism. The decline in consumption, based in turn on the decline in real wages, has been the product of wage controls imposed on a labour force which has historically been highly organised but since 1973 almost entirely defenceless. Accompanying the fall in real wages has been the growth of unemployment in Montevideo until the second half of 1977 (Table 5.3). Although the data for Montevideo probably exaggerate national unemployment and the size of the economically active population has been increased by the fall in real family incomes, probably a further 5 per cent are employed less than thirty hours per week and the size of the labour force has been diminished by the massive emigration of the early 1970s. The regressive redistribution of income during this period is shown in Table 5.8, from which it emerges that the benefits of the redistribution have been concentrated in the second decile of income receivers. A notable aspect of this process, in its political dimension, is that unlike the case of Chile there was no mass working-class involvement in either of the radical political movements – Frente Amplio and *Tupamaro* guerrillas – which preceded the military coup. The decline in living standards is therefore to be seen primarily as a technical adjustment inspired by an ideology which extols the businessman and private sector profitability, rather than – as Whitehead suggests for Chile[32] – an attack on working-class collectivism.

TABLE 5.8   Income distribution 1973–6 (percentiles of Montevideo household incomes)

	Top 10%	10%	30%	30%	Bottom 20%
1973[a]	25·3	15·8	31·6	20·2	7·1
1976[b]	24·7	20·0	31·0	18·3	6·0

Source: Dirección General de Estadística y Censos, *Encuesta de Hogares*, quoted in *El Día*, Montevideo, 8 August 1977.
Notes: [a] First half.
         [b] Second half.

The centrepiece of the new model, and the area in which the achievement has been greatest, has been the growth and structural change of the industrial and export sectors. The industrial strategy of the National Plan adopted by the military in 1973 sought 'fundamentally the expansion and diversification of exports of industrial products',[33] and although there is no available breakdown of industrial output by market, there can be no doubt that the crushing of the domestic market and deployment of incentives for exporters has been effective. Between 1973 and 1977 the industrial product grew in real terms by 22 per cent,[34] a modest enough rate of growth by international comparison, but quite impressive in the Uruguayan context. Sectors showing the lowest rates of growth were typical wage goods: beverages, tobacco, footwear and clothing. Those with the highest growth included non-metallic minerals, rubber products, electrical equipment and textiles – industries which have all participated in the growth of non-traditional exports (though this is true equally of footwear). The new industrial policy has been organised under the Law of Industrial Promotion of 1974, which grants credit facilities and tax exemptions to industrial projects which are deemed to be of 'national interest'. This status, which may be granted to existing as well as new enterprises, may be acquired on a number of grounds, including greater efficiency, use of raw materials of national origin, and employment creation. In practice, the most important appear to have been the growth and diversification of exports. For the eighty-three projects approved by the end of December 1977, export earnings in the first five years of production were expected to yield US$130 million in excess of investment requirements in foreign exchange of US$80 million.[35]

Non-traditional exports

Exports have been characterised by rapid growth since 1972, a result of very high prices for traditional exports, especially beef, during 1973–4, and an expanding volume of non-traditional exports during 1975–7. The distinction between traditional exports (basically beef and wool) and the non-traditional group, lies essentially in the inability of the latter to compete in the world market. To enable them to do so, they have been eligible since 1968 for tax rebates (*reintegros*), which have effectively subsidised the new export industries and enabled them to penetrate new markets. The growing importance of the rebates may be seen in terms of the ratio of their value to the value of exports, which averaged 1 per cent during 1969–72, but reached nearly 13 per cent in 1975[36] (or approximately one-half of the central government current expenditure deficit). Non-traditional exports increased their share of total exports from about 25 per cent in 1972–3 to 55 per cent in 1976–7. The principal commodities exported include rice, leather goods, fish, textiles, cement, malted barley, citrus fruit, motor vehicle tyres and glass and ceramic products. The diversity of Uruguay's export trade in the last two years has been impressive. It has been assisted by treaty arrangements with Brazil (1975) and Argentina (1974). The contribution of the latter has in fact been almost negligible, but the Brazilian market is of fundamental significance, absorbing 15 per cent of total exports in 1975–6, of which 73 per cent were non-traditional. The US market, also, which took only US$7 million of Uruguayan exports in 1972, was worth US$59 million in 1976, largely as a result of the rapid growth of footwear and leather goods. The EEC, with one-third of exports in 1975 and 1976, has retained its traditional position as the most important regional market, in spite of the ban on imports of Uruguayan beef during 1974–7.

In spite of the impressive export performance of the last three years, there is room for doubt whether it can be sustained. First, restrictions have been placed on the import of Uruguayan leather footwear into the US market as a result of the subsidies they receive. It is true that the *reintegros* are seen as a transitional measure designed to give exporters temporary assistance in achieving efficient production and/or market acceptance, and over the last three years have been reduced by some 30 per cent. None the less – the second point – it is extremely doubtful that the export effort could be maintained if the subsidy were to be substantially withdrawn.[37] There is a danger that some of the new export industries will become as dependent on state protection as were some of the home market industries, or – if the liberalisation model is finally adopted – that the rate of growth of exports will fall and the degree of diversification decline. The third point is that in spite of the diversification which has occurred, the agricultural base of the export trade remains emphatic (about 85 per cent in 1977). Exporting is, therefore, tied to a source of supply which in the livestock sector has historically shown a very low rate of growth, and which in all sectors is vulnerable to climatic conditions. The problem was experienced in acute form in 1977 by the tanning and leather goods industry, the most important of the non-traditional exporters, whose rate of expansion was restricted by a shortage of raw material in spite of the importing of 400,000 hides from the USA.[38] It is interesting to notice, therefore, that while exporters are subsidised, the sectors producing exportable output or raw materials have experienced the effects of liberalisation in the form of a continuous and sharp adverse movement in the internal terms of trade since 1974. The situation of the livestock sector in particular was very severe by 1977. Decapitalisation was evident in the decline in the size of cattle stocks and in a 20 per cent reduction in the area under improved pasture between 1974 and 1977.

Foreign investment

There is no doubt that foreign capital was expected to play a major part in the construction of the export-oriented industrial economy. The privileges which became available to foreign capital by the Law of Foreign Investment of 1974 appear to have had their origin not in the National Plan, but in the conclave at San Miguel in October 1973. While the authors of the proposal are not known, it is interesting that the Law was criticised by Végh in 1975 as a discriminating and illiberal measure.[39] Végh claimed

that new foreign investments were tending to reject the advantages of the Law because the obligations they entailed were too
onerous. In the absence of general information on direct foreign
investment in Uruguay, it is difficult to verify the claim. But there
is a widely held belief that the participation of foreign capital in
industry since 1974 has been very limited, and confidential
information on the operation of the 1974 regime confirms that the
number of contracts has been small, for a relatively insignificant
volume of investment, and that they show no special preference
for the dynamic sectors of industry. The essential provision of the
Law is for a bilateral contract (*Contrato de Radicación*) to be
negotiated between the government and investor, which specifies
the valuation of the capital and the terms on which remittances
may be made. By the end of 1977 sixteen enterprises had signed
contracts with an agreed capitalisation of approximately US$15
million. Of these three were banks, while other activities represented include a dry dock, an enterprise for the manufacture of
surgical thread, foodstuffs (Nestlé), locks, and photocopiers
(Xerox). In nine cases the company was already operating in the
country; one of these proposed to open a new plant. In the
remaining seven cases, five intented to establish themselves by the
acquisition of an existing plant. Only four of the sixteen are
believed to have a direct interest in exporting. The contracts are of
course secret, but what is known of them suggests that in at least
some cases foreign capital has secured extremely generous treatment.

In view of this, it seems unlikely that foreign capital has decided
to abstain from the advantages to be secured under the Law; but
rather, that in spite of the achievement of internal peace and
security, the small and slowly growing domestic market of
Uruguay was scarcely more attractive to direct foreign investment in the 1970s than it had been in the 1950s. The Law of
Foreign Investment has had little impact in attracting new capital, in spite of the increasingly cheap labour supply, the export
subsidies, and the fact that the privileges of the Law are additive
to those of the Law of Industrial Promotion. It is true that foreign
capital has had some participation in non-traditional exports —
the largest firm in the leather industry is foreign-owned, for
example — but it is probably national capital, in the main, which
has benefited from the growth of exports.

The Law of Foreign Investment has therefore been largely

irrelevant as an instrument for restructuring the economy. As far as the securing of international support is concerned – in which its authors evidently placed their faith – multinational enterprises showed little interest. Eventually the unexpectedly rapid growth of exports[40] reduced the requirement for direct investment and once the effects of the oil price rise were felt, the need was for short-term financial assistance. The decision was taken in 1974 to maintain the fundamentals of the new economic strategy, in spite of deteriorating world conditions, using the relatively high level of gold and foreign currency reserves to attract a massive inflow of loans to finance the trade gap. The import regime was liberalised to the extent required to permit the expanding supply of capital goods and raw materials needed to sustain a higher rate of investment and growth (Table 5.9). Quotas were removed on imports of consumer goods, but the increase in their supply was limited by the imposition of prior deposits. The essence of the strategy, however, was to secure external support and the effect was to produce an abrupt increase in the level of external indebtedness (Table 5.10). In 1974 and 1975 loans were contracted on hard terms, resulting in a sharp rise in debt service obligations. Since then, however, the repayment profile has improved, easing the short-term service problem.

TABLE 5.9   Composition of imports 1973–6

	1973	1974	1975	1976
Consumer goods	9·2	7·7	5·0	3·2
Oil	19·2	33·0	32·9	31·0
Raw materials and intermediates	63·7	52·7	49·1	48·0
Capital goods	7·9	6·6	13·0	17·8
	100	100	100	100

Source: *El Día*, Montevideo, 8 August 1977.

Fiscal policy

During 1974 the instability of the economy was emphasised not only by the trade gap but also by a deteriorating fiscal performance. The fiscal policy of the regime has had as its principal

TABLE 5.10   External public indebtedness 1971–6 (US$m)

	Total public debt, beginning of year	Interest and amortisation payments	Debt service as % of export of goods and services
1971	267·0	56·6	22·3
1972	290·8	107·2	34·3
1973	324·4	93·8	22·6
1974	344·1	156·1	31·0
1975	516·0	228·0	45·5
1976	614·5		

Source: World Bank, Latin America and the Caribbean Regional Office, *Economic Memorandum on Uruguay*, December 1977, Table 4.2, p. 1.

Note: Unguaranteed suppliers' credits and short-term reserve liabilities are excluded from this calculation. To that extent the data indicates a level of indebtedness substantially lower than that reported in Banco Central del Uruguay, *Endeudamiento Externo del Uruguay*, May 1977. None the less, the World Bank calculation (and that of the BCU) includes all dollar-denominated government bonds sold to the private sector. These have been taken up by Argentine residents in particular, attracted by the favourable rate of interest, but some (unknown) proportion of such bonds is held by Uruguayan residents.

objectives the reduction of the ratio of government spending to GDP while altering its composition in favour of investment, and of the level of the budget deficit. As Table 5.5 above shows, these aims, complementary to each other and necessary to short-term stabilisation and long-term restructuring, have proved elusive, though provisional data for 1977 suggests some improvement in that year. Throughout the period the share of total central government spending allocated to investment increased, from 10·1 per cent in 1974 to 12·0 per cent in 1977. But the ratio of total spending to GDP, though lower in 1975–6 compared with 1974, did not indicate an important reduction in the burden of public spending, and even the figure for 1977 at 14·7 per cent was higher than the average for 1966–70. The financing of current expenditure out of income also proved impossible until 1977. The difficulty lay both in the stagnation of government income, and in restraining current spending. On the revenue side, the reduction of taxes on trade and the suppression of other taxes was barely compensated by increases elsewhere, due to the effects of declining consumption on sales taxes and depressed world agricultural product prices on the minimum land-yield tax. The deficit left by inadequate revenue, traditionally financed by credits from the official banks, was covered to a growing extent by Treasury Bond issues up to 1975, but in 1976 less than 40 per cent was met in this way.

Government spending has proved extremely difficult to contain. In spite of declarations that the size of the enormous bureaucracy was to be reduced, the achievement has been largely confined to the dismissal of those suspected of left-wing sympathies, and the loss of security of tenure of those who remain. Wages in the public sector have not declined more sharply than the national average. Indeed, although the regime is dedicated to the diminution of the state sector, the only important enterprise to be hived off has been the urban transport system AMDET, formerly owned by the municipality of Montevideo. Apart from such evidence that the regime's practice is a long way distant from its supposed liberal principles, the explanation of sustained high central government expenditure appears to be the very high level of spending on the armed forces and other security services. This has resulted from their growing size and level of remuneration. In 1973 budgetary provision was made for the army to double its numbers, and in 1976 the manpower of the armed forces and police was estimated at 45,000,[41] more than 3 per cent of the economically active population. Since 1972, when a state of (internal) war was declared, the incomes of members of the armed forces have been automatically increased by 40 per cent above their peacetime level, and this level has in turn been raised substantially in real terms, in spite of opposition, principally from Végh. It is notable, for example, that in a speech made in 1975 to the Instituto Militar de Estudios Superiores (IMES), Végh emphasised two points: that experience of government confirmed his belief in the value of economic theory (of which the armed forces have limited knowledge); and that the budget deficit posed greater problems than the oil crisis and the balance of payments.[42] The military were not so impressed as to reduce the scale of their spending, which on the basis of two unofficial estimates made in 1976 accounted for at least 49 per cent of total central government expenditure.[43]

Political viability of the model

The appropriate level of remuneration for the armed forces was only one of the factors giving rise to disagreement between Végh and the military high command. A second was his persistent support for the view that there should be a limited resumption of political activity by the traditional parties during a transitional phase, leading after a period of a few years to the full restoration of liberal democratic forms of government.[44] It was in fact the replacement of the formally 'independent' judiciary by a Ministry of Justice, as part of the executive, which provided the occasion for Végh's resignation late in 1976. It should be borne in mind that Végh is regarded as a leading contender for nomination as presidential candidate in the single-candidature 'election' due to be held in 1981, a nomination which, it is believed, would carry the support of the USA.

The third and most fundamental disagreement between the *técnicos* and at least some members of the armed forces concerns the general validity of liberalisation and the restructuring model. The adoption of the model was due originally to its ideologically sound nature in the eyes of a regime concerned as much with the prosecution of the anti-communist cause as with plans for national recovery. Whilst the model has achieved a degree of success, notably in export growth, it has done so at a cost in terms of external debt, lower standard of living, greater inequality, and exclusion of some sectors of the capitalist class, to which the armed forces are probably more sensitive than the authors of the model. Indeed, in spite of the liberal ideology of the model, the application of economic liberalism in post-1974 policy has been distinctly uneven,[45] and there are areas – notably the promotion of non-traditional exports – in which the policy has been actively to interfere with the free operation of the price mechanism. In early 1978 a major policy issue concerns the general reduction of protectionist barriers, which is to occur over a period of five to eight years but with a starting date yet to be announced. While Uruguay's own 'Chicago boys' urge the case,[46] the resistance of some sectors of domestic capital evidently has effect within the executive.

The further issue arises as to the identity of the interests on whose behalf the present model is constructed. The military coup was fundamentally a response to the long-run crisis of hegemony within the domestic capitalist class, its timing dictated by the unprecedented strength of radical or revolutionary political movements in 1971–2. Stabilisation and restructuring, on the basis of a closer integration with the international capitalist system and with massive external financial support, won acceptance with the military as a way out of the crisis of 1974; and the new regime and its model won the support of the capitalist class as a whole, since it guaranteed the principle of the private ownership of the means of production. However, such support can only be provisional: in the long-run a regime which confirms the private ownership of capital but condemns it to unprofitability ceases to enjoy unqualified approval. Clearly, non-traditional exporters have benefited enormously from the new policy. Landowners, on the other hand, exposed to low world prices for beef and wool and receiving a rate of exchange which is overvalued by the effect of subsidies for non-traditional exports, were by the end of 1977 in open confrontation with the regime. Manufacturing industry producing for the domestic market, especially the mainly nationally owned wage–goods sector, has been severely affected by the contraction of demand, which in turn has hit the mainly petty-bourgeois retail sector. The construction industry has recovered from the low level of 1973–4, but very much on account of Argentine-financed development at the resort of Punta del Este.

CONCLUSION

In the absence of normal forms of political expression, and while power is concentrated in the armed forces, relieving the capitalist class of the structural necessity to organise a ruling alliance, it is possible for public policy to be organised in the interests of a relatively small fraction of the domestic capitalist class. The logic of the process appears to be to use the present exceptional period to impose on producers the need to export, thus strengthening the sector of the dominant class linked to external markets and ensuring its domination over other sectors when a representative political process is resumed in the 1980s. For this reason the task of liberalisation is seen as urgent, at least by Végh and his supporters, and long-term restructuring takes precedence over short-term stabilisation. Success will depend on the growth and efficiency of the export industries. Otherwise there must remain the risk for the regime that the impasse of the post-ISI period will reassert itself.

NOTES

* The author is grateful to many friends in Uruguay, who must unfortunately remain anonymous, for advice and assistance in the preparation of this paper.

1 For such an approach to the first two stabilisation efforts, see F. Pazos, *Chronic Inflation in Latin America*, New York, Praeger, 1972.

2 For a more complete account, see M. H. J. Finch, 'A Political Economy of Uruguay 1870–1970', typescript.

3 Julio Millot, Carlos Silva and Lindor Silva, *El Desarrollo Industrial del Uruguay*, Montevideo, Universidad de la República, 1973, p. 169.

4 'The Measurement of Latin American Real Income in US Dollars', *Economic Bulletin for Latin America*, vol. XII, no. 2, 1968, Table 11.

5 Millot, Silva and Silva, op. cit., p. 209; *Banco de la República Oriental del Uruguay (BROU), Cuentas Nacionales*, Montevideo, 1965), p. B30.

6 The analysis in this and the following section is drawn from Finch, op. cit., Chapter 2.

7 The ratio of cash and bank deposits to GDP fell from 35·3 per cent (1957–9) to 26·9 per cent (1960–1).

8 *Cuentas Nacionales*, op. cit., p. B162.

9 Calculated from data in Ministerio de Ganaderia y Agricultura – CIDE Sector Agropecuario, *Estudio Económico y Social de la Agricultura en el Uruguay*, Montevideo, 1967, vol. I, pp. 182, 479.

10 It is illustrative that between 1955 and 1961 the proportion of the total population employed by the government or public sector, or in receipt of a state pension, is estimated to have increased from 15·5 per cent to 18·7 per cent: see Comisión de Inversiones y Desarrollo Económico (CIDE), *Estudio Económico del Uruguay*, Montevideo, 1963, vol. I, p. 117. On the implications for the stabilisation policy of the elections of 1962, see Juan Eduardo Azzini, *La Reforma Cambiaria*, Montevideo, Editorial AMF, 1970, pp. 151–84.

11 That is, assuming that net emigration during the period was zero. During the intercensal period 1963–75 the rate of net emigration was approximately 0·7 per cent, but most of this population loss occurred during the 1970s: see Dirección General de Estadística y Censos, *Encuesta de Emigración Internacional*, Montevideo, 1976, pp. 15–16.

12 Instituto de Economía, *Uruguay: Estadísticas Básicas*, Montevideo, Universidad de la República, 1969, Tables 90, 91.

13 Instituto de Economía, *El Proceso Económico del Uruguay*, Montevideo, Universidad de la República, 1969, p. 289.

14 Banco Central del Uruguay (BCU), *Boletín Estadístico Mensual*, July 1968.

15 BCU, *Boletín Estadístico Mensual*, March 1977.

16 Instituto de Economía, *Estudios y Coyuntura 3*, Montevideo, Universidad de la República, 1973, p. 39.

17 Alejandro Végh Villegas, *Economía Política: Teoría y Acción*, Montevideo, Ediciones Polo, 1977, pp. 44, 70.

18 Presidencia de la República, Oficina de Planeamiento y Presupuesto, *Plan Nacional de Desarrollo 1973–77*, Montevideo, 2nd edition 1977.

19 The communiqués, reproduced in *Cuadernos de Marcha* No. 68 (March 1973), included as a 'basic objective . . . to establish a wage and price policy which ensures the maintenance of the real incomes of all levels' (p. 31).

20 Presidencia de la República, Oficina de Planeamiento y Presupuesto, *Definición de Políticas y Estrategías del Gobierno Uruguayo y Análisis de la Instrumentación del Plan Nacional de Desarrollo*, Montevideo, October 1973, p. 4.

21 *Plan Nacional de Desarrollo 1973–77*, vol. I, p. 24.

22 Ibid., vol. I, p. 36.

23 Ibid., vol. I, pp. 14–17, 37–8.

24 Report to Comisión de Economía y Finanzas of the Consejo de Estado, 22 July 1974, reproduced in Végh Villegas, op. cit., p. 33.

25 Interview with Végh Villegas, *Búsqueda*, Montevideo, no. 34, April 1975.

26 Speech to Cámara Nacional de Comercio, 26 April 1976, reproduced in Végh Villegas, op. cit., p. 92.

27 None the less, the rate of inflation in the twelve months to March 1976 was 49·9 per cent, greatly in excess of the undertaking given to the IMF that the rate would be reduced to 30 per cent. Bank of London and South America, *Review*, vol. 9. no. 7/75, July 1975, p. 420.

28 BCU, *Boletín Estadístico Mensual*, March and September 1976, Tables IV 4 and IV 5.

29 BCU, *Indicadores de la Actividad Económico – Financiera*, March 1978, p. 12.

30 World Bank, Latin America and the Caribbean Regional Office, *Economic Memorandum on Uruguay*, Washington DC, December 1977, pp. 5–7.

31 Interview with José Gil Díaz, president of the Central Bank, *Búsqueda*, no. 57, March 1977.

32 See this volume.

33 *Plan Nacional de Desarrollo*, vol. I, p. 495.

34 BCU, *Indicadores*, March 1978, p. 71.

35 *El Día*, Montevideo, 27 February 1978. For an analysis of the Law, see A. P. Ricaldoni, J. E. Santías and Lindor Silva, *El Régimen de Promoción Industrial*, Montevideo, Fundación de Cultura Universitaria, 1975.

36 Information for 1976–7 is not yet available.

37 'On various occasions I have declared that industry needs the continuation of the regime of *reintegros* to give it the incentive to go on with the process of winning markets abroad' (Helios Maderni, president of the Chamber of Industry, quoted in *El País*, Montevideo, 8 April 1978).

38 Eduardo Lanza, vice-president of the Chamber of the Tanning Industry, *El Día*, 26 December 1977.

39 Végh Villegas, op. cit., p. 83.

40 The plan projected a doubling of exports between 1970 and 1977 (*Plan Nacional de Desarrollo 1973–77*, vol. I, p. 152), against an actual increase by a factor of 2·6.

41 *El Día*, Mexico, 17 December 1976, quoted in Grupo de Informacion y Solidaridad Uruguay (GRISUR), *Informaciones*, Geneva, no. 61, 11 January 1977.

42   Speech of 5 August 1975, quoted in Végh Villegas, op. cit., pp. 72–3.

43   Ibid.; and the Economist Intelligence Unit, *Quarterly Economic Review: Uruguay*, 1976, no. 1, p. 2.

44   'I believe that the armed forces should gradually return to their traditional and most recent role which we might call "the supreme arbiter of the Nation" or "last resort of the Republic".' The only other solution would be 'a permanent technocratic-military system, with power rooted in the armed forces and its exercise in the charge of a group of technocrats. I see grave defects and an inherent instability in such a system'. Among the risks envisaged are a political vacuum opening the way for a resurgence of clandestine Marxist activity ('to suppose that this tendency can be counter-balanced by repressive measures is an error'), and the deepening of internal divisions within the armed forces leading either to the suicide of the military government or the emergence of a military *caudillo* (quotations from 'Memorandum de Végh Villegas sobre las Perspectivas Políticas del País, principios de 1976', typescript).

45   'After 32 months it is clear that the programme of liberalisation of the economy is out of balance. Good progress has been made in money and banking, foreign trade, the capital market, external financial relations, and reduction of the fiscal deficit. Progress has been much slower as far as the allocation of resources is concerned. The balance of payments gives a good indication of the situation. The commercial account is "sealed up": extremely high protectionist barrier, "implicit taxes" on traditional exports, subsidies to non-traditional exports' (president of the Central Bank, *Búsqueda*, no. 57, March 1977).

46   See Juan José Anichini, Jorge Caumont and Larry Sjaastad, *La Política Comercial y La Protección en el Uruguay*, Montevideo, Banco Central del Uruguay, 1977. The work was prepared under the auspices of AID and the Banco Central.

6 The Economic Policies of Argentina's Labour-based Government (1973–6)

GUIDO DI TELLA*

INTRODUCTION

The economic evolution of Argentina from 1973 to 1976 has to be viewed against a background of persistent economic and political instability over a period of more than forty years.[1] During this period, the labour-based party has won the only two relatively free elections, while parties with middle-class support were successful in the two where the former was banned. Conservative groups have taken power four times through military interventions.[2]

This instability should not hide Argentina's considerable economic and social development – an intermediate level of $2200 *per capita*. While its rate of economic growth has not been negligible and has increased over the last decade, (to 4 per cent per year) it has probably lagged compared with the significant increase in social mobilisation. The middle classes since the First World War, and the working classes since the Second, have erupted into the social, economic and political life of the country. Argentina has been one of the few countries in Latin America which has attempted a mass democracy with full participation, a fact that may – paradoxically – be at the root of the political and economic conflicts of the last fifty years.

Whatever the reason, the fact remains that the political stability which the country had enjoyed since the end of the last century was lost around the 1930s, while economic stability, which proved to be more resilient, was lost some time during the 1940s and 1950s.

In this paper we shall analyse the economic problems faced and the policies carried out by the four successive governments which came into power, as a result of free elections, from May 1973 to March 1976. They include the presidencies of H. Cámpora, R. Lastiri, of J. D. Perón himself, and of Isabel Perón.

We will have to refer briefly to the political scene in order to understand, if not the nature of the economic problems - which parallel those encountered in previous stabilisation programmes – then their extraordinary intensity. To a large extent, these problems were connected with two departures from the tradition-al, mildly reformist attitude of the Government Party. The first one, towards the extreme left, took place during the electoral campaign, and coloured the short-lived presidency of H. Cámpo-ra. This problem created serious strains and Cámpora's presiden-cy was predictably brought to an abrupt end after less than two months. After a caretaker government, Juan Perón was elected by a landslide in September 1973. He was President until his death in July 1974, and followed a broadly middle-of-the-road course. He was then succeeded by the Vice-President, Isabel Perón, who started the second major departure, this time towards the extreme right. The consequence was a head-on collision with the union movement, which staged an open revolt, forcing a partial retreat towards more moderate policies during the second half of 1975. A second more moderate right-wing attempt occurred at the begin-ning of 1976, which continued until the military coup in March.

While the initial left-wing twist had very serious political consequences, to the point of forcing a change of president, it did not seriously affect the economic scene. In fact the initial economic programme was carried out to a large degree indepen-dently of the general policies of the Cámpora period, being regarded at the time as a 'concession' to the middle-class sectors of the party. Thus the first Minister of Economics, a member of the small business organisation, the CGE, lasted seventeen months and served under all four Presidents, following basically the same economic policy.

This comprised a stabilisation programme and a set of refor-mist measures. The stabilisation scheme, as we shall see, had a characteristic two-stage sequence. The first and initially rather successful stage was based on a 'social pact' which tried to enforce a certain distribution of income. It involved a price freeze and the lowering of certain prices – in real terms – which in turn gave rise to some of the tensions that later destroyed the whole scheme. The consequent decrease of industrial and agricultural profits (and of private investment) and the maintenance of a fixed and increasingly overvalued exchange proved to be crucial factors in the failure.

The initial success of the scheme was, to some extent, the consequence of the strong authority exercised by a popularly elected government, and particularly by the presidency under J. Perón. This gave credibility to the programme, so reducing inflationary expectations. Another equally crucial factor was the improvement in the international situation, where a windfall gain helped initial distributionist policies.

The deterioration in the terms of trade which occurred after 1973, the very significant external inflationary pressures and the increasing incongruity of a price freeze accompanied by expansionary monetary and fiscal policies, gave rise to increasing economic difficulties: internal shortages, reduction of investment and a loss of reserves which characterised a situation of repressed inflation. Meanwhile, the accompanying reformist measures antagonised established groups, even though few of them were implemented.

By the time of Perón's death, in July 1974, the middle-of-the-road programme was showing obvious strains. While a significant change was necessary, the fact that it was made after the loss of a forceful leader, and accompanied by a drastic political move to the right, led to a period of unprecedented instability. Isabel Perón had five Ministers of Economy. Whereas the currency had been stable during the first twenty-two months of the populist government, during the last twelve months the dollar increased its peso price by 1330 per cent and the price level rose 731 per cent. But the last period is not unrelated to the first. We shall argue that it can be seen as an inevitable, if exaggerated, consequence.

The movement towards the right on the economic front required a degree of allegiance to the Justicialista Party so extreme as to be unattainable. The unions staged an open rebellion, which nearly brought down the government, a conflict which was at the root of the extraordinary intensity of the price explosion. This conflict marks the end and the failure of the initial stabilisation programme. What follows is its converse: the rebalancing of the economy. We would argue that any programme implies this 'second stage', which must also be included in the analysis – though it frequently is not. Thus, a reversal of a whole set of relative prices was to be expected. What was abnormal in this case was the intensity of the reversal. It became clear that the price mechanism was the principal battle-ground for the distribution of income, and that this was at the root of the inflationary process. There was a marked oscillation of relative prices, and the parallel changes in distribution had a self-feeding character, a phenomenon associated with the non-competitive behaviour of significant sectors.

The price outburst was accompanied by a reduction of money in circulation in real terms, brought about by the price increases and by the flight from money. The outburst was in large measure the consequence of the political struggles, but also increased their intensity and created a climate of chaos. One of the more immediate consequences was that the President lost all arbitrating power, surviving as a figurehead only. Her leading supporters were removed from the government, which was taken over by the moderate middle-of-the-road, strongly supported by the unions.

The second half of 1975 was coloured by the aftermath of the price explosion while a gradual correction was made of some of the most distorted relative prices. These policies were soon hindered by an attempted come-back of the right wing of the Government party, producing a stalemate by the year-end. By January 1976 the forthcoming military coup became rather obvious, heralded by the business and agricultural sectors and by a good part of the intelligentsia. The President gained control of the government, and attempted a more moderate right-wing programme. But the imminence of the coup – which became a fact in March – meanwhile destroyed the government's credibility and led to a new price explosion.

The political and economic turmoil of these years was connected with the tremendous difficulty of creating a popularly based government that could still exert restraint on the economic front. The personalist leadership of Peronism, its emergence after a political ban lasting more than seventeen years, the spontaneous character of its support and its extremely wide appeal to rather dissimilar groups contributed to a weak organisational structure. The period also shows how even moderate changes in power and in income can generate enormous resistance from vested interests.

We shall analyse, first, the immediate background, particularly since the 1967–9 stabilisation programme, tackling afterwards in some detail the six peiods into which we have divided the thirty-four months of the popular governments.

THE IMMEDIATE BACKGROUND

Since the war, the performance of the Argentine economy, although uneven, has been significant. It had recurrent problems in the foreign sector while it experienced one of the most persistent inflations of any country. The economy suffered a succession of stop-go policies (Brodersohn, 1974, Canitrot 1976). Growth was negative in 1952, 1959 and in 1962–3, negligible in 1966 and again negative in 1975 (see Table 6.1). These were years of serious balance-of-payments problems, which prompted stabilisation programmes. After the serious political and economic crises of 1962–3 some improvements became noticeable. The country was able to maintain a continuous rate of growth from 1964 until 1974, averaging 5·2 per cent per year,[3] which, given a population growth rate of 1·4 per cent, allowed a modest but significant increase in *per capita* income. This was largely attributable to the adoption of more subtle economic policies, both during the 1964–5 revival[4] and during the 1967–70 stabilisation programme, than those of 1958–60 (de Pablo, 1974). The 1967 programme, following the accession of the new military government, achieved for a while a reduction in the rate of inflation to about 10 per cent per year, without a reduction in the level of activity, maintaining the share of wages at around 44 per cent of GDP (see Table 6.6). It was not a classically orthodox policy–contrary to initial interpretations on both sides: see Braun 1970. A significant devaluation was carried out, with the idea of maintaining thereafter a fixed exchange rate, something which was to become one of the stumbling blocks of the whole programme. The novelty was that the devaluation was accompanied by *ad valorem* taxes on agricultural exports, avoiding the typical initial abrupt transfer to the agricultural sector. These taxes were then gradually eliminated, although this barely compensated for the increase in internal prices, given the fixed exchange rate. Another novel element was the expansionist monetary policy, based on a tight fiscal programme but a generous credit policy, particularly towards the private sector (Van

Rijckeghem, 1972). An incomes policy (involving the freezing of wages at 95 per cent of their historical real values) was imposed, together with a rather flexible price agreement with the 500 leading firms.

Unfortunately the reliance of the programme on a fixed exchange rate, while contributing substantially to the initial reduction in the rate of inflation, inevitably built up tensions, depressing the agricultural and the new industrial export sectors, reducing net effective protection to industry while bolstering imports. The result was a poor performance by the external sector – only helped by significant foreign borrowing which compensated for the rather small amount of direct investment. In this programme one can detect a clear emphasis on expectations and on the cost side of the inflationary process, setting it apart from the more standard monetarist solutions. There are even some similarities with the 1973–4 stabilisation programme (see de Pablo, 1978). The initial successful stage, very much affected by the change in expectations, and based on the depression of certain sectors, nevertheless created such pressures that an inevitable second stage followed, with the bouncing back of relative prices completing the full circle of economic policies.

The riots of 1969, followed by the change of President in June 1970 (Onganía to Levingston), revealed the wide discrepancies within the military and destroyed the credibility of their claim to an indefinite stay in government. Its most immediate economic effect was to impair the foreign borrowing potential which had been one of the bases of the 1967–70 stabilisation programme. In 1970 the new Minister of Economy, A. Ferrer, attempted a 'developmentalist' policy (see Ferrer, 1977). But many of the measures were an inevitable consequence of the previous programme. The administration had inherited an overvalued currency and a depressed agricultural sector, with the cattle-raising industry faring very badly and practically in a state of revolt. On the other hand, the cattle crisis had helped, through low beef prices, to keep down nominal wages, which was crucial to the whole programme.[5] A substantial devaluation was clearly necessary, and was carried out in a succession of small steps. Although this new policy was considered by many people to have been the means of destroying the previous stabilisation, it was in fact largely its consequence, aggravated by the beginning of political discord.[6]

The further change of President that took place in 1971

(Levingston to Lanusse) and the new open-handed economic policy[7] aggravated inflationary pressures and worsened the economic outlook. Inflation reached an annual rate of 100 per cent during the first five months of 1973 – affected by the uncertainty caused by the electoral process. While the beef cycle had helped the Krieger Vasena stabilisation, the sharp turn-up of the cycle now hurt. The fiscal deficit increased from the low levels of 1968 – 70 (less than 2 per cent of GNP) to over 5 per cent by 1972 (Table 6.9) and to a projected rate of more than 6 per cent of GNP in 1973 as a consequence of pre-election commitments in 1973, for which no financing was provided.

The external situation, on the other hand, improved, reflecting developments in the international economy. There was an extraordinary increase in export prices between late 1971 and early 1973, exceeding the increase in import prices by nearly 20 per cent. The country negotiated an agreement with the IMF when the external situation was still bleak. By the end of the year the improvement became noticeable, while the fears regarding the external situation were removed by early 1973. The rate of growth had been falling since the high figure of 8·5 per cent in 1969, reaching 3·1 per cent in 1972 (Table 6.1), but it now appeared that exports had a good chance of leading a revival.

However, at the close of the military government in 1973 all indicators were pointing to a delicate situation regarding the inflationary process, since the higher import prices would eventually transmit themselves to the rest of the economy, as would the high export prices of agricultural goods – which make up nearly half of worker consumption – while both the fiscal deficit and the evolution of the monetary supply gave cause for concern.[8]

The mounting economic problems began to affect the political situation. The situation reached the point where even an eventual return of the Peronista Party began to be considered as an acceptable outcome – a rather surprising conclusion, in view of the ban of more than seventeen years imposed on the party by the military. There was a growing awareness of the advantages of having the labour unions and their sympathisers within the political system, instead of on the fringe, more prone to radical infiltration.

The ground was thus prepared for the 1973 elections, which despite the personal banning of Perón, were won by the Peronista Party's candidate, initiating Argentina's second experience with a labour-based government.

THE SIX PHASES OF THE LABOUR-BASED GOVERNMENT

We divide the thirty-four months of the labour-based government into the following periods, which we will now discuss in detail:

(i)   June–December 1973. The initial economic policies; the stabilisation programme, the social pact and the price and wage freeze; the reformist measures.

(ii)   January–September 1974. Mounting problems of the price freeze and the contradictory expansionist policies; problems in the foreign sector.

(iii)   September 74–May1975. Partial 'flexibilisation', the introduction of financial restraint and the crisis in the foreign sector.

(iv)   June–August 1975. Drastic readjustment, social conflict and the beginning of recession.

(v)   September 1975–January 1976. The gradualist approach, the redressing of relative prices, partial indexation of the economy, the anti-recessive measures and the balance-of-payments crisis.

(vi)   January–March 1976. The attempt to 'cool' the economy and the effects of the imminent military intervention.

(i) June–December 1973: the initial economic policies

The early days of the new government were strongly influenced by its left-wing groups, ranging from evolutionary to radical. The moderate labour unions had surprisingly little influence, although they were able to appoint the crucial Labour Minister, a long tradition within the party. On the other hand, the Minister of Economy, J. B. Gelbard, and the bulk of appointments in the economic area were members of the CGE, the confederation of small businesses, mildly nationalistic in outlook.[9]

The new economic programme was correspondingly diverse, comprising both reformist measures and a stabilisation scheme. Although they were never fully enforced, the reformist measures were the keynote in the initial period.[10] They included, among other measures: (1) a tax reform, increasing the progressiveness of the tax system, requiring identification of ownership of shares and other financial assets (this was never enforced); (2) a foreign investment law, which restricted some areas to local ownership, restricted the transfer of dividends and required approval by law of all major investments; (3) an agrarian law, allowing, among other things, expropriation of unproductive estates; (4) greater interference of the state in export trade, with as official policy the development of trade with the Eastern Bloc (an initiative that at the time—oddly enough—was rather controversial); and (5) a 'nationalisation' of credit, which really meant a greater degree of Central Bank interference with the credit system, but no outright expropriation of banks.[11]

It must be pointed out that the reformist programme was part of a general left-of-centre mood prevalent in several countries of South America. In Argentina it affected many institutions and political groups: the army, the Church, and most political parties. After creating some tensions within these organisations it faded away while the inevitable backlash to the radicalisation of the Cámpora period gained momentum. This was exacerbated by the persistence and violence of the subversive organisations.[12] For most of the traditional left the reformist programme was seen as falling far short of a 'true' change. The sharp contrasts with both the Chilean and the Peruvian experiment were frequently pointed out. The programme sufficed, however, to antagonise the establishment—alarmed more by the dangerous overtones of the general political context than by any specific measures.

The reformist programme was soon overshadowed by the stabilisation scheme and by the 'social pact' which was an integral part of it. The control of the inflationary process was of greater concern to most people than the more grandiose and distant 'structural' reforms. At the time of the new government, inflation appeared in danger of running out of control.

On the one hand an improvement in the trade balance, with improved terms of trade and strong export demand, provided a favourable backdrop to the programme. On the other, the government deficit was growing and could be expected to grow more given the distributive aims of the new government. Real wages had fallen during 1972 to one of the lowest levels in the last ten years (see Table 6.5). Upward pressure on wages was inevitable with a strong cost-push effect, and inflationary expectations were very high.

The basic idea of the programme was to induce, or even force under state auspices, an agreement on the distribution of income (i.e. on relative prices and taxation), between wage-earners and business as represented by their respective central organisations.[13] This *política de concertación*, or 'social pact' (Ayres, 1976) was essential to the Peronista tradition of inter-class co-operation. It was implemented through a strict wage and price freeze, with fiscal, and particularly monetary, measures very much out of the picture. The price freeze included an actual reduction in the prices of a select group of fifty-seven firms and of a list of products. Prices for all other firms and products were frozen at their prevailing levels. Wages were to be frozen for two years after an initial rise of 20 per cent. This rise was much less than that demanded by the union leaders, although it allowed real wages to increase 13 per cent above the 1969 level. The rise in wages and a slight reduction in unemployment allowed an increase in the share of wages of more than 4 percentage points, reaching 47 per cent of GNP, somewhat above the level of the previous stabilisation programme. One of the factors contributing to the initial success of the wage and price freeze was the fact that many firms had made anticipatory price increases before the new Government had come into office and so were able to absorb the wage increase. The impression was that at last a government with strong arbitrating power had arrived and that, at a price, each sector had received a not untenable share of income. The business sector had been alarmed by the runaway inflation and even more so by the political outlook and the initial pre-eminence of radical groups. In the circumstances, the programme was received with a sense of relief. This explains the initial strict compliance with the price freeze, which helped to put a sudden brake on expectations.[14] Probably the best indication of this was the downward movement in the black market rate from 12.5 pesos to the dollar, to about 10 pesos, almost the official rate of exchange. Indeed, the absolute level of prices actually decreased in June by 2·8 per cent.[15] From July to December it increased by only 4 per cent, creating excessively optimistic expectations that inflation had come under control: the Government began to use the expression 'zero inflation' as a political slogan. (This term was eventually to become a straitjacket, leading to the continuation of rather rigid price policies well beyond the optimum point.)

Another factor contributing to the initial success was the very great improvement in the international situation. Argentina was taking advantage of the tail-end of the international prosperity of

1972 and 1973 (see Table 6.15). During 1973 the country had record exports of $3.266 million, 65 per cent higher in value than in 1972. The volume of imports initially decreased substantially, reflecting relatively uncertain investment conditions and the devaluation. They picked up, however, towards the end of the year, following expansionary internal policies and the gradual overvaluation of the exchange rate. Imports for the whole year increased in value by 16 per cent, reflecting the large price increase. By the end of 1973 the country was able to accumulate a significant current account surplus of $704 million (about 3 per cent of GNP) compared with a deficit of $218 million the previous year.

While the external situation was good, the Government allowed the currency to become overvalued; at the same time it was engaging in an expansionary policy, a dangerous combination in view of the coming reversal of the international situation. (Even in the last quarter of 1973, the oil crisis brought an abrupt shift in the terms of trade, which fell by over 20 per cent.) This expansion is seen in the increase in the expenditure of the Central Treasury compared to receipts (see Table 6.10). The increased expenditure reflected the increase in real wages and in the number of public employees (see Table 6.11). The increase far outweighed the rise in revenue, the latter being partly due to the tax reform, but more to the beneficial effect of the stabilisation of prices, which eliminated the 'fiscal lag'.

On the monetary side, there was a strong expansion (see Table 6.7) reflecting a passive policy, the drastic curbing of inflationary expectations and a corresponding increase in the demand for money.[16] While from May 1972 to May 1973 money and prices had grown roughly by 70 per cent, during the whole of 1973 money increased by 93 per cent, while prices increased by 30·8 per cent.

The rate of interest was decreased in nominal terms (cheap credit had been one of the slogans of the CGE, even with negative interest rates). Paradoxically, the reduction in the rate of inflation was so drastic that the real rate of interest, which had been −27 per cent in 1972, became +8·5 per cent in the second half of 1973.

The impact of the external situation and of expansionary internal policies was almost to double the real rate of growth in 1973, while unemployment fell. The role of the external sector is seen in the sharp increase in agriculture (13·5 per cent) while industry increased by 6·4 per cent (Table 6.1). On the other hand, construction declined by 5·1 per cent reflecting the depression of investment, which decreased from 23·6 per cent to 22 per cent of GNP in 1973. Public investment fell from 8·8 per cent to 7·7 per cent of GNP, while private investment was practically unchanged at 14·1 per cent of GNP. Foreign capital was intentionally discouraged; while local capital was officially preferred, both the price freeze and the increased cost of credit began by the end of the year to cause a downturn in private investment.

This makes clear the flaws within the programme. As a transitory policy, the social pact proved its worth, in so far as inflationary expectations were dramatically cut off. But by the end of 1973, the international reversal and local expansionary policies began to create some of the first strains. Moreover, it was not clear whether the price freeze was intended as a permanent policy or even how it would be followed up, a problem that was to prove to be the stumbling block of the whole programme.

(ii) January–September 1974: the mounting problems

By the end of the year it was clear that the relative price structure that had prevailed since the date of the freeze was not rational. Those who had repriced just before the freeze had been able to make good profits, while others suffered. At the same time, it was increasingly true that monetary and fiscal policies were out of line. The absorption of the wage increase had penalised the more labour-intensive industries. Moreover, imported prices had risen by nearly 30 per cent from June to December, official policy still requiring that they should be absorbed by profits. In many sectors this became impossible, particularly where the import content was high and unsubstitutable. Some industries began to incur losses, reducing or stopping production altogether, while others began to violate price controls, selling at a premium, collected in black-market money.

It was therefore rather clear by the end of 1973 that some degree of price flexibility had to be introduced. The government was very hesitant, as this would imply an abandonment of the 'zero inflation' scheme and risk re-creating inflationary expectations. The first attempt was made in December 1973 and clearly exemplifies this ambivalent attitude. The government announced that the higher costs of imported products could be transferred to prices: before the decision was put into effect it was cancelled and replaced by a revaluation of the currency for a select list of imported goods, mainly raw materials.[17] Some 'flexibilisation' – as it was called – was, however, introduced during 1974 and particularly after September when a new Minister of Economy took office.

By March the pressures of the unions became very strong despite the fact that the decrease in real wages was still small. Although the initial social pact had specified no changes in wages for two years, an increase was granted, representing a rise of about 20 per cent for unskilled workers, less for skilled workers. This wage increase, compounded by a gradual 'heating' of the economy, pushed up prices in the second quarter by 10 per cent, compared with 3 per cent in the first quarter, a trend that was to continue throughout the year. Zero inflation had become a thing of the past.

The unemployment rate, having been reduced to about 5 per cent in the second half of 1973, moved down to an all-time low of 2·3 per cent in April 1975 (Table 6.12). (It may be wondered whether it was approaching a 'natural' rate of unemployment, in which case the inflationary consequences would be significant. It would seem, however, that at least in the short-run the inflationary process was affected more by changes in expectations than by the unemployment rate.)[18]

One of the crucial variables that goes a long way to explain the end of the social pact, was the sharp reversal of the terms of trade. Export prices were maintained at the level of the end of 1973, but one of the most important problems was the ban on meat imports imposed by the EEC in about July 1974 (considered by the IMF as an infant industry protective measure and therefore not qualifying as trade discriminatory!). Import prices, on the other hand, increased a further 35 per cent, while their volume also rose. The current account moved from a surplus of $704 million in 1973 to a deficit of $286 million in the second half of 1974.

Despite the price increases and the reversal of the external situation, the exchange rate was not changed. The overvaluation of the currency (see Table 6.14) meant a significant increase in imports and a huge loss of reserves. The reserves were again being used to postpone the dreaded devaluation, for fear it would add fuel to the inflationary process. But it is fair to say that at the time it was unclear how far the export problems were temporary.

The depression in meat exports accelerated the downward movement of the cattle and meat cycle (though helping the cost-of-living index, where meat accounts for 22 per cent). The situation, moreover, stirred strong sectoral unrest, that would later have serious political repercussions.

The government's expansionary policies are evidenced by the increase in the deficit, the result of increases on both current and capital accounts. The government was evidently acting as if it accepted an extreme cost-push interpretation of inflation, expanding the money in circulation, increasing current expenditures and the number of public employees and pushing investment projects as if there were no need to watch the demand side.

The renewal of inflationary expectations reduced the demand for money, so increasing inflationary potential even had the money supply been held constant. In fact money moved from 20 per cent of GNP in the second half of 1973 to 24·5 per cent during 1974 (see Table 6.8). The government deficit represented 32 per cent of total money creation, 80 per cent corresponding to credit creation (see Table 6.7). The real rate of interest now fell, reaching −17·6 per cent in the second half of 1974, as the annual rate of inflation accelerated to about 40 per cent (see Table 6.3). The argument used was that higher interest rates would increase costs, offsetting the dampening effect this would have on the demand side.[19]

In reality the renewal of inflationary expectations now had the reverse effect of the initial 'virtuous' circle: they now led to a decrease in the demand for money with an extremely dangerous inflationary potential.

Profits of the large companies were seriously affected until the policy reversal of the last quarter of 1974. The smaller companies, which were not subject to detailed control, did not follow this pattern, a result which coincided with the political base of the CGE. On balance, however, private investment fell quite sharply (see Table 6.2). But contrary to the view commonly held at that time, total investment was not going down (in absolute terms). Public investment rose strongly and total investment rose from 19·4 per cent of GNP in 1973 to 20·6 per cent in 1974. The government was pursuing both distributionist *and* developmentalist policies, and both of them in the short run, a process which could not continue.

The rate of growth of the economy was excellent, at 6·5 per cent, slightly up from the previous year, sustained by the increase in the level of effective demand. But the demand expansion and the maintenance of the price and wage freeze gradually began to produce shortages. The most serious was the shortage of foreign exchange, the consequence of overheating the economy while maintaining a 'frozen' exchange rate.

The lessons from this period are rather clear. A price freeze is a possible policy *only* if it is adopted at the right time so as to brake expectations (which was the case), but then it can *only* be undertaken as a temporary measure, for it introduces a serious degree of rigidity, with pernicious longer-term effects. It is also clear that it *cannot* bring under control cost-push pressures and can only delay them for a while, with the danger of making them worse in the future. It *must* be accompanied by coherent management of the demand side of the economy. The more stringent and the longer the freeze is, the more serious the demand restraint should be.

Unfortunately this was not appreciated at the time. It was a policy easier to embark upon than to end. In retrospect it can be seen how some of the intrinsic weaknesses of the policy were compounded by the international reversal and by the particular domestic policies which were adopted.

(iii) September 1974 – May 1975: 'flexibilisation' and financial restraint

While the economic clouds were gathering, larger ones were accumulating on the political front. The death of General Perón in July 1974 meant a significant reduction in the arbitrating power of the executive, a particularly serious problem in such a loose political alliance. The problem was compounded by the unexpectedly strong identification of the new president, Isabel Perón, with the right wing of the party, headed by the Minister of Social Welfare, J. López Rega. This group favoured a straightforward right-wing programme, an essential part of which was a drastic shift towards an orthodox economic line and a forceful attempt to curb the power of the unions.

While on the political front the measures were taken soon after the death of Perón,[20] on the economic and labour fronts there were delays. In September, a respected middle-of-the-road Minister of Economics was named, A. Gómez Morales. This was a compromise solution reached rather reluctantly, as it meant the postponement of the full implementation of the right-wing programme to a later stage; in fact, until the second quarter of 1975.

As described in the preceding section, some important shifts in economic policies were clearly necessary. Two different approaches were now put forward by business groups and political sectors. One – the more common view – emphasised the need for a more flexible price policy, and the second a general 'cooling' of the economy. The tendency appeared to be to view the matter as if a price approach and an income approach were alternatives rather than complementary policies.

The new economic authorities took an intermediate position: it was thought that under the circumstances a freeing of all prices could result in an enormous jump in the price level. Further, a non-explosive and partial freeing of the economy would be possible only if accompanied by a policy of financial restraint.

Many price adjustments were now allowed. Prices accelerated, increasing by 12 per cent in the last quarter of 1974 and by 25 per cent in the first quarter of 1975, while inflationary expectations increased significantly. Wages were increased in November by 13 per cent, and could be transferred to prices, as part of a policy of increasing business profits. Wage readjustments took place again in March, with increases of about 20 per cent. (In both instances, the increases were granted before any significant real loss had taken place, as if the inflationary process had made the unions over-zealous in their defence of the real wage.) The higher real wage rates may in part be related to the high demand for labour and the low unemployment rate. But it is also true that despite the more orthodox outlook of the economic policy it did not count on a reduction of wages as one of its tools. However, one important price was not freed: the exchange rate was frozen until March 1975, while very significant losses of reserves took place. The black market rate started to move above the official rate, more than doubling it by February 1975. At last, the currency was devalued: from 10 to 15 pesos to the dollar, reducing but not eliminating the overvaluation (see Table 6.14). (These wide fluctuations in the real value of the exchange rate were a major reason for the difficulty experienced in developing a consistent export policy for anything other than land-intensive goods.)

The fact that the official exchange rate was not devalued decreased the level of net effective protection,[21] and consequently increased the value of imports, by more than 50 per cent. But with the anticipation of devaluation, speculative imports began in significant amounts by the end of the year. The problem was compounded by the abrupt fall in export prices which gave rise to a deterioration of over 20 per cent in the terms of trade between the first and second halves of 1975. All this contributed to an impressive reversal in the trade balance and in the reserves, as shown in Tables 6.16 and 6.17.

The profitability of agricultural exports was diminished by the overvaluation of the currency and by the policy of applying *ad valorem* export taxes. The cattle sector was additionally affected by the closing up of the European Common Market, and by the world cattle crisis. Not surprisingly the internal terms of trade shifted against agriculture (Table 6.4). It was only after November 1974 that they fell below the 1967–9 level, reaching an all-time low by the middle of 1975. But the real problem was that these figures were based on industrial prices which were also low. By the end of 1974 the problem was not so much one of relative prices, but of absolute prices, that is, of low output prices relative to input prices.

On the demand front, a strict programme to reduce current government expenditure began, particularly expenditure on personnel. A reduction of some of the rather over-ambitious government programme, including cheap housing, was attempted, creating strong opposition. At this stage the money supply was seen, and rightly so, as having an important impact on the inflationary situation. Attempts were made to curb the rise of money in circulation, with the deficit in the foreign sector making a significant contribution there (see Table 6.7). At the same time a policy was undertaken to settle some of the conflicts with foreign capital that had arisen in the previous period, while a study was started in order to liberalise the foreign investment law. All these measures were part of a strategy to attract capital for investment in the hope of offsetting the planned reduction in public investment – a hope that was not in fact realised. The actual outcome was that private investment declined even further, while public investment reached an all-time high. Total investment, however, fell from 23·4 per cent of GNP in the last quarter of 1974, to 20·8 per cent in the first quarter of 1975.

Throughout this period the Minister of Economics faced continued opposition from the extreme right wing of the party, who took an ambivalent attitude, criticising some of the proposed actions, only to push them in an even more drastic form when their candidate eventually displaced him.

While quite a few of the measures described above were clearly necessary, they should surely have been started much earlier. They were at least six months late and were milder than the situation warranted, particularly those concerned with the foreign sector. Further, at least some necessary measures concerning both prices and incomes were not taken. Probably the reliance on the effects of financial restraint was pushed too far, i.e. to a point where it was supposed to replace the need for direct price adjustments, in particular the need for devaluation. Thus, when the adjustments finally took place, they had to be that much more drastic and abrupt, a fact which explains the final convulsions of the Peronist period.

(iv) June–August 1975: the drastic readjustment

While the protests of several groups had already become quite vocal (particularly in the agricultural and industrial sectors), it was the very delicate situation in the foreign sector that finally forced a change. The devaluation and wage increases in March 1975 had created new cost-induced inflationary pressures. These developments, coupled with rumours of imminent political changes aimed at strengthening the right wing, caused destabilising speculation on the exchanges, increasing the spread between the black market and the official rate for the peso.

The Cabinet shuffle took place in June 1975. C. Rodrigo (a member of the inner circle of the right wing) became the new Minister of Economy. The new group aimed to bring in a realistic exchange rate, to improve agricultural prices, to encourage private investment, to increase prices of public services and public goods, to diminish the fiscal deficit, to keep down wages and to curb the power of the unions. Within this rather orthodox framework the role attributed to money was not completely clear, except that a reduction in its rate of increase was implied in the reduction of the fiscal deficit; however, at the same time more credit to the private sector was envisaged. The main exception to the general line of the plan was an insistence on the continuation, and even increase, of the low-cost housing programme, since this was the main project of the Welfare Minister, Jose López Rega, who was the political leader of the right-wing faction.

In order to explain the acceleration of inflation, from 67·7 per cent in the twelve months to May 1975 to 87·7 per cent in the following twelve months, and to explain the conduct of the government, it should be understood that the period was over-shadowed by an all-out fight between the union-based sector of the party and the right-wing faction, a struggle for power and political domination which was fought around the readjustment of relative prices.

The new government devalued from 15 pesos to 30 pesos to the dollar. Prices of public goods were increased in many cases by more than 100 per cent, reaching 200 per cent in the notorious case of petrol. Meanwhile a wage increase of less than 40 per cent was offered to workers. This left public opinion in a state of shock. The direction of the changes was expected, but not their intensity. One may suspect that the government's object was to create an impossible situation for the union leaders. The union leaders in consequence felt that they were fighting not so much for a wage adjustment as for their very political survival. A tentative settlement was nearly reached on the basis of a 50 per cent immediate wage increase to be followed by two 15 per cent increases (not compounded) in August and October. But the unions finally rejected the agreement, maintaining a state of political mobilisation. One of their main problems was that, as the economic policies had been wholeheartedly supported by the President, their opposition could bring about the downfall of the government. At this point they were divided on whether to press their claims regardless. In the event the unions displayed such strength that they were granted wage increases, negotiated union by union in a tumultuous fashion, ranging from 60 per cent to more than 200 per cent, and averaging about 160 per cent. Successful wage claims of this magnitude can only be understood as a means of bringing about the downfall of the right wing of the party. This objective was in fact attained, amidst military unrest, but the authority of the government was very much hurt. The prospect of its overthrow became an element of calculation which made the economic situation even more delicate.

The immediate effect of the wage explosion was a drastic increase in the cost of living (102 per cent in June–July–August) with, in addition, the prices of imports increasing in real terms by 30 per cent compared to domestic prices, while, unintentionally, agricultural prices decreased a further 10 per cent. Real wages increased by 50 per cent, although this was swiftly eroded to the pre-disturbance level: none the less it meant a significant once-and-for-all transfer of about 4 per cent of the yearly wage bill.

Another very important transfer of 3·7 per cent of GNP took place from creditors to debtors as a consequence of the halving in value of debts contracted with an expectation of a 4–5 per cent monthly rate of inflation (Table 6.13).[22] Another consequence of the price increase was that money in circulation decreased from 13·7 per cent of GNP in the first quarter to 8·1 per cent in the third. This was also the consequence of a rapid flight from money, coupled with the short-term effects of an explicit policy of the Central Bank, which, acting largely alone, avoided a worse price explosion, and contributed to the toning down of the inflationary rate in the following months.[23]

The economy moved abruptly from an overheated situation in April to a situation of near-crisis in July and August. Unemployment shot up from 2·3 per cent to 6 per cent in the Greater Buenos Aires area and to 7·5 per cent in areas like Córdoba, where the automobile industry was hit hard. Something very near to a collapse of manufacturing activity was feared. Output fell during the third quarter by 5·6 per cent.

The external situation also continued to be very delicate. The devaluation had been very significant but its effect was not felt until the beginning of the following year. However, in the short run, the situation was eased by a massive increase of 'swaps' – i.e. foreign short-term loans, with Central Bank forward coverage (see Table 6.18).[24] During the year short-term loans increased to an all-time high of $2,124 million, of which 60 per cent were in swaps, which had become an essential factor in the balancing of the external situation. The reliance on short-term financing was due to the increasing difficulties in negotiating medium-term loans.[25] Despite the increase in the real price of several government services, the fiscal situation deteriorated sharply, mainly owing to the effect of the very rapid inflation on the fiscal revenues. Treasury income fell from 6·6 per cent of GNP for 1974 to 4 per cent and 3·8 per cent for the second and third quarters of 1975 (see Table 6.10).

Summarising the aftermath of this drastic attempt to overhaul the economy, there was an effective real devaluation of the currency and an increase in some public sector prices, while money in circulation was drastically reduced as a consequence of the flight from cash. Contrary to what was intended, real wages were not reduced, but a significant difference between various labour groups appeared, the tax system was disrupted, industrial activity collapsed, and unemployment increased, while agriculture's position continued to worsen contrary to the explicit wishes of the government. Within months the economy had veered between the dangers of hyperinflation and of recession, although the full effects of the convulsion were not to be felt until the end of the year.

The turmoil of this period brought about the downfall of the right-wing factions. The unions, with the support of the middle-of-the-road politicians, were able to remove both López Rega and Rodrigo from the Cabinet. The unions moved into the centre of the political scene, reconstituting something like the alliance which had prevailed during the presidency of J. Perón. A caretaker Minister was named, who devalued a further 20 per cent. The economy was in a situation of chaos and paralysis, and there were persistent rumours of a split within the army, raising the possibility of a military coup.

(v) August 1975 – January 1976: the gradualist approach

The previous economic 'fiasco' had deeply hurt the authority of the President, who had obviously lost the fight against the unions. The military situation was settled within the army, with the strengthening of the so-called professional group and the removal of the sector that had tried to bring the army into the support of the right-wing programme of the government.[26] The commander-in-chief of the army, General Numa Laplane, was replaced by General J. R. Videla. The new Minister of Economy, A. Cafiero, who took over at the end of August, had been closely associated with the trade unions for a long time, and had poor relations with most members of the right wing.

There were three pressing problems that required immediate attention. The first and most critical was the redressing of the external situation. The second alarming problem was the increasing depression in the industrial sector which, together with rising unemployment, was giving rise to tremendous social unrest and to strong protests from both the business sectors and the trade unions. The third problem, and not the least important, was the need to damp down the inflationary outburst of the previous months. While it was improbable that inflation would continue at the same extraordinary rate, it was not clear that it could be brought back to pre-shock levels. It is clear that these three objectives were in large measure contradictory. Moreover, the new economic team was determined to move towards meeting these objectives through rather gradual measures. They considered that the extraordinarily high price increases, the jump in unemployment, the collapse of the external market, the tripling of the rate of exchange, the halving of credit in real terms and the abrupt income transfers had deeply shocked the economy, and that the system could not withstand further shocks.

Inflation at this stage was not viewed primarily as a consequence of monetary disequilibria. The inter- and intra-sector distributional struggles had become the basic element propagating the inflation. These conflicts were in turn exacerbated by the inflationary process and by its differing impact in different sectors, by its leads and lags. If inflation can be characterised by the degree of divergence between the relative prices of the various sectors and products, the 1975 inflation was clearly one of great relative price oscillations (see Table 6.4). Unfortunately this type of inflationary process is much more resistant to orthodox treatment than more uniform inflations.

It must be realised that the conflict over income shares was waged not only between the larger groups – i.e. wage earners, industrial and agricultural groups – but also among different sub-groups within these categories.[27] One of the most serious consequences of the previous shock was that the government lost the strong arbitrating power it had at the time of the social pact. Under these conditions any attempt to stop inflation altogether was thought unrealistic. A sufficient achievement would be to reduce it to 'somewhat below 100 per cent per year', as was deliberately and ambiguously stated, and to avoid abrupt lurches in the rate of inflation, which were thought to worsen its effects even more.

The wage structure had emerged grossly distorted, those unions that had been the first to sign new agreements during the outburst having fared worst. These groups now began to press for a reconsideration of their 'special cases', requesting a return to the traditional differentials, while those which had fared better thought that any allowance to one group should be extended to all.[28] The government proposed a compromise solution, but without success. Some unofficial increases began to take place and by November 1975, when the real wage had moved below the pre-shock level, the government granted a general rise of about 27 per cent. More important was the agreement that wages would be indexed: quarterly adjustments were intended to guarantee an average real wage of about 95 per cent of the previous year. A special institute to check on the figure and police the indexing of wages was to be created with worker and business participation. Under the peculiar situation created by the mid-year crisis, it was felt that keeping down wage demands to previous price increases would in itself be important in toning down expectations.

A readjustment of some significant relative prices of goods and services was also considered an essential part of the new policy, but while this was undoubtedly necessary for the longer-term it would be hard to make such adjustments without giving a new impetus to the overall rate of inflation. Here was another instance of the recurring conflict between shorter-term, mainly anti-inflationary considerations and longer-term, mainly efficiency considerations. Nevertheless prices of agricultural products clearly had to be increased, and were. The policy was to maintain the real price of agricultural products, from sowing to harvesting, but allowing for changes in real prices from year to year. The plan was to move to international prices over a period of three years,[29] the time thought necessary to effectively establish a tax system, based on the potential productivity of land, which had been made law but not been implemented. In addition the prices of some public services were formally indexed, while, in the case of loans and tax debts, the ground was laid for the indexation of medium- and long-term obligations. These instances were part of a general indexation of the economy, which was advocated as one of the few ways of diminishing the disruption that a continuous inflationary process would otherwise cause. Not all prices were indexed, of course.

An important consequence of the wide variation and leads and lags in relative prices, was that arbitraging became at that time extraordinarily profitable. A speculative climate developed, particularly noticeable in government bonds. The policy was to allow this arbitrage, but to reduce its profitability, by equalising the nominal cost of money with the rate of inflation. The nominal rate for deposits was in fact increased several times but even so remained below the rate of inflation. However, the part of the market where interest rates were free, i.e. bank acceptances, was enlarged and the rates were soon practically in line with inflation, at least until the end of 1975.

A tax reform was also attempted, reducing some tax rates, which were thought to be so high as to encourage an increase in the already high level of evasion. Firms were to be required to depart from traditional accounting practices and report on a 'real' basis. This tax package was sent to Congress but was never approved, for it became part of the intense political bickering which was already going on even within the government party.

Meanwhile the external situation became really desperate, although some of the basic measures had been taken by the previous administration, in particular the large devaluation of the peso. The immediate problem was tackled by departing from the traditional anti-IMF attitude of the Peronista Party. A negotiation was started with the Fund, in order to draw on the 'compensatory financing', the oil facility and the first tranche, which required the presentation of a coherent plan, but with less stringent conditions than the Fund would attach to subsequent tranches. The Fund did not, however, like the plan that was presented, as it included no drastic reduction of wages, aimed at full employment and only sought to reduce the public sector deficit to about 6 per cent of GNP. After intense negotiations, where crucial US State Department co-operation was sought,[30] an agreement was reached, which increased the chance of obtaining other short-term financing. The Fund provided £250 million. The private banks initially responded well, but after two months increasing political difficulties and the lukewarm support of the Fund induced some of the lending groups to retract.

This short-term 'breathing space' was accompanied by a firm decision to maintain the real exchange rate reached after the previous shock. The method used was small devaluations at intervals of ten to twenty days, each time by 3–5 per cent. At the same time, a scheme of multiple exchange rates was maintained as a transitional measure, that would permit more subtle devaluations, as categories of goods were reclassified from lower to higher rates. These measures and other indirect devices used to increase the cost of imports were supposed to diminish adverse expectations and the immediate repricing of goods that had followed previous spectacular devaluations.

By these means the real weighted rate of exchange was maintained at the very devalued level reached after the mid-year outburst, about 50 per cent below the real rate prevailing during the six previous months. The policy was to maintain a relatively devalued currency as a basis both for the external balance and for rational industrial protection. As early as the first quarter of 1976 these policies allowed the appearance of a surplus in the current account, for the first time in five quarters.

The other fundamental problem was the greatly reduced level of activity, amounting to what seemed nothing short of an industrial breakdown. The intention was to ease this situation, by allowing a modest increase in the amount of money, the chief hope residing in relative price adjustments. In fact the money supply (M_2) remained stable at 11·8 per cent of GNP. It is not easy to appraise the significance of this, since in the early part of the year expectations were below out-turn, while later on they were well above the actual rate of inflation. Prices had changed so abruptly that the business sector and consumers were utterly confused as to what to expect next. As for interest rates, despite several rises, as we have seen, inflation was so high that real rates continued to be negative. The increase in nominal money supply was caused by an extremely high Treasury deficit, a combination of a high level of expenditures and a further fall in income due to the fiscal lag. Despite these trends on the monetary front industrial production continued to slide, with −5·6 per cent in the third quarter and −8·9 per cent in the last. GNP, which had gone down by 3·2 per cent in the third quarter, went down by 6·3 per cent in the last quarter of the year. It was not until the first quarter of 1976 that any recovery could be detected, and by January 1976 an increase in inflationary pressures could also be observed, compounded by the very serious destabilising effects of the political crisis with which the new year started.

In fact the political situation had begun to deteriorate again before the end of 1976, when the President staged a partial comeback: she was able to make some changes in the cabinet, but without touching the middle-of-the-road coalition led by the Ministers of the Interior and of Economics. A stalemate developed between the two groups, creating a difficult political situation and a complete loss of authority by the government. In this situation the trade unions jockeyed for position in a rather anarchic way, making the normal management of the economy very difficult. Two lock-outs carried out by the cattle sector, several producers' strikes, and the creation of a new business organisation, the APEGE, with the avowed purpose of creating a pre-revolutionary climate, all contributed to an atmosphere of chaos. An aborted rebellion in one of the air garrisons, in December, gave the impression that the end of the regime was at hand. In January 1976 the President attempted a full comeback, so opening the last act of this story.

(vi) January–March 1976: the end

The President dismissed all the middle-of-the-road ministers and made new appointments further to the right, including E. Mondelli as Minister of Economics, who up to that moment had been head of the Central Bank. The trade unions were shocked by the abrupt political change and initially they reacted violently. For a while they were undecided whether to opt out again, as in mid-1975. This time, they settled for accommodation, as the end of the regime was clearly in sight and an open fight did not seem worth while.

The military had reached the point where their strategy was to let the situation deteriorate until the need of a coup became evident to all. While this objective was obtained, the pre-coup climate, coupled with the stalemate within the government coalition, the unchecked power of the unions and the opposition of business sectors, created a very anarchic situation. The phenomenon of an 'expected' coup contributed greatly to the price explosion that again more than doubled prices from February to April. Wholesale prices increased more than consumer prices. This was a repetition of the previous outburst, suggesting that in both cases the cost-push factor was dominant. All sectors were frantically jockeying for an improvement in their relative positions, ahead of the imminent change of government. Although the increase in prices appeared to repeat the experience of the previous year, the causes were different, as this time the disintegration of the government and the pre-coup atmosphere were the crucial factors.

There was a general change of attitude regarding indexation, which apparently was considered partly responsible for the increase in inflationary pressures. This was reflected in wage and exchange rate policy, and in the abandonment of other plans for indexation. Wages were increased by 20 per cent in early March, real wages being expected to contract, and frequent small devaluations were replaced by larger jumps. Money in circulation fell from 11·8 per cent of GNP in the last quarter of 1975 to 8·4 per cent in the first quarter of 1976. This was partly caused by the drastic price increases, which, as in mid-1975, produced an intensification of the flight from cash. The Treasury deficit, at 12·9 per cent of GNP, was again affected by the price jump and the erosion of receipts caused by the fiscal lag. The level of activity continued low, at 4·4 per cent below the same quarter of the previous year. Manufacturing activity showed a small improvement while construction and investment continued at extremely low levels.

Despite the internal recession the external situation continued to be extremely precarious. Closer collaboration with the IMF was therefore attempted, this time going all the way in order to qualify for the third tranche. Reserves were low, particularly since the private foreign banks had curtailed their lines of credit, a policy which was continued up to the day of the military coup, but reversed directly after. The economic measures were thus basically right-of-centre, repeating, but more moderately, some of the mid-1975 policies. Despite this, the loss of authority of the government, the anarchic behaviour of the members of the coalition and the very high price increases created a sensation of chaos and doom. The opposition, both economic and political (excluding the Radical Party), had succeeded in the creation of the right political climate for the military coup, which finally took place at the end of March.

CONCLUSIONS

The hectic experience of these years provides some interesting lessons regarding the economic problems created by rapid inflation. At the same time it throws some light on the viability of reformist regimes in countries like Argentina. The 1973 stabilisation programme was only possible because of the initial conditions created by a political change and by the international situation. In this respect, and in its typical two-stage development, it followed a similar pattern to previous ones. The first stage was relatively successful at the expense of increasing the distortion of some relative prices. Profits, agricultural and industrial, were depressed, which in turn had a negative effect, first on investment and, later on, on the external situation. The second stage, when the inevitable readjustment of relative prices took place, was more violent than in previous cases, showing very clearly the interplay of economic and political factors. What sets the 1973 stabilisation programme apart from earlier ones, is the extraordinary intensity of the problems of the second stage.

The stabilisation programme was associated with the imposition of a certain distribution of income by the middle-of-the-road coalition, but the government did not have the power, the cohesion or the discipline to enforce it for long. While at the beginning the problem was one between the government and previously established interests, at a later stage it became a fight between the various groups of the Peronist alliance, mainly between the trade unions and the party's right wing, which tried to impose a very orthodox programme. This attempt alienated the support of the Peronist rank and file, without winning the support of the conservative forces, whose policies the Peronist right was trying to apply. It can be said that the inflationary process was, in large measure, the consequence of the political conflicts *between* sectors and *among* them. These conflicts can also be viewed as attempts to increase – or to maintain – the income shares captured by oligopolistic groups of various kinds, not only the trade unions. Firms, for example, compounded their pricing behaviour with the lobbying power of their trade organisations. In the industrial sector they were even able to organise lock-outs, and in the agricultural sector, traditionally considered as the typical competitive sector, several producer strikes were staged. While this lobbying was not very successful at the beginning, by the end it had a considerable destabilising influence, with pernicious effects on the inflationary process.

But conflicts among sectors were not the only damaging ones. Intra-sectoral struggles to improve a relative position within the same social or economic group were as damaging, or even more so, than the inter-sectoral ones. The conflicts varied in intensity. At the beginning they were damped down by the social pact, which included both inter- and intra-sectoral agreements. Later on, after the 1975 price outburst, they were toned down, for a brief period, by the short-lived deflationary process. A deflationary policy is an alternative to a social pact but requires equivalent qualities of cohesion and discipline.

When relative price shifts were attempted as part of the policies of the government, they proved difficult to sustain, particularly when they did not accord with the relative power of the groups affected. Price shifts, which were necessary to improve efficiency, increased inflationary pressures in the short term, generally from the cost side. The obverse was also true: cost-push pressures were checked at times by methods that would make the problems worse at a later stage. But buying time was tempting on economic and, particularly, political grounds.

Indexation was one of the few ways of allowing some kind of efficient allocation of resources under these conditions. It is not clear to what extent it was a factor contributing to the inflationary process. It may be true that if a certain sector's income can be squeezed for a time this may help to slow down the inflationary process. But if this squeezing cannot continue for long, either because of the deleterious effect on production, or because of the political resistance that may arise, it may be better to protect that sector from wide fluctuations in its income share. In the long run and with efficiency considerations in mind, the advantages of indexation are indeed clearer than in the short run and when the sole concern is an anti-inflationary policy.

Monetary policy proved to be an important but not decisive tool, its role being relatively passive. An active monetary policy is possible when the government is strong and active in areas other than the purely monetary realm, and is therefore able to reduce the sources of monetary expansion. Such conditions did not typically obtain in Argentina during our period. In real terms the amount of money in circulation was fundamentally determined by expectations and by the rate of interest (Salama, 1977). An important policy tool – though it was not correctly used – should therefore have been the determination of the rate of interest and the consequent demand for cash balances. The role of expectations proved to be extremely significant, helping when they were reduced, but viciously compounding the inflationary process as they regained momentum.

Foreign exchange policies played a very active role. But most sectors became overly sensitive to price changes. Devaluations, among other price changes, were very soon counteracted by repricing in the rest of the economy. In fact, it was not at all easy to devalue in real terms. It was clear that devaluation, if not accompanied by an explicit policy to reduce absorption, would be insufficient, risking the possibility of never-ending devaluations.

A concept such as 'velocity of adjustment' to relative price changes may be necessary in order to understand the process. This velocity depends on the degree of awareness of the various sectors, which in turn is related to past experience, and on the level of effective demand and the intensity of the departure from the previous equilibrium. Obviously, the higher this velocity, the more difficult it will be to control the inflationary process. Small changes from the equilibrium situation may have, in these situations, a disproportionate effect. In the same way that a small reduction in the level of unemployment below a natural rate may have a very high inflationary effect, it may also be true that moderate increases in effective demand beyond a certain point, or moderate additional price distortions, also beyond a certain range, may have disproportionate effects. Thus in Argentine conditions an initial wage increase in real terms of 10 per cent, an increase in the government's deficit from 2 per cent to 6 per cent of GNP, an overvaluation of the currency of around 20 per cent – each could give rise to a very high rate of inflation.

The economic evolution of these years, despite some important local peculiarities which exacerbated the cycle, were also influenced to a substantial extent by the international situation. The rather propitious beginnings were closely related to the tail of the pre-1973 international prosperity. While the international situation was good, that made possible the initial stabilisation programme and some of the distributionist policies. When it was reversed – a fact compounded by the closure of the European Common Market to meat imports – that helped to precipitate the 1975 crisis. The way in which the deterioration of the terms of trade took place (i.e. with import prices increasing fast relative to export prices) led both to a reversal of the external balance and to an immediate upward pressure on imported prices and consequently on prices in general. This diminished the profitability of business, particularly for those sectors relying on imports, making impossible the continuation of the price freeze. Nevertheless it is clear that internal policies which might have dampened the effects of the changes of the international economy in fact made them more severe. One lesson from this experience is that, despite, or because of, the diminishing quantitative importance of international trade, the Argentine economy has become more vulnerable to further reductions in imports. In other words, indiscriminate import substitution can lead, paradoxically, to an increased 'dependency' on the smaller quantum of trade.

Our last comment, inevitably, has to do with the viability of reformist regimes in the Argentine context. Reform, despite its intrinsically moderate character, cannot be implemented through the weak policies of weak governments. On the contrary, it requires a great degree of firmness, not only in dealing with opposed groups, but particularly in dealing with its own base of support. And this strength is not easy to muster in a country where the government has been traditionally weak and where the reformist forces are a rather loose and undisciplined alliance. Some of the initial mild attempts to make some small transfers of income met with an extraordinarily bitter opposition. But it is also true that the flamboyant rhetoric in which these mild measures were shrouded hindered the possibility of successful reform. Also, the lack of discipline of the various groups making up the government alliance and the difficulty of imposing any sort of authority acceptable to them all, made the functioning of the government in general very difficult.

The initial strongly left-leaning twist hindered the acceptability of the new government and harmed its inner cohesion, even after the deviation had been corrected. The lack of self-restraint by the unions, during the two brief periods when they exercised effective control – particularly during the second – prevented a consolidation of the middle-of-the-road groups. The character of the right wing, headed by the President herself, does much to explain the intensity of the conflicts during the latter part of 1974, the whole of 1975 and up to the end.

The attempts to put across an orderly reformist programme based on the unions and on a populist alliance did not meet with success. Reform, despite its mildness, is a most difficult affair and requires a degree of determination and cohesion no less than that required for radical change. The bulk of the governing coalition, based on trade unions and on middle-class sectors, showed a rather strong tendency towards a middle course and its resistance to extreme movements gave a certain anchorage to the whole social situation. The fact that the alliance was subject to opportunistic shifts at the top was undoubtedly a serious structural weakness. The author believes, however, that, even though it may be a long and hard road before a more viable reformist group can be constructed, it will still require a similar broad social base. Easier alternatives do not seem to exist. Learning by doing, even if by doing the wrong things, may be the only way, although a painful one. No easier solution was, or for that matter is, at hand.

NOTES

* This essay is part of a larger one on Argentina's recent history. Although there are some marginal references to the political situation necessary to understand the economic developments, an analysis of the political aspects will be the subject of a separate essay. Likewise the analysis of the nature and the workings of the inflationary process, and in particular the role of oscillations of relative prices, will all be treated more fully in future essays.

This essay was written while the author was at the Centre for Latin American Studies, at St Antony's College, Oxford, an institution which has given generous support to the project. The author also wants to thank A. Conte, J. C. de Pablo, H. Dieguez, E. Gaba, A. Guadagni, A. Petrecolla, L. Reca, J. Villanueva and E. Zalduendo for their help in improving significantly some parts of this chapter, and C. Piccinini for his help in the compilation of the statistical appendix.

Finally, the author has no intention of hiding the fact that he has been associated with one of the periods into which this paper is divided, namely the fifth (August 1975 – January 1976). This has given him a better knowledge of the facts but unavoidably a greater bias, which he hopes, however, to have decently disguised.

1   Over a period of thirty-three years (1943 – 76) there have been five military governments and four civilian ones. There have been ten appointed and seven selected Presidents, only one of whom, however, completed the constitutional period in office.

2   It has to be said that the 1943 coup, which brought Perón to power, was a significant exception, giving rise to the idea that military governments could be associated with 'Nasserist', 'developmentalist' or even 'populist' regimes. This was a view more typical of the 1950s and 1960s.

3   This figure slightly overrates the performance of this particular ten-year period, as it starts with a trough and ends with a peak year. But if we take the period from 1965 up to 1975, the average becomes 4·3 per cent, not strikingly different.

4   During the 1964/65 revival, a periodically adjusted exchange rate was introduced, avoiding thereby the wide oscillations in relative prices that had affected previous policies. By 1966 it had created certain inflationary pressures and some balance-of-payments problems, which were, however, rather mild, compared with the earlier and later experiences (Mallon and Sourrouille, 1977).

5   The crisis has to be viewed in the context of the typical cattle cycles. While some of the measures probably exacerbated the cycle, the downward phase helped the stabilisation policies of the Krieger Vasena period, while the upward phase made a significant contribution to the renewal of the inflationary pressures, particularly during the Ferrer period.

6   It is still open to question whether the Krieger Vasena programme could have continued if the political troubles had not occurred. A devaluation of the exchange, an increase in beef prices in particular and a new inflationary round were inevitable, it would seem. Probably the 1971 – 2 developments would have taken place in any case, but in a less extreme form. The argument that the political troubles were a direct consequence of Krieger Vasena's economic policies seems unwarranted, considering the wage figures and the distribution of income shares.

7   The loose and imprecise policies of the Treasury, headed by Quillici, lacked a minimum of coherence. But the external situation was managed rather independently and in a much more coherent line – with a strong orthodox flavour – by the Central Bank under the chairmanship of C. Brignone.

8   Money in circulation had fallen from 21·6 per cent of GNP in 1971 to 16·7 per cent in 1972. Despite this reduction money probably had a greater inflationary potential, as the demand for cash balances diminished, increasing its velocity.

9   The CGE tended to represent newcomers who were at odds with the larger Union Industrial Argentina, which represents more established, more efficient and larger firms, including many of the foreign ones.

10 An analysis of the longer-term aims and of the nature of this reformist programme will be the subject of a separate paper. Probably its image as an extreme left-wing programme is the consequence of its being launched at a moment when the government was in the hands of the left wing.

11 Other measures taken later on, rather haphazardly, included some expropriations of foreign enterprises, in banking, in manufacturing and in service sectors, each event being heralded as the beginning of a structural change. These measures affected some banks which had become foreign-owned in the immediately preceding period. Two very large contracts for telecommunications with the local subsidiaries of ITT and Siemens were cancelled and a messy negotiation was started, including a variety of odd solutions implying the elimination of the telecommunications side of both companies. Much later, a law was passed nationalising the petrol stations of Esso and Shell, which had about 40 per cent of the petrol market, leaving them the processing side. Later still, the concession of the Swiss-owned electrical utility company was abruptly cancelled, antagonising many European banking groups with which it was connected. These last three measures were taken during the Isabel Perón period and were in clear contradiction to her general right-wing political and economic lines.

12 While we refer to these subversive organisations only marginally, it has to be emphasised that their existence, strong connections with the Peronista left and deliberately provocative behaviour poisoned the political climate of these years. Some of what may seem excessive reaction to and distrust of the specific measures of the left-wing programme has to be attributed to the complicity or, at least, the leniency of the Cámpora backers in regard to these groups.

13 The CGT and the enlarged CGE, which now included the old Union Industrial Argentina.

14 As mentioned, the emphasis on braking inflationary expectations was also a characteristic of the 1967–70 programme. In both cases, the political change which preceded them helped for a while to give some credibility to the new policies.

15 Despite the price controls, the statistical office, INDEC, used prices effectively paid in the market rather than official prices as its basis. A certain bias remained, but probably not a significant one. For a different view and a debatable but interesting estimate, see de Pablo (1977).

16 This again was a repetition of the 1967–9 experience, when the reduction in the rate of inflation from 22·7 per cent to 7·2 per cent allowed an increase in the liquidity coefficient from 0·20 to 0·26 without adverse effects.

17   The decision to cancel was taken by the President, pressed by the CGT. The CGT leadership was being harassed by some radical elements within its rank and file, who considered the 'social pact' a sell-out, and thought that they could not withstand a price increase of any kind without asking for an immediate wage increase.

18   J. C. de Pablo has pointed out to me that the reduction of unemployment was partly due to the increase in state employment, something which is not considered in the Philips curve. Although the unemployment rate may have been poorly correlated with the various inflationary outbursts, it may be a good indicator of the degree of heating of the economy, which, with varying and significant lags, and in a roundabout way, may have something to do with the level of expectations. For a very negative view on the role of unemployment as an explanatory variable of the price increases see Brodersohn (1977).

19   This is a typical case when government has to choose between measures that will feed the inflationary process, either from the demand side or from the supply side. The choice is usually made against measures which imply a cost push, particularly because of their more immediate impact.

20   The political side of the programme was based on the elimination of the left wing in the educational system, on the organisation of semi-legal anti-subversive groups and on the attempt to get the active support of the army, the so-called *'profesionalismo integrado'*. The programme advanced quite well on the three fronts but was shattered when the economic side faltered because of the firm opposition of the unions.

21   Which sometimes depends much more on the value of the exchange than on explicit tariffs (Corden, 1971; Berlinsky, 1977).

22   The figure refers to the whole year, but the bulk of the transfer took place between July and August 1979. This income effect was probably at the root of the early revival of instalments sales. See Feldman (1976), Gaba (1977).

23   The Central Bank, headed by E. Mondelli, who was to become the last Minister of Economics, deserves credit for a tight monetary policy, which in this particular instance avoided an even greater disaster.

24   In fact this practice of extending forward coverage had originated before 1973 during the Ferrer administration, and was the consequence of nationalistic policy which differentiated between locally owned and foreign-owned firms as far as local credit was concerned. Foreign firms were forced to use foreign financing, for which exchange coverage was granted, equalising the cost of money from both sources. This discriminatory treatment, however, was more apparent than real. During certain periods, the availability of credit was much greater for the foreign firms, as the Central Bank could not regulate the granting of forward coverage owing to the tight external situation, while during others it even had to make foreign borrowing cheaper in order to boost the flow of funds. This is but another instance where piecemeal policies can have the opposite results from those originally envisaged.

25   An interesting exception was the government's deal with the local motor-car manufacturers, the largest single importers of manufactured goods. This allowed them to free their prices before anyone else, provided they

agreed to obtain medium-term financing for their supplies. A total credit of £200 million was accordingly built up.

26 It may seem surprising that the army gave so little support to a programme which in the economic field as well as in its attitude *vis-à-vis* the guerrilla movement was apparently very much in line with military inclinations. This reflected a deep lack of confidence in the leaders of the right wing, Isabel Perón and J. López Rega, partly owing to their past political records and their personal peculiarities.

27 This could be seen, for example, in cases like the metallurgical and the motor-car unions, which concentrated their efforts on the improvement of their relative position. The same was true in many other instances, including business groups. These sub-groups were not so much in favour of a general improvement of the broadly defined group to which they belonged, as sensitive to measures that improved the position of their particular sector. This attitude was to some extent the consequence of the awareness that the income of some of the broader categories – i.e. wage earners, capitalists – was to some extent fixed and could not be changed easily in real terms. Instead, a change in the relative position of a specific sector relative to the income of the broader sector, of which it was part, was seen as possible. Of course, we are implying that these sectors behaved in an oligopolistic manner.

28 The electricity workers' and the car workers' unions pressed more than others for a reconsideration of their special cases, as their wages had risen by 80 and 100 per cent, respectively, while the metallurgical union, which had obtained 160 per cent, closing the traditional gap with the competing car workers' union, led the group which was opposed to any change.

29 Prices of products fixed by the government were increased to pre-shock levels, those of grain to somewhat above, while meat, despite the reduction and finally the elimination of export *ad valorem* taxes, continued at a very low level until the very end of the period, when a significant increase took place, reaching one of the highest levels of the 1975–7 period. Two lock-outs by the cattle sector took place, each time suspending deliveries to the stockyards for a week. While the lock-outs were caused by the economic situation of the sector, they were part of a political plan to bring down the government, particularly the second one.

30 The sympathetic attitude of Albert Fishlow, Under-Secretary for Latin American Affairs, was instrumental in the conclusion of the negotiations.

REFERENCES

Ayres, R. (1976), 'The Social Pact as Anti-Inflationary Policy. The Argentine Experience since 1973', *World Politics*, July.

Bajraj, R. (1976), 'La Inflación Argentina en los Años 70', paper presented at the Seminario sobre la inflación reciente en América Latina, Cáracas, November.

Berlinsky, J. (1977), 'La Protección Efectiva de Activadades Seleccionadas de la Industria Manufacturera Argentina', mimeo, Buenos Aires, September.

Braun, O. (1970), 'Desarrollo del Capital Monopolista en la Argentina', *Tiempo Contemporáneo*, Buenos Aires.

Brodersohn, M. (1977), *Conflictos entre los Objectivos de la Política Económica de Corto Plazo de la Economía Argentina*, Documento de trabajo no. 77, Instituto Torcuato Di Tella, Centro de Investigaciones Economicas.

Canavese, A. J., and Montuschi, L. (1975), 'Efectos Redistributivos del Pacto Social', paper presented at the tenth annual meeting of the Asociación Argentina de Economía Política, Mar del Plata, November.

Canitrot, A. (1976), 'La Experiencia Populista de Redistribución de Ingresos', *Desarrollo Económico*, no. 59, pp. 331–51.

Corden, M. (1971), *The Theory of Protection*, Clarendon Press, Oxford.

de Pablo, J. C. (1974), 'Relative Prices, Income Distribution, and Stabilization Plans: The Argentine Experience, 1967–1970', *Journal of Development Economics*, I, pp. 167–89.

de Pablo, J. C. (1977), 'Estimadores de la Inflacíon Reprimida: Argentina 1973–1976', IDEA, research papers no. 92.

de Pablo, J. C. (1978), *Inflación*, in *Cuatro Ensayos sobre la Economía Argentina*, Ediciones Macchi, Buenos Aires.

Feldman, M. (1976), 'Comportamiento de la Demanda de Bienes Durables en un Período de Alta Inflación: Argentina 1974–1975', paper presented at the twelfth meeting of Central Bank Economists, Ottawa, Canada.

Ferrer, A. (1977), *Crisis y Alternativas en la Política Económica Argentina*, Fondo de Cultura Económica, Buenos Aires.

Gaba, E. (1977), Indexación y Sistema Financiero, *Revista Argentina de Finanzas*, Buenos Aires, no. 2, pp. 33–67.

Hicks, J. (1974), *The Crisis in Keynesian Economics*, Blackwell, Oxford.

IMF, *International Financial Statistics*, Washington.

Mallon, R., and Sourrouille, J. (1977), *La Política Económica en una Sociedad Conflictiva: El Caso Argentino*, Amorrortu, Buenos Aires.

Nun, J. (1966), 'América Latina: La Crísis Hegemónica y el Cambio Militar', *Desarrollo Económico*, nos 22–3, pp. 355–415.

Olivera, J. (1967), 'Money Prices and Fiscal Lags: A Note on the Dynamics of Inflation', *Banca Nazionale del Lavoro Quarterly Review*, September.

Van Rijckeghem, V. (1972), 'Políticas de Establización para una Económia Inflacionaria', *Desarrollo Económico*, no. 46, pp. 245–52.

Salama, E. (1977), 'La Velocidad del Dinero y el Diseño de la Política Económica', *Revista Argentina de Finanzas*, Buenos Aires, no. 1, pp. 97–116.

Sommer, J. (1977), 'La Deuda Externa Argentina, entre 1972 y 1976', paper presented at the fourteenth meeting of Central Bank Economists, Bariloche, Argentina.

Statistical Appendix

TABLE 6.1 Argentina: Percentage rate of change of GDP and investment, 1966–77

	GDP	Agriculture	Industry	Construction	Investment
1966	0·6	−3·7	0·7	6·2	−7·2
1967	2·7	4·3	1·5	12·9	4·5
1968	4·3	−5·4	6·5	18·1	10·6
1969	8·5	5·5	10·8	19·1	21·5
1970	5·4	5·6	6·3	9·4	7·4
1971	4·6	−5·0	9·7	−3·4	10·2
1972	3·1	−7·9	6·0	4·9	5·2
1973	5·8	13·5	6·4	−5·1	−1·3
1974	6·5	6·2	6·1	12·2	3·9
1975	−1·3	−3·5	−2·8	−9·6	−7·2
1976	−2·9	3·5	−4·5	−14·1	−6·2
1977	4·4	7·1	3·8	13·3	19·5

Source: Banco Central de la República Argentina (BCRA), Departamento de Cuentas Nacionales.

TABLE 6.2 Investment as a percentage of GDP, 1966–76

Years	Total		Private	Public
	Including stock variation	Not including SV	Not including SV	
1966	17·9	17·8	11·7	6·1
1967	18·2	18·1	11·0	7·1
1968	19·3	19·5	11·6	7·9
1969	21·6	21·7	13·6	8·1
1970	22·0	21·5	13·3	8·2
1971	23·1	22·5	14·0	8·5
1972	23·6	23·0	14·2	8·8
1973	22·0	21·8	14·1	7·7
1974	21·4	21·2	11·3	9·9
1975	20·2	20·0	8·5	11·5
1976	19·5	19·6	7·7	11·9

Source: BCRA, Departamento de Cuentas Nacionales.

TABLE 6.3   Argentina: Rates of change of consumer and wholesale price indices, 1966–77

	1966	1967	1968	1969	1970	1971	1972	1973	1974	1975	1976	1977
Rate of change of consumer price index (seasonally adjusted) (Dec. to Dec.)	29·9	27·3	9·6	10·7	12·2	39·2	64·2	43·7	40·0	335·0	364·0	160·0
Rate of change of wholesale price index (Dec. to Dec.)	22·7	20·6	3·9	7·2	26·9	48·2	75·9	30·8	36·1	348·7	386·0	147·0

Source: Instituto Nacional de Estadísticas y Censos (INDEC).

TABLE 6.4   Relative price movements (1960=100)

	1972	1973	1974	1975	1976	1977
Cost of living/wholesale prices	105	112	116	112	125	112
Agricultural/industrial prices	129	120	106	85	93	101
Imported/national prices	96	105	121	149	200	185
Grain+linseed/cattle prices	58	61	73	91	86	92

Source: Instituto Nacional de Estadísticas y Censos (INDEC).

TABLE 6.5   Real wages, 1966–76 (1973=100)

Year	Yearly average		
	(a) Unskilled married workers, hourly rate	(b) Skilled married workers	(c) All workers, wage drift included, test firm
1966	107·1		
1967	100·2		
1968	99·7		
1969	103·7		
1970	103·7		
1971	108·0		
1972	97·0		
1973	100·0	100·0	100·0
1974	109·2	105·4	114·8
1975	105·6	100·7 (109·4, with	117·6
1976	63·3	57·8 wage drift)	88·3

Source: Fundación de Investigación Económicas Latino Americanas (FIEL), Ministerio de Economía and private sources.

Note: These are some of the more highly contested series, particularly in view of the importance of the wage drift, over and above the official rates, something which was important in the second half of 1975 and first quarter of 1976. Series (c), actual payments, was supplied by A. Mayoral to whom we owe our thanks. It allows us to analyse a single case, but one which we think is quite representative of the metallurgical industry. Figures for 1977 are available but are not given here as they are even more dubious due to the enormous increase in wage drift.

TABLE 6.6 Share of the national income accruing to wage earners, 1950–75

1950	49·7	1969	44·6
1955	47·7	1970	45·8
1960	38·0	1971	46·6
1965	40·6	1972	42·7
1966	43·8	1973	46·9
1967	45·5	1974	46·7
1968	44·9	1975	44·8

Source: Ministerio de Economía.

TABLE 6.7 Sources of money creation 1967–77 (changes, in million pesos and as a percentage of the total increase in M_2)

	Foreign sector		Government sector		Private sector		Banks net worth and other		Total increase in M_2
	$m	%	$m	%	$m	%	$m	%	
1967	1153	35	230	7	2322	71	−423	−13	3282
1968	323	8	249	6	4234	102	−651	−16	4155
1969	−609	−21	439	15	4014	130	−945	−33	2899
1970	771	17	697	16	3770	84	−768	−17	4470
1971	−1080	−13	2232	26	9364	110	−1976	−23	8540
1972	1004	6	4999	31	15399	95	−5151	−32	16251
1973	5736	12	15398	33	26415	57	−1448	−3	46101
1974	4317	8	20383	39	40793	77	−12619	−24	52874
1975	−14420	−8	118525	63	174154	92	−88914	−47	189345
1976	387144	35	113782	10	922612	82	−304405	−27	1119133
1977	886145	25	554444	16	2400352	91	−1137265	−32	3543359

Source: BCRA.

	M_1 as % GNP	M_2 as % GNP	M_3 as % GNP	M_4 as % GNP
1966	12·7	19·3	—	—
1967	13·1	20·0	—	—
1968	14·9	23·4	—	—
1969	15·6	25·8	—	—
1970	14·7	25·0	—	—
1971	12·5	21·6	—	—
1972	9·5	16·6	17·5	—
1973	10·3	17·8	19·8	20·0
1974	13·8	24·5	27·5	27·4
1975	9·0	13·7	15·2	16·1
1976	6·2	8·4	9·4	12·4
1977			14·4	16·8

Source: BCRA.

Notes: M_1 = Currency and demand deposits.
M_2 = M_1 + Interest yielding deposits.
M_3 = M_2 + Bank acceptances.
M_4 = M_3 + VNA (indexed government bonds) + treasury bonds.

TABLE 6.9 Public sector operations (central government's treasury, provinces and state enterprises, as a percentage of GDP)

	Revenue		Expenditures			Deficit	Borrowing		Deficit financing
	Total	Taxes	Total	Current	Investment		External	Internal	
1966	26·7	15·9	31·3	25·3	6·0	-4·6	0·3	—	4·3
1967	30·3	19·0	32·3	25·2	7·1	-1·9	-0·3	0·1	2·1
1968	30·2	18·4	32·3	24·6	7·7	-2·1	—	0·4	1·7
1969	29·5	17·3	34·2	23·6	7·6	-1·6	0·3	0·5	0·8
1970	29·4	18·0	31·1	23·3	7·8	-1·7	0·8	0·1	0·8
1971	26·7	16·1	31·0	23·3	7·7	-4·3	1·1	0·7	2·5
1972	25·0	14·3	30·2	22·1	8·1	-5·2	1·0	0·9	3·5
1973	26·5	16·2	33·8	26·5	7·3	-7·3	0·1	0·9	6·3
1974	30·2	19·3	38·0	29·4	8·6	-7·8	0·9	1·0	5·9
1975	25·7	14·3	41·7	32·4	9·3	-16·2	0·1	1·7	14·4
1976	30·0	17·5	41·1	28·2	12·9	-11·1	0·6	2·6	7·9
1977[a]	35·4	20·9	40·5	27·6	13·4	-5·6	1·6	1·2	2·8

Source: IBRD, *Argentina, Reconstruction and Development*, 1977.   Note: [a] Estimated.

TABLE 6.10   Central government's Treasury operations (as a percentage of GDP)

Year and quarter	Expenditures (a)	Income (b)	Deficit (a−b)
1972	8·64	6·21	2·43
I	7·79	5·69	2·10
II	8·65	7·00	1·65
III	8·84	6·28	2·56
IV	8·96	5·84	3·12
1973	10·95	5·54	5·43
I	8·75	4·89	3·86
II	9·41	4·39	5·01
III	11·93	6·35	5·58
IV	13·24	6·31	6·93
1974	13·12	6·58	6·54
I	11·37	5·94	5·43
II	13·22	7·87	5·34
III	13·32	6·77	6·55
IV	14·06	5·82	8·24
1975	15·98	4·27	11·71
I	12·15	5·03	7·12
II	12·22	4·40	6·92
III	13·81	4·06	9·75
IV	20·17	3·80	16·38
1976	13·66	5·65	8·01
I	16·97	4·03	12·94
II	11·34	4·32	7·02
III	13·91	6·13	7·79
IV	13·90	6·73	7·18
1977	10·41	6·74	3·67
I	12·62	6·80	5·18
II	10·50	7·25	3·73
III	10·59	7·33	3·26
IV	9·11	5·89	3·23

Source: BCRA.

TABLE 6.11 Percentage variation in the number of government employees, 1967–76

	Central administration	Special accounts	Decentralised accounts	State enterprises	All national authorities	All provincial authorities	All public employees
1967	−0·2	1·5	3·3	−3·5	−0·7	1·3	−0·1
1968	0·4	12·3	1·7	−5·6	−1·5	−0·6	−1·2
1969	−0·1	20·7	−1·8	−2·8	−1·3	0·7	−0·6
1970	−2·6	27·9	−4·0	−1·3	−1·9	0·1	−1·2
1971	−0·1	5·0	5·5	−0·4	1·3	2·1	1·6
1972	4·5	−17·3	5·2	2·3	3·5	2·5	3·2
1973	5·8	10·4	−3·1	10·9	5·5	16·5	9·4
1974	−13·4	12·3	1·2	20·3	3·3	8·5	5·3
1975	5·5	3·4	11·7	5·3	6·8	12·2	8·9
1976	−1·4	18·7	−0·8	1·0	0·2	1·4	0·7

Source: Ministerio de Economía, Informe Estadístico no. 10.

TABLE 6.12 Unemployment, 1971–7 (as a percentage of total employed)

	1971		1972		1973		1974		1975		1976		1977	
	Apr.	Oct.	Apr.	Oct.	Apr.	Oct.	Apr.	Oct.	Apr.	Oct.	Apr.	Oct.	Apr.	Oct.
Total	6·1	—	7·8	6·1	6·1	5·4	4·7	3·1	3·2	3·5	5·3	4·5	—	—
Greater Buenos Aires	5·7	—	7·4	5·8	6·1	4·5	4·2	2·5	2·3	2·7	4·8	4·2	3·4	2·2
Córdoba	5·0	4·4	7·2	5·2	5·3	6·1	7·0	5·4	7·2	7·5	6·5	5·6	5·9	—
Tucumán	11·7	12·2	14·2	11·7	12·5	11·3	10·5	7·5	8·6	6·8	7·4	5·5	7·2	—

Source: INDEC.

TABLE 6.13   Transfer of income from debtors to creditors, 1966–76

	Rate of interest on deposits (%)	Implicit tax on interest-yielding deposits (%)	As % of GDP
	(1)	(2)	
1966	−15·2	17·2	1·18
1967	−13·5	15·5	1·13
1968	0·3	1·7	0·15
1969	3·0	−1·0	−0·10
1970	−9·8	11·8	1·27
1971	−18·8	20·8	2·03
1972	−27·1	29·1	2·42
1973	−17·1	19·1	1·61
1974	−16·7	18·7	2·15
1975	−72·4	74·4	3·70
1976	−65·1	67·1	1·66

Source: Gaba (1977).
Note: (2) derived from (1) assuming a positive equilibrium rate of 2 per cent.

TABLE 6.14   Nominal rates of exchange, 1966–77 (pesos per US$; real rate of exchange, July 1973=100)

Year	Average					
	(a) Free exchange rate	(b) Commercial exchange rate	(c) Financial exchange rate	(d) Financial special rate	(e) Black market rate	(f) Estimate of the real rate for imports
1966	2·08	—	—	—	2·44	96·90
1967	3·31	—	—	—	2·42	123·60
1968	3·50	—	—	—	3·50	122·50
1969	3·50	—	—	—	3·51	119·20
1970	3·28	—	—	—	3·86	117·80
1971	4·19	5·00	7·51	—	6·14	104·70
1972	—	5·00	9·85	—	11·50	100·50
1973	—	5·00	9·98	—	11·30	99·90
1974	—	5·00	9·98	—	16·25	100·30
1975	—	21·36	30·67	699·40	72·15	122·60
1976	246·58	140·33	69·53	99·00	257·80	146·10
1977	409·90	—	—	—	423·10	132·30

Sources: (a), (b), (c), (d): BCRA; (e) Boletín Informativo Techint no. 207; (f) estimate derived from BCRA (weighted average of import rates, divided by wholesale prices and accounting for the American inflation).

TABLE 6.15 Terms of trade, 1966–76

Year and quarter	Export prices	Import prices	Terms of trade
1966	95·8	94·9	118·1
1967	90·7	93·0	114·1
1968	88·0	93·8	109·8
1969	139·0	99·5	104·3
1970	100·0	100·0	100·0
1971	101·0	96·4	104·9
1972	121·5	103·5	117·4
1973	180·3	165·5	108·9
1974	195·7	272·3	71·9
1975	170·2	239·0	71·2
1976	179·0	256·0	69·3

Sources: 1966–9: BCRA, based on the 1958 trade mix; 1970 onwards: Fundacion de Investigaciones Economicas Latino Americanas, and IMF, *Interational Financial Statistics*, based on the 1970 trade mix.

TABLE 6.16 Argentina's balance of payments, 1970–7 (yearly figures; US$m)

	1970	1971	1972	1973	1974	1975	1976	1977
I Merchandise account	79	−128	37	1031	435	−985	852	1727
Exports	1773	1740	1941	3266	4005	2960	3762	5677
Imports	1694	1868	1904	2235	3570	3946	2909	3950
II Services	−225	−258	−255	−327	−190	−304	−287	−182
III Current transactions (I+II)	−156	−386	−218	704	245	−1289	565	1545
IV Non-compensatory transfers	414	−190	−75	25	−172	502	380	934
International payments (III+IV)[a]	260	−560	−285	729	73	−787	945	2479
International reserves (variation)	185	−385	167	921	−51	−791	945	2227
Compensatory transfers	75	−175	−452	−192	124	4	—	252

Source: BCRA and INDEC.
Note: [a] Includes unilateral transfers and errors and omissions.

TABLE 6.17   International reserves, 1966−77 (end year; US$m)

1966	251·1
1967	763·4
1968	792·4
1969	560·2
1970	724·7
1971	316·7
1972	529·0
1973	1412·4
1974	1446·4
1975	678·0
1976	1943·9
1977	3862·0

Source: BCRA.

TABLE 6.18   External debt 1972−6 (US$m)

	1972	1973	1974	1975	1976
TOTAL DEBT	5788	6233	7968	9149	9738
Public sector	3089	3426	4558	5295	6648
Less than 180 days	162	243	379	717	675
More than 180 days	2922	3183	4179	4578	5973
Private sector	2699	2807	3410	3854	3090
Less than 180 days	930	1230	1759	2124	1066
More than 180 days	1769	1577	1651	1730	2024

Source: 'La deuda externa argentina entre 1972 y 1976', Sommer, J. (1977).

7 Brazil and the post-1973 Crisis in the International Economy

JOHN R. WELLS

INTRODUCTION

The aim of this paper is to examine the circumstances in which the so-called Brazilian 'economic miracle' appears to have been blown off-course in the period since 1973–4 and the response of Brazilian policy-makers to the recent return of two problems which have beset Brazilian economic development historically: severe balance-of-payments disequilibrium and accelerating inflation.

The principal conclusion is that, although[1] policy-makers have been largely unsuccessful in solving these basic problems, Brazil has, nevertheless, by and large avoided the severe deflations imposed on other Latin American economies in the wake of the recent crisis in the international economy–deflationary action which Brazil itself experienced during a period of external disequilibrium and inflationary pressure between 1963 and 1967.[2] What has stood out in the Brazilian case has been the willingness of foreign bankers to finance what have been, by any standards, extremely large balance-of-payments deficits between 1974 and 1977 and to permit a spiralling level of public and private sector foreign indebtedness. Such finance has been forthcoming largely because of a basic satisfaction in international financial circles with the economic and social policies being pursued by the regime and a certain bullishness about the economy's medium-term prospects (especially its export performance post-1980 and its capacity to service the foreign debt). This is not to suggest that leverage has not been exerted, but it has been mainly in the direction of pressing Brazil to *moderate* its rate of growth (from 10 per cent a year to, say, around 6 per cent) and to persist with the main elements of the economic model developed between 1964 and 1973, eschewing more radical solutions to the country's economic, social and political problems. It must be emphasised that stabilisation measures have not been dictated from abroad, nor have Brazilian policy-makers voluntarily pursued the orthodoxies propounded by foreign bankers: the gradual shift towards protectionism is one example of the degree of relative autonomy exercised by Brazilian policy-makers. Some fortuitous events, such as the large rise in coffee prices in 1976–7, have also obviated the need for really deflationary stabilisation policies.

It might be useful to start with a review of the period of 'miraculous' economic growth, 1967–73.

THE PERIOD OF 'MIRACULOUS' GROWTH, 1967–73

Using standard performance criteria, the Brazilian economy's record during the period 1967–73 was most impressive, both in terms of Brazil's historical experience and in terms of the good performances achieved by other non-socialist less-developed countries during this period. The economy was able to combine extremely high rates of growth of GDP (averaging 10 per cent a year, but accelerating to 11·4 per cent by 1973) and gently decelerating rates of inflation (down from 27·1 in 1967 to 17 per cent in 1972) (see data in Table 7.1); growth was not constrained by foreign exchange, as net foreign capital inflow continually exceeded the current account deficit, with the result that foreign exchange reserves rose from US$200 million in 1967 to US$6·4 billion in 1973.

The 'leading' sector during this period was manufacturing industry and the principal sources of industrial growth during the period were:

(i) the rapid growth in demand for manufactured consumer durable goods, stimulated by increased household indebtedness, rising real incomes amongst urban middle-income groups, growing urbanisation, market-deepening and favourable relative price movements, due to the exploitation of economies of scale; the consumer durables sector was the leading sector within manufacturing, grow-

TABLE 7.1   The Brazilian economy: selected indicators and annual rates of change

Year	Money supply[a] (%)	Loans to private sector[a] (%)	Government expenditures[a] (%)	(A)[a] (%)	(B)[a] (%)	(C) (%)	GDP (%)	Agriculture (%)	Industry (%)
1965	79·5	67·1	57·5	34·5	31·4	55·4	2·7	13·8	−4·7
1966	13·8	29·8	44·4	38·8	42·1	38·8	5·1	−3·1	11·7
1967	45·7	58·3	23·8	24·3	21·2	27·1	4·8	5·7	3·0
1968	39·0	62·4	43·1	25·4	24·8	27·8	9·3	1·4	15·5
1969	32·5	44·5	27·9	20·2	18·7	22·3	9·0	6·0	10·8
1970	25·8	36·3	28·7	19·2	18·7	19·8	9·5	5·6	11·1
1971	32·3	45·5	46·1	19·8	21·3	20·4	11·3	11·4	11·2
1972	38·3	42·7	38·3	15·5	16·1	17·0	10·4	4·5	13·8
1973	47·0	46·4	37·4	15·7	15·6	15·1	11·4	3·5	15·0
1974	33·5	59·3	38·7	34·5	35·4	28·7	9·6	8·5	8·2
1975	42·8	56·4	30·8	29·4	29·3	27·7	4·2	3·4	4·2
1976	37·2	57·3	73·8	48·2	44·9	n.a.	8·8	4·2	10·9
1977	37·6	54·4	n.a.	38·6	35·4	n.a.	4·7	9·6	3·9

Sources: Central Bank; *Conjuntura Econômica*, Fundação Getulio Vargas.
Notes: [a] December to December changes; (A) general price index, *Conjuntura Econômica*, column 2; (B) wholesale price index, *Conjuntura Econômica*, column 12; (C) GDP implicit deflator.

ing at 23·8 per cent p.a. between 1967 and 1973, compared
with an all-sector manufacturing average of 14·7 per cent
p.a.;[3]

(ii) the rapid growth of the construction industry, facilitated
again by expanding credit facilities and heavy public
sector investment;

(iii) an acceleration in the rate of fixed-capital formation, with
the share of gross fixed-capital formation in GDP rising
from under 20 per cent in the mid-1960s to 23 per cent by
1973 (see Table 7.2). Much of the increased investment
demand (construction apart) was satisfied by the domestic
capital goods industry, which grew at an average rate of
20·5 per cent p.a. (1967−73), accelerating to 30 per cent
p.a. in 1972−3;[4] there was also a marked increase in the
import-content of investment in machinery and equipment, rising from 18·3 per cent in 1966 to 27·1 per cent in
1972, due to the growth of import-liberalisation in capital
goods between 1969 and 1973.[5] Massive long-term foreign
direct investment inflows (almost US$1 billion a year by
1972−3), as well as state and local capital, all played an
important part in this investment boom;

(iv) the growth of manufactured exports, which was an additional, though subsidiary source of growth, contributing in
the aggregate to no more than 8 per cent of the increase in
total manufacturing sales between 1968 and 1972.[6] The
importance of external markets was much greater in the
'traditional' non-durable manufacturing sectors, but, in
the aggregate, manufactured exports were mainly important as a growing source of foreign exchange earnings.

TABLE 7.2   Main macro-economic aggregates (as a percentage of GDP at
market prices)

	1949	1959	1967	1970	1973	1975
Personal consumption	75·3	69·4	69·8	66·7	64·3	68·8
Government consumption	10·9	10·7	10·9	10·2	9·6	9·8
Government investment	4·0	3·7	4·4	4·1	3·8	4·3
Enterprise (public and private) investment	8·9	14·9	14·9	18·1	19·2	21·1
Stockbuilding	1·0	2·2	—	1·2	4·3	—
Exports of goods and services	8·6	5·8	5·5	6·6	8·1	7·4
Imports of goods and services	8·8	6·6	5·6	7·0	9·3	11·4

Source: *Conjuntura Econômica*, July 1977.

Several important factors contributed to the achievement of a decelerating rate of inflation and the absence of an external constraint, which accompanied and facilitated the achievement of this rapid growth spurt. First, the repression of the trade union movement and the consolidation of an authoritarian political system enabled the government to pursue a strict wage policy, in which the real minimum wage declined sharply and increases in average real earnings in manufacturing constantly lagged behind productivity growth, permitting a shift in the functional distribution of income in manufacturing in favour of profits:[7] this not only reduced the inflationary pressure from the side of costs but, at least in the early stages of the cycle, permitted the rise in the rate of investment to be financed in a relatively non-inflationary fashion. Second, strict control over government current expenditures with negative effects on government salaries, the value of transfer payments, the supply of urban social services and the quality of the urban infrastructure, combined with buoyant tax and social security revenues, served to transform the government sector into an important source of savings in the economy, thus contributing to the financing of investment from domestic savings.[8] Third, the existence of widespread spare capacity in the industrial sector at the beginning of the cyclical upswing permitted relatively easy non-inflationary output growth to take place—spare capacity contributing roughly 6 per cent a year to the growth of industrial output between 1967 and 1973.[9] Fourth, the international environment was particularly favourable during this period, allowing Brazil to experience a substantial improvement in its capacity to import. On the trade side, though export promotion policies did play a role in facilitating the diversification of Brazilian exports (both manufacturing and agricultural) and in slightly raising Brazil's share of world trade, the extraordinary rapid growth of world trade in this period was a major factor in the rapid growth of exports; the terms of trade also experienced a slight improvement, taking 1967 as base year (see Table 7.4 below). In addition, Brazil was the principal borrower from the official international financial institutions during this period and captured a lion's share of the foreign currency loans made available to peripheral capitalist countries by the Euro-dollar market.

The huge transfer of foreign resources (as measured by current account deficits) permitted growth to continue unconstrained by foreign exchange scarcity, and this, together with rising domestic savings, tended to reduce inflationary pressure below what it would otherwise have been in a situation of such rapid growth of both private consumption and investment.[10]

While this explanation for the economic 'miracle' has emphasised a variety of *special* factors during 1967–73 – namely, the rapid growth of world trade and international liquidity, ample idle capacity in the industrial sector and strict wage control – both government officials and, paradoxically, the government's most radical critics would argue that the stabilisation measures imposed between 1964 and 1967 under Planning Minister Roberto Campos *laid the foundations* and, thus, created the possibilities of the resumption of growth. This is an important issue in the context of the general theme of this book. Government officials point to the reduction in inflation, to the elimination of price distortions (abolition of subsidies and rationalisation of the foreign exchange regime), to institutional reforms (particularly those affecting the capital market) and to the increased role played by 'incentives' as the fruit of the period of tough stabilisation; extreme left-wing critics argue that stabilisation brought about a 'restructuring' of capital (through the elimination of the weak), was responsible for a rise in the aggregate rate of profit and was accompanied by a regressive redistribution of personal income, which stimulated the durables industries to renewed growth.

This is not an easy issue to resolve. Certainly, the reduction in inflation from the hyperinflationary levels of 1964 stands to the credit of the stabilisation policies, but even here policy was only partially successful, because of the re-emergence of cost pressures in 1966. On the other hand, while the political repression which accompanied the regressive redistributional changes was certainly essential for the maintenance of Brazilian capitalism, the distributional changes themselves were probably largely redundant (in the sense that the rate of profit was already very high by international standards and that the growth of the durables sector can be ascribed more to the growth of credit than to the regressive changes in size distribution). Furthermore, the capital market reforms made very little difference to the operation of the financial sector, and, as we shall argue below, did little to increase the ability of the monetary authorities to control the monetary system. To conclude, we would emphasise the elements of *continuity* in the development of Brazilian capitalism between the mid-1950s and the mid-1970s and would not accept that the stabilisation of the mid-1960s was responsible for a radical restructuring of the system, which laid the foundations for the 'miracle'.

THE MIRACLE OUT OF CONTROL

Despite the favourable macroeconomic indicators, however, such unbridled and unbalanced growth began to generate severe disequilibria in 1972 – even before the oil price rise and the ensuing international economic recession. It is difficult to believe that annual rates of GDP growth of the order of 11·3 per cent (achieved in 1971), 10·4 per cent (1972) and 11·4 per cent (1973) could be continuously sustainable in any economy, even given the sharp rise in the investment–GNP ratio which occurred, or that industrial output growth could have continued at the compound rate of 14·7 per cent p.a. achieved between 1967–73. By 1972–3, the industrial sector was clearly showing signs of intense overheating, under the pressure of excessive monetary expansion (fuelled by foreign currency inflows), rapidly growing consumption expenditures and buoyant investment expectations. Widespread shortages of many industrial inputs and components began to appear, due to the lack of balance between the expansion of capacity in the durable consumer goods sectors and in those producing intermediate inputs. The shortages generated inflationary pressure and were also responsible for a large rise in net imports of many intermediate inputs (steel and chemicals, in particular) (see Table 7.3). Given that the margin of spare capacity built up by accumulation in the early 1960s had been thoroughly eroded by 1972, the very rapid growth of demand could only be satisfied by a phenomenally high rate of accumulation. Although the domestic capital goods sector grew at 30 per cent p.a. in 1972 and 1973, investment also became, of necessity, increasingly import-intensive.

It can be argued that such disequilibria were virtually inevitable in an unplanned economy, attempting to use the rapid expansion of a particular sector of consumption (durable goods) as a lever to raise the rate of investment - leading to rapid rates of growth of *both* consumption *and* investment expenditure. The shortages ensuing from the creative tension induced by unbalanced growth in excess of the economy's maximum potential rate

TABLE 7.3   The structure of merchandise imports 1973–6 (US$m)

	1973	*1974*	*1975*	*1976*
Consumer goods	1104	1598	1293	1348
Wheat	335	468	321	530
Other non-durables	411	630	521	418
Durables	358	500	451	400
Oil and derivatives	711	2840	3073	3740
Crude oil	606	2558	2674	3490
Derivatives	105	282	399	250
Intermediate goods	2235	5084	3871	3442
Fertilisers	139	405	304	205
Steel	493	1536	1263	555
Copper	164	329	182	220
Aluminium	51	131	100	68
Zinc	41	76	44	42
Other metals	75	128	122	91
Paper	135	295	200	130
Rubber and plastics	159	422	252	277
Chemicals	718	1283	1135	1304
Other	260	479	269	550
Capital goods	2142	3119	3932	3510
Machinery and equipment	1708	2484	3238	2910
Transport material	434	635	694	600
Total (FOB)	6192	12641	12169	12040

Source: Banco Central do Brasil.

of growth could be met by foreign resources and the momentum could possibly have been sustained, but only if the economy had access to virtually unlimited foreign savings – a theoretical fantasy which was certainly entertained by Brazilian policy-makers in 1973, but which has no place in reality.

However, the implications for external equilibrium of the economy's growing import-dependence were masked in 1973 by the world primary commodity boom and its effects on Brazilian export earnings: a 10 per cent improvement in the terms of trade, a 15 per cent rise in export volume and a 55 per cent rise in the US$ value of exports in that year produced a small trade surplus for the first time since 1967 (see Table 7.4). However, such strong external demand increased the pressure on the local supply of foodstuffs, adding a further twist to inflationary pressure.[11] It was not until 1974 that the full implications of overheating became more visible, with a trade deficit of US$ 4·7 billion and a service deficit of US$ 2·4 billion summing to a current account gap for that year of US$ 7·1 billion (which amounted to about 6 per cent of Brazilian GDP) (see Table 7.4). Of course, the quadrupling of oil prices and the rising cost of imported machinery (as primary commodity price rises fed through into the price structure of the advanced countries) partly contributed to this: however, of the US$ 6449·1 million rise in imports between 1973 and 1974, only US$ 2 billion could be attributed to the increased oil deficit. Taking full account of the rise in other international prices, it can be concluded that the volume of imports rose by 34 per cent in 1974. Speculative stockpiling played a role, but such large marginal import requirements reflected the demands of an overheated industrial sector.

Thus, by 1974, ironically, it appeared that the Brazilian economy exhibited many of the features identified by the *Cepalino* economists of the 1960s as 'structural' impediments to growth —features which the years of the Brazilian economic 'miracle' were supposed to have shown to be a mirage: severe import-dependence in certain sectors, a huge overhang of external debt, inelasticities in domestic food supply and accelerating inflation (the rate of inflation rose to an annual rate of 50 per cent a year during the first half of 1974). In addition, the years of automobile-led growth had greatly accentuated Brazil's dependence on imported energy supplies and worsened urban problems, while the deliberate fostering of increased inequality made Brazil's social and political conflicts even more intractable. As a meningitis epidemic swept through Greater São Paulo in 1974, the public's attention became better focused upon the sharp cuts in public current spending and on the attitude of blithe neglect, adopted under the regime of Delfim Netto, towards the standard of living of the mass of the people.

OVERVIEW OF ECONOMIC PERFORMANCE 1974-7

Since 1974 policy-makers have had to deal with two economic problems which were largely absent during the period of the so-called Brazilian economic 'miracle': accelerating rates of inflation, and external disequilibrium.

Between 1967 and 1972, the rate of inflation appeared to be on a

TABLE 7.4 Exports and imports: price and quantum indices; terms of trade and import capacity 1970, 1972–7

	Exports			Imports			Terms of Trade		Import Capacity
	Value US$ m	Quantum	Price	Value US$ m	Quantum	Price	Including coffee	Excluding coffee	
1970	2739	100·0	100·0	2507	100	100	100	100	100
1972	3991	134·5	108·9	4235	146·4	111	98·2	105·4	132·1
1973	6199	155·1	149·6	6192	178·6	139	107·9	118·0	167·4
1974	7951	152·3	189	12635	239·1	214	88·3	97·2	134·5
1975	8670	165	189	12169	215·2	217	87·1	99·1	143·7
1976	10128	172	229	12347	216·5	219	104·6	105·9	179·9
1977	12139	n.a.	n.a.	11999	n.a.	n.a.	n.a.	n.a.	n.a.

Source: *Conjuntura Econômica*, indices 128, 117, 154, 141; Non-coffee terms of trade from IMF, *International Financial Statistics*.

declining trend, ending somewhat below an annual rate of 20 per cent. As measured by a variety of prices indices (see Table 7.1) above), it rose to about 30 per cent in 1974 and remained at the same level during 1975. In 1976, the rate of inflation accelerated sharply to over 40 per cent, and, in 1977, it appears to have stabilised at that level once more (there is, however, some divergence between the movements of alternative price indices in this year). Thus, in general terms, the rate of inflation has moved up to much higher levels than those experienced in the recent past – a movement which took a somewhat step-like form from year to year, without any apparent hyper-inflationary tendencies.

Between 1974 and 1977, the current account of the balance of payments experienced much larger deficits than those which came to be regarded almost as a 'structural' feature of the economy in the post-war period. The current deficit rose to US$ 7·4 billion in 1974, but experienced a steady decline to the still very substantial figure of US$4·3 billion by 1977. This trend (1974–7) is made up of two contradictory movements: a steady improvement in the trade balance (which moved into surplus in 1977) and a steady deterioration in the services account (see Table 7.5).

On the trade account, the movement in 1974 into a deficit of US$ 4·7 billion from a small surplus in 1973 can be ascribed to the following factors: a 34 per cent rise in import volume, an 18 per cent deterioration in the terms of trade and stagnation in export volume. The steady improvement in the trade balance since 1974 reflects a reversal of these tendencies. The volume of imports fell by 10 per cent in 1975 and has remained roughly constant ever since, while the volume of exports has shown a steady growth of roughly 6 per cent a year. In addition, import unit values have stayed constant since 1974 and export prices increased sharply after 1975 (partly, though not wholly, due to the frost-induced rise in coffee prices), with the result that the overall terms of trade (including coffee) are now at as favourable a level as in the 'golden' year of 1973. Increased coffee earnings explain only US$1662 million of the US$4824 million improvement in the trade performance between 1974 and 1977 – about 34 per cent. The rest must be ascribed to the relative success in reducing and then stabilising the volume of imports (albeit at a higher level than in 1972–3), as a result of import controls and the expansion of domestic capacity (see the discussion below), and to the growth

TABLE 7.5   Balance of payments 1969, 1972–7: Summary accounts (US$ m).

	1969	1972	1973	1974	1975	1976	1977
Trade balance	+318	−244	+7	−4684	−3499	−2218	+140
Exports (FOB)	+2311	+3991	+6199	+7951	+8670	+10128	+12139
Imports (FOB)	−1993	−4235	−6192	−12635	−12169	−12347	−11999
Balance of services (including transfers)	−630	−1250	−1722	−2463	−3213	−3919	−4425
Non-factor services	−322	−689	−988	−1547	−1478	−1781	−1725
Factor services	−308	−561	−734	−916	−1735	−2138	−2700
(Net interest payments)	(−182)	(−359)	(−514)	(−652)	(−1463)	(−1758)	(−2200)
(profits, dividends)	(−81)	(−161)	(−198)	(−248)	(−235)	(−380)	(−500)
Current account balance	−312	−1494	−1715	−7147	−6712	−6137	−4285
Capital account	+871	+3492	+3512	+6235	+5912	+8066	+4945
Net direct investment	+177	+318	+940	+887	+877	+1010	+800
Loans and financing	+1023	+4299	+4495	+6886	+5177	+10094	+8345
Amortisation	−493	−1202	−1672	−1940	−2088	−2888	−4100
Overall balance[a]	+549	+2439	+2179	−938	−1052	+2392	+460
Financing requirement = current account plus amortisation of external indebtedness	−805	−2696	−3387	−9087	−8800	−9025	−8385

Source: Banco Central do Brasil.
Note: [a] Including errors and omissions.

in export volume (which was very rapid in 1977). Nevertheless, the volume of imports is still twice the level of 1970, and much remains to be done, either by way of eliminating or of adjusting to the rapid import-penetration of the early 1970s.

On the services account, non-factor service payments were roughly stable in nominal terms between 1974 and 1977, after experiencing a phenomenally rapid growth between 1967 and 1973: this stability appears to reflect some success in import-substitution of freight services, as well as the fall in the volume of imports. The most rapidly growing items on the services account are interest payments on the external debt (which, net of receipts, increased from US$ 652 million in 1974 to US$ 2·2 billion in 1977) and outflows of profits and dividends, which doubled between 1974 and 1977 (Table 7.3).

Turning to the capital account, the size of capital inflows since 1974 has tended to dwarf even the substantial inflows of the early 1970s. The basic foreign financing requirement (i.e. current account deficit plus amortisation on loans) trebled between 1972–3 and 1974 and has remained about US$ 8 billion or US$ 9 billion a year ever since, the effect of a steadily improving current account being virtually negated by the steady growth of amortisation payments on the external debt. Net long-term direct investment has provided between US$ 800 million and US$ 1 billion annually; foreign exchange reserve loss provided about US$ 1 billion a year in 1974 and 1975, but this was offset by reserve gains totalling roughly the same amount over 1976 and 1977. The rest of the foreign capital requirement has been made up of a truly massive inflow of foreign currency loans, suppliers' credit and loans from international financial institutions: US$ 6·9 billion (gross) in 1974, US$ 5·2 billion in 1975, US$ 10·1 billion in 1976 and US$ 8·4 billion in 1977. From time to time, doubts have been expressed about Brazil's ability to be able to raise foreign loans on this scale, but though there has certainly been an increase in shorter-term borrowing (relative to the position in 1972–3) and a consequent deterioration in the maturity structure of the debt, foreign financiers appear to have been willing to finance transfers which are currently of the order of 4–5 per cent of Brazil's GDP. Meanwhile, total external indebtedness (both public and private sector debt) increased from US$ 12·6 billion at the end of 1973 to US$ 31 billion by the end of 1977; despite the rapid increase in interest and amortisation payments on the debt, a 50 per cent rise in the value of exports of goods (between 1974 and 1977) has ensured that the debt service ratio has remained rather stable (rising from 39·2 per cent in 1974 to about 44 per cent by 1977) (see Table 7.6). Two points should, however be noted: first, as the trade account moved into surplus in 1977, Brazil is currently borrowing principally in order to service its large external debt and to finance dividend and profit outflows (these amounted to 81 per cent of the basic foreign saving requirement in 1977). Second, the external account remains extremely vulnerable to external shocks, such as changes in primary commodity prices (notably coffee) and harvest fluctuations.

TABLE 7.6   External indebtedness, debt–service ratio and foreign exchange reserves, 1973–7 (year-end)

	Total external indebtedness (US$ b)	Public or publicly guaranteed (US$ b)	Foreign exchange reserves (US$ b)	Gross debt–service ratio	Public gross debt–service ratio
1973	12·6	6·5	6·416	39·2	n.a.
1974	17·2	8·5	5·269	38·7	15·2
1975	21·2	11·5	4·041	42·9	16·7
1976	26·0	14·9	6·544	45·6	18·7
1977	31·5	n.a.	7·004	n.a.	n.a.

Sources: *Conjuntura Econômica*; Banco Central, *Boletín*.
Notes: Gross debt service ratio defined as ratio of debt service (amortisation plus gross interest payments – i.e. excluding receipts) as a percentage of goods and non-factor services.

In response to inflationary pressures and external disequilibrium, the government has, in general, pursued less expansionary fiscal and monetary policies than during the 'miraculous years'; for the reasons discussed below, policy has actually assumed a 'stop-go' character. The effects of this on the growth of manufacturing output can be seen in Table 7.7: the growth of manufacturing output halved in 1974 (from 15·8 per cent in 1973 to 7·6 per cent), fell again to 3·7 per cent in 1975, recovered to 12·9 per cent in 1976 and virtually stagnated in 1977 (+2·3 per cent). Output growth was much stronger in sectors, where there has been considerable import-penetration prior to 1974 (steel, chemicals and capital goods), and the main source of the poor industrial performance was the sharp deceleration in output growth in the industries producing consumer durable goods. Despite the unfavourable evolution of exports, the so-called 'wage' goods industries (textile, clothing and shoes) performed somewhat better than the durable goods sector. Overall, this particular pattern of output growth has been consistent with industrial policy aims, though the sharp fall in the output of the mechanical engineering sector in 1977 indicates that the government has not been wholly successful in maintaining the rate of accumulation (linked to import-substitution) in the face of the weak growth of demand for consumer durables.

TABLE 7.7   Manufacturing sector growth rates, 1972–7

	1972	1973	1974	1975	1976	1977
Non-metallic minerals	19·1	16·4	14·8	9·0	12·0	8·3
Metallurgy	17·8	4·9	6·7		13·5	7·2
Engineering	17·0	26·9	11·7	8·4	14·8	−7·2
Electrical goods	25·7	28·7	10·5		18·4	1·4
Transport equipment	32·3	27·6	18·9	0·5	7·3	−2·6
Paper	14·5	10·1	4·3	−14·6	20·8	2·5
Rubber	19·1	12·4	10·8	2·7	11·2	−2·0
Chemicals	11·6	23·6	5·4		17·8	6·5
Pharmaceuticals	—	—	—	2·9	19·1	−13·8
Perfume	8·3	6·6	11·5		19·2	9·3
Plastics	30·6	28·3	23·2		17·8	−0·6
Textile	11·3	7·0	−3·4		6·2	0·5
Clothing, Shoes	5·5	14·1	2·1	3·2	8·3	5·2
Food	20·0	8·3	5·4		11·3	5·6
Drinks	19·6	17·8	8·4	1·2	13·5	13·6
Tobacco	6·4	6·4	12·8		9·1	5·3
Total	18·2	15·8	7·6	3·7	12·9	2·3

Source: Instituto Brasileira de Geografia e Estatística (IBGE) and *Conjuntura Econômica*.

POLICY RESPONSES

This section discusses the policy-measures, adopted by the new government of General Geisel which came to power in March 1974, to deal with the problems of accelerating inflation and external disequilibrium which became apparent by early 1974. It would be wrong to regard policy-measures adopted since 1974 as if they were part of a consistently-applied stabilisation strategy. Certainly, the search for an appropriate balance between growth and price and balance-of-payments stability has been a major pre-occupation of the Geisel government, but there have been quite sharp changes in the direction of policy from time to time, and it was only by 1977 that there was an acceptance of the need for a much more moderate rate of growth (6 per cent at most) than during the years of the 'miracle'.

During much of 1974, Brazilian policy-makers, in their public utterances at least, appeared to assume that Brazil could continue repeating the performance of the 'miraculous' years. The new Finance Minister, Simonsen, declared that Brazil would remain 'an island of sanity and economic progress' within the depressed international economy, and the second National Development Plan forecast that GNP would grow at a compound rate of 10 per cent through 1978, accompanied by rates of inflation of no more than 15 per cent. It was apparently assumed that Brazil would traverse quite rapidly its balance-of-payments problem, which was *exclusively* the product of external factors. Such complacency was bred by the government's wish not to break the cycle of prosperity presided over by their predecessors, by a fear of the political consequences of lowering popular growth expectations and by the absence of immediate external pressures; Brazil had a large cushion of foreign exchange reserves (US$ 6·4 billion as of December 1973) and, although the rate at which the current account was in deficit would have eliminated these reserves in twelve months, Brazil succeeded in obtaining new loans.[12]

The political background

It is important to realise that economic measures adopted during 1974 and afterwards need to be interpreted in the light of the President's commitment, at least during the first half of his administration, to a series of steps leading to political re-democratisation: relatively free congressional elections (in 1974) and municipal elections (in 1976) leading up to direct elections for the state governorships in 1978. The political model which the regime appears to have had in mind is the one subsequently pursued in Spain and Greece; that is to say, a shift away from authoritarian rule, under the aegis of a conservative party's political leadership. In order to try to ensure that ARENA (the government party) was the main beneficiary of the electoral process, the government felt the need to sustain growth and was obliged to adopt certain measures of income redistribution. For example, in both 1974, 1975 and 1976, the government-decreed urban minimum wage was increased slightly in real terms, and constancy was achieved in 1977; also, government-imposed wage adjustments for workers above the minimum exceeded cost-of-living increases up to June 1976; more resources were directed to social welfare programmes, and new benefits and programmes were introduced. Such measures undoubtedly marked a significant shift away from the wage and social policies pursued under Delfim Netto. However, these measures completely failed to achieve their expected electoral pay-off, and in late 1976 and early 1977 the government abandoned its re-democratisation policies, due to the substantial electoral gains made by the opposition party in both congressional and municipal elections. Of course, it is arguable that some relaxation of wage and social policies was inevitable by 1974, the meningitis epidemic indicating perhaps that total workers' consumption (comprising the social wage and private consumption) had been pushed below the reproduction costs of urban labour power. But, for whatever reasons, the need for more liberal wage and social policies blocked one possible line of response to the solution of internal and external disequilibria (i.e. that the working class should bear the brunt of anti-inflationary policies and that working-class consumption should bear the burden of increasing net exports).

Meanwhile, beneath the surface complacency, conflicting views were being aired within the government over the most appropriate strategy to deal with the severe external disequilibrium.

The import-substitution strategy

Groups in the Ministry of Planning and the National Development Bank (BNDE) planned for Brazil to maintain its rate of growth and escape potential balance-of-payments constraints by switching to an import-substitution strategy, based on exploiting the market opportunities in the production of intermediate inputs and producers' goods, which rapid import-penetration in 1972–4 had shown to exist. This strategy was quite explicit about the beneficiaries of this new model of development and about certain aspects of the institutional framework designed to facilitate the process: state enterprises and local industrial groups were supposed to be the principal beneficiaries. In addition to plans for a renewed wave of import-substitution, the idea was mooted that the automobile sector should shift to the production of smaller cars and mass-transportation systems, and other investments designed to reduce dependence on imported energy (for example, in the railway sector) were contemplated. Further, in the face of pessimistic forecasts concerning the likely growth of demand for Brazil's manufactured exports (especially of 'traditional' manufactures, such as textiles and shoes), it became fashionable in some official circles to advocate the need for a redistribution of personal income in order to stimulate the internal market for manufactured wage goods and shift the focus of growth away from the consumer durables and export sectors.

It was virtually inevitable that the change in international economic conditions should give rise to pressures for a shift in economic strategy away from the increased internationalisation which had characterised the years 1964–73, but there were certain crucial defects to these plans for a more 'nationalist' solution to the country's problems. At a technical level, the defects were as follows: first, the strategy would hardly have led to an immediate reduction in foreign exchange requirements, as the new wave of import-substitution in producers' goods and intermediate manufactured inputs would itself have been very import-intensive, in the early stages at least; second, by examining the degree of import-penetration in producers' goods, at what, in retrospect, appears to have been the peak of the investment cycle, the planners were probably overestimating the possibilities for a renewed cycle of import-substitution. The more important defect of the plan was that it was somewhat idealistic, with a lack of correspondence between its goals and those of some important economic groups – particularly those in the international sector of the economy; for example, it was not clear whether a more extensive transfer of producers' goods production fitted into the global strategies of the multinational corporations, whose predominance in these areas of production made their co-operation essential to the new investment plans; furthermore, increased international specialisation and, thus, greater dependence on imports appears to have constituted an integral part of the production strategies of many multinational corporations in the early 1970s. Nor, as it quickly became apparent, were car-makers particularly enthusiastic about substituting mass-transport equipment for individual car production. In addition, income redistribution did not have much support amongst élite groups either. Given the lack of support for this alternative economic strategy amongst the leading economic groups, it is not surprising that it was never really adopted *as a whole*.

Nevertheless, further import-substitution investments – which are crucial to Brazil's ability to break out of its current external disequilibrium – were undertaken between 1974 and 1978, and probably provided an important stabilising influence on the overall level of activity during the period. Mid-way through the plan period (1975–9), the following achievements could be noted. The expansion of capacity of local petrochemical production (which will be competitive with imports) is proceeding according to schedule. The output of nitrogenous and phosphate fertilisers increased by 76 per cent between 1974 and 1976, and plan targets for 1979 look as if they will be exceeded by 60 per cent. Steel output has lagged way behind plan targets, but because demand growth has been below the projected level, the share of local production in total consumption increased from 62·2 per cent (1974) to 89·4 per cent (1976). Import-substitution in petroleum is lagging badly, however, with the import-coefficient rising from 78·5 per cent (1974) to 83·2 per cent (1976) and domestic consumption rising by 17·9 per cent between 1974 and 1976; furthermore, efforts to utilise alcohol from domestic sugar and manioc production have not proceeded very far (partly because locally produced alcohol is not efficient at present world prices). Import-substitution in capital goods production also seems to have lagged badly (as might have been expected from the foregoing analysis), with official estimates of output growth of only 13·6 per cent between 1974 and 1976 – way below the targeted increase of 70 per cent for the period 1975–9 as a whole. Increasingly progressive import controls (see below) have been adopted to stimulate increased local production of capital goods.

As a result of these investment activities, it seems that the rate of public investment was actually stepped up in 1975 and 1976 (increasing by 13 per cent in real terms in that year) from the already high levels of the early 1970s. Although there are no published statistics, it appears that the savings-investment gap of the public sector (*as a whole*), which fluctuated between 1 and 2 per cent of GDP in the early 1970s, increased to 5–6 per cent of GDP in 1976 – partly as a result of a recession-induced slowing down in receipts and a more liberal wage policy for public servants. As a consequence, the government came under intense pressure both from local groups – alleging increasing state control (*estatização*) – and from the international financial institutions – arguing that public enterprise investments were a major source of continuing inflationary pressure. As a result of such pressure, public enterprise investments were scaled down in 1977 and held down in real terms to the level of 1976. This is an interesting example of the way in which a more self-reliant solution to the problems of external equilibrium has been partially thwarted by a coalition of private and international interest groups.

Increased internationalisation

The other main strand of thought, entertained in government circles, was that represented by the Finance Minister, Mario Simonsen. He appears to have rejected the emphasis on import-substitution, on developing the internal market and on altering the supply structure of the economy, arguing that the best approach to external disequilibrium was a more rapid growth of exports. This appeared to imply that the broad strategy of increasing internationalisation, pursued during the previous ten years, and the composition of output growth, associated with it, would continue unchanged; Simonsen also seemed to accept the need for further increases in external indebtedness. In view of the high level of incentives to exporters already in existence and the growth of protectionist measures (particularly those oriented towards Brazilian exports) in advanced country markets, it was not clear precisely *how* rapid export growth was to be achieved; however, the strategy seemed to imply the need for a substantial devaluation.

As things turned out, Brazil failed to adopt an aggressive policy of competitive exchange rate depreciations during the period 1974–8. Using Brazil's general price index, the cruzeiro experienced an effective depreciation of 4 per cent in 1974, was held constant in 1975 and actually appreciated by 3·2 per cent in 1976. While additional export incentives were introduced, it is clear that trade policy has not been particularly conducive to encouraging a more rapid expansion of manufactured exports in depressed world conditions. It is not easy to analyse the performance of Brazilian manufactured exports, since many processed agricultural exports (such as soluble coffee, refined sugar, orange juice, etc.) are included in the Brazilian totals. Nevertheless, the data in Table 7.8 show that, while the momentum of manufactured exports was maintained between 1973 and 1975, exports in real terms actually declined in 1976, though there seems to have been something of a recovery in 1977.

TABLE 7.8   Real rates of growth of Brazilian manufactured exports 1973−6

	Machinery	Electrical equipment	Transport equipment	Textiles	Shoes
1973−4	+52	+61	+118	+9	+25
1974−5	+40	−14	+29	+8	+25
1975−6	−7	−0·2	+0·3	−2	−12

Source: *Conjuntura Econômica*, February 1978, p. 315, and February 1977, p. 118.

It is interesting to speculate on why the government failed to adopt a large 'step' devaluation or a series of larger mini-devaluations as part of its policy measures designed to achieve external equilibrium. The most frequently mentioned reason is that a large devaluation would have imposed a heavy burden on companies and financial institutions with large, outstanding foreign currency debts. Furthermore, competitive devaluations would also have discouraged the continued smooth inflow of currency loans, given the ceilings on local interest rates (imposed up to 1976). The government was unwilling, it seems, to accept the degree of intervention implied, either by the establishment of dual rates of exchange (for trade and financial transactions) or by its adoption of the currency risk on foreign loans. If this line of reasoning is true, it implies that the extremely high level of foreign indebtedness has imposed additional constraints on government policy-making – impinging on the government's ability to balance the commodity account and thus making for further dependence on foreign loans. Other reasons advanced for the failure to pursue a vigorous devaluation strategy are: (i) the appearance in advanced country markets of quantum restrictions on the growth of Brazilian exports (shoes, textiles, steel); (ii) an appreciation that incentives to exporters were already sufficiently generous; (iii) an unwillingness to turn the terms of trade further to Brazil's disadvantage; (iv) a fear of induced inflationary pressures resulting from large-scale devaluation; and (v) a certain elasticity pessimism about the demand for Brazilian exports.

Import controls

Curiously, despite the preferences of the Finance Minister, Brazil chose increasingly between 1975 and 1977 to rely on direct import controls and discretionary measures to curb the trade deficit, backed up by restrictions on aggregate demand expansion (see the discussion of these measures below). This option was, however, probably inevitable given depressed world trade conditions and the deterioration in the external terms of trade in 1974 and 1975.

It is clear that such measures (combined with the effects of growing capacity in import-substituting sectors and a slower growth of demand on average) have been largely responsible for successfully reducing Brazil's import bill both in nominal and in real terms. Such unorthodox policy measures could probably not have been implemented had Brazil needed recourse to the IMF, but given that other more radical policy options were ruled out, they were the only sensible way of moderating *somewhat* the scale of foreign currency borrowing.

Conclusions on policy options

Thus, as things have turned out, neither of the two major policy options floated in 1974 – redistributive, import-substitution-with-growth *or* devaluation-cum-export-led growth – have been adhered to. Policy has been one of wait-and-see, relying on the use of generalised import restrictions together with the use of orthodox fiscal and monetary policies to dampen down the rate of growth of demand – though the latter have not been consistently applied. Massive capital inflow and a favourable turn in coffee prices in 1976–7 have allowed Brazilian policy-makers to escape the need to adopt more thoroughgoing solutions.

MONETARY AND FISCAL POLICY AND THEIR EFFECTS

In assessing monetary policy during this period, it is as well to remember that the monetary authorities have only gradually sought to mobilise all the instruments at their disposal, that conflicting aims have frequently been pursued simultaneously, that control over certain important financial intermediaries is extremely partial and that there are important constraints on the imposition of a sharp credit squeeze. One feature of the system concerns the use of open-market operations. Prior to 1974, the authorities had placed great reliance on open market operations to counter the effect on the money supply of large additions to the foreign exchange reserves resulting from heavy foreign currency borrowing; but recourse to open-market sales has had to be limited since 1975 due to illiquidity in the market, resulting from the widespread use of so-called 'repurchase agreements', establishing both the price and term of repurchase of government debt and the government's wish to avoid raising short-term interest rates. In addition, Treasury bills (sold in the open market) are, because of their high degree of liquidity, used as near-money in the Brazilian economy – their sale therefore, having little or no impact on the general liquidity situation. A second feature of the monetary system has been the rapid growth in recent years of the special lending programmes of the monetary authorities and of state financial intermediaries: agricultural credit, loans to small and medium-sized industry, agricultural price support, urban development funds, etc. etc. There is no doubt that the growth of these special credit programmes has frequently run counter to overall monetary goals. To quote a recently leaked Ministry of Planning document: 'the housing finance system and the National Development Bank control 27 per cent of all credit by the financial system. An additional 25 per cent goes through the Bank of Brazil. This means that 52 per cent of credit is outside the direct reach of policy instruments of the Central Bank. The Central Bank alone, therefore, cannot carry out a stabilisation policy'.[13]

To give one example of the effect of these aspects of the monetary system: in 1976, a number of highly restrictive measures were taken to counter monetary expansion, including increases in commercial bank reserve requirements, the raising of Central Bank discount rates, the freeing of money market lending rates and curbs on instalment and real estate credit. Nevertheless, these had only a marginal impact on the rate of monetary expansion during that year, due to the large rise in foreign exchange reserves and the continued rapid growth of official credit lines: the overall expansion of the money supply (M_1) was 37 per cent – significantly in excess of the 25 per cent target set by the monetary authorities.

Monetary and fiscal policy in 1974

The aim of monetary policy in the first year of the new administration was to slow the growth of the money supply below what were

considered the wildly inflationary levels of 1973. Two factors
worked in favour of this policy: a significant loss of foreign
exchange reserves (US$ 936 million or 6·4 per cent of the money
supply) and the continued strong growth of government receipts:
the federal government accounts showed a surplus of 5 per cent of
total receipts. On the other hand, there was a strong growth in the
lending activities of certain public agencies: the BNDE providing
finance to new import-substitution activities (loans increased by
223·2 per cent) and the Banco do Brazil, whose loans principally
for agricultural credit, increased by 77·5 per cent. There is no
doubt that the monetary authorities were somewhat hampered in
their restrictionist activities by the over-exposed and illiquid state
of some of the more adventurous financial institutions, and a
couple of major bankruptcies produced an undesirable contraction in commercial bank liquidity which forced the authorities to
moderate their policy and provide special rediscount facilities.
Superficially, the restrictive policy appeared successful: cash
emissions rose by 28·2 per cent (compared with 46·7 per cent in
1973) and M_1 rose by 35·5 per cent (47 per cent in 1973) (see Table
7.9). But the major factor responsible for the slower growth of
loans (from both banking and non-banking institutions) to the
private sector (52·1 per cent compared with 65·9 per cent in 1973)
was the sharp reduction in the demand for hire purchase finance
(a growth of 28·9 per cent compared with 82·8 per cent in 1973).
While the authorities temporarily reduced the repayment period
of HP credit, real factors on the *demand* side were more prominent:
first, a drop in real personal disposable income, due to the sudden
acceleration of inflation (partly induced by government policy
following the period of 'repressed' inflation in 1973), and the
lagging growth of money incomes; second, the large rise in the cost
of running a car following the oil price rise; third, the negative
effect of the deteriorating domestic (and world) economic situation on expectations and a certain rebound from the wild euphoria
of 1972–3; and finally, it has been suggested, the reaching of a
certain limit on household indebtedness – a limit which was, of
course, not independent of the factors mentioned above.

The other components of demand appeared to continue to grow
strongly: there was a slight deterioration in the overall quantum
growth of exports (from 14·2 per cent in 1973 to 9·6 per cent in
1974), but exports from the metal-working sector accelerated
strongly, reflecting orders placed in the peak of the world boom.

Similarly, total investment continued to grow strongly (recent national accounts estimates show that the investment: GDP ratio rose from 23 per cent in 1973 to 24·2 per cent in 1974): this reflected the building capacity commissioned in the boom and new import-substituting investment in bottleneck sectors.

The outcome of these divergent tendencies was almost a 50 per cent fall in industrial output growth (from 15 per cent in 1973 to 8·2 per cent in 1974; see Table 7.1 above) with the most marked reduction occurring in the consumer durables and non-durables sectors.[14] However, an exceptionally good harvest (principally

TABLE 7.9 Some monetary statistics (percentage change from December to December)

	Rate of inflation	Cash emissions	M_1	M_2	M_3	Bank and non-bank loans to private sector	Hire purchase acceptances
1973	15·1	46·7	47·0	n.a.	n.a.	65·9	82·8
1974	28·7	28·2	35·5	20·2	32·8	52·1	28·9
1975	27·7	42·8	42·8	44·8	47·4	56·3	32·0
1976	41·3	45·7	37·2	51·4	50·5	57·3	28·9
1977	42·7	39·2	37·6	45·9	48·8	54·4	28·8

Source: Banco Central do Brasil.
Notes: M_1 = cash with public plus current accounts with banks (commercial banks, Central Bank, Banco do Brasil).
M_2 = M_1 + current accounts with savings institutions + Treasury Bills outside banking system.
M_3 = M_2 + 50% of deposits accounts in banks, savings associations, acceptances, etc.

due to a 45 per cent rise in the coffee harvest) moderated the fall in the overall rate of GDP growth from 11·4 per cent to 9·6 per cent. Thus, the so-called Brazilian economic 'miracle' came to an end, amid deteriorating industrial performance, accelerating inflation and internal disequilibrium. But its end was not surrounded by the cataclysm some had predicted. Instead, more as a result of good luck than good management, continued high investment levels and the market afforded by previous extreme import-penetration provided important demand-stimulating factors to keep industrial growth going.

Monetary and fiscal policy in 1975

Prompted by the slowdown in economic activity apparent in late 1974 and early 1975, the government relaxed both monetary and fiscal restraint from the second quarter of 1975. There are strong parallels here with the 'stop-go' pattern which characterised the earlier prolonged stabilisation attempt between 1964 and 1967 – relaxing policy when recession threatened, tightening when inflationary pressures increased.[15] The money supply rose by 42·8 per cent (compared with a monetary budget projection of 30 per cent) and loans to the private sector increased by 56·4 per cent (compared with a projection of 40 per cent). On the fiscal side, as a result of a cut in sales and income taxes and higher civil service salaries, a 5 per cent surplus over current revenue in 1974 was transformed into a 3 per cent deficit in 1975. The 50 per cent cut in sales tax – on textiles, shoes, furniture and domestic appliances – appears to have played a significant role in stimulating industrial recovery; a more liberal wage policy, which in November 1974 granted an advance on future pay rises and permitted small but nevertheless positive real wage gains in the course of 1975 in both the minimum wage and 'arbitrated' (actually government-decreed) wage rises, must also have contributed to stimulate demand. In addition, gross fixed capital formation rose to 25·4 per cent of GDP (Table 7.2 above), reflecting the implementation of capital spending programmes in the second National Development Plan. While stimulating domestic activity, the government opted for direct controls to begin scaling down the current account deficit.

In July 1975, an interest-free 180-day advance import deposit of 100 per cent was imposed on certain goods, representing 26 per cent of the 1974 import total. In October 1975, the government decreed for 1976 a reduction in public enterprise non-petroleum imports of 15 per cent compared with 1975. Tariff rates on selected consumer goods were increased by 100 per cent and by 30 per cent on various intermediate products, and the coverage of import deposits was extended. There was also a further increase in petroleum prices of 25 per cent, making a 67 per cent increase since late 1974. Other measures required a more rigorous application of the Law of Similars, affecting capital goods. This gamut of measures must have played at least some role in reducing merchandise imports from US$ 12·6 billion in 1974 to US$ 12·2 billion in 1975 (a 10 per cent decline in quantum). Another factor was, of course, the reversal of speculative import-purchases. These policy moves were followed by even more far-reaching measures: in December 1975, the advance import deposit was extended from 180 to 360 days and the coverage embraced about 40 per cent of the 1975 level of total imports.

Whatever the short-run effect of import-controls, the reflationary monetary and fiscal policies, adopted in 1975, did not prevent a severe industrial recession (growth of only 4·2 per cent in 1975), whose negative effects on GDP growth were compounded by the effect of frosts and floods on agricultural output growth (3·4 per cent in 1975); overall GDP growth (at 4·2 per cent) was the lowest recorded since 1965.

Monetary and fiscal policy in 1976

In 1976, the authorities again became more concerned with accelerating inflation and attempted to restrict credit, but the attempt does not appear to have been very successful: on the one hand, there was a large rise in foreign exchange reserves (+ US$ 2·2 billion), which was mainly due to to an accelerated level of foreign borrowing (net inflow of financial loans of US$ 4·4 billion). Increased coffee earnings were almost solely responsible for a US$ 1·4 billion narrowing of the trade gap (Tables 7.10 and 7.5 above), but debt interest and profit remittances swallowed up half of the improvement, so that the current account deficit only fell by US$ 0·6 billion to US$ 6·1 billion. Other expansionary factors were the large lending programmes of the monetary authorities themselves. On the other hand, the authorities engaged very actively in short-term open-market operations and the sale of long-term government debt, and the import deposit scheme was responsible for a large once-and-for-all reduction in private sector liquidity. In addition, the government activated a series of restrictive controls which had long been dormant, mainly affecting the commercial banks. In April and July 1976, commercial bank reserve requirements were raised progressively from 27 per cent to 35 per cent of demand deposits. The composition of reserve requirements was also changed, effectively raising the cash component from 2·6 per cent to 14·9 per cent and limiting the amount of Treasury securities used to discharge reserve requirements.

TABLE 7.10   Merchandise exports, 1973–7 (US$ m; volume in 'ooo tons, unit price US$/ton).

		1973	1974	1975	1976	1977
Basic products (value)		4203	5036	5437	6129·2	6972·9
Coffee	Value	1344	980	934	2397	2642
	Volume (m. 6okg. bags)	19·8	13·2	14·6	15·6	10·2
	Unit price (¢/lb.)	51	56	49	—	—
Sugar	Value	559	1322	1100	153	277
	Volume	2820	2357	1731	—	—
	Unit price	198	561	635	—	—
Soybeans	Value	494	586	685	789	708
	Volume	1786	2730	3333	—	—
	Unit price	277	215	206	—	—
Soymeal	Value	423	303	465	795	1150
	Volume	1582	2031	3134	—	—
	Unit price	267	149	148	—	—
Cocoa	Value	88	210	220	219	436
	Volume	83	130	177	—	—
	Unit price	1069	1617	1248	—	—
Corn	Value	3	139	151	165	137
	Volume	41	1109	1148	—	—
	Unit price	77	125	131	—	—
Iron ore	Value	363	571	921	994	908
	Volume (m. tons)	45	59·4	72·5	—	—
	Unit price	8·1	9·6	12·7	—	—
All others (value) Semi-processed (value)		476	634	645	840	1044
Soy oil	Value	24	2	152	175	274
	Volume	61	2	263	453	487
	Unit price	388	830	579	386	563
Manufactured	Value	1359	2086	2379	2776	3845
Other	Value	161	195	209	—	—
Total		6199	7951	8670	9747	11,861·5

Source: Banco Central do Brasil.

Central Bank rediscount rates were raised from 22 per cent (March 1976) to 28 per cent (May); in addition, the Central Bank fixed lending rates 'on many investment and commercial bank operations. Curbs were also placed on instalment and real estate credit.

The effectiveness of the policy can perhaps be judged by comparing the targets established by the monetary authorities for the 1976 Monetary Budget and the actual out-turn. The money supply (M_1), forecast to rise by 25 per cent, actually increased by 37·2 per cent. Loans to the private sector increased by 57·3 per cent against a forecast rise of 42·8 per cent. Also, commercial bank lending, in spite of the new credit restrictions, rose by 52·1 per cent. The principal factor responsible for this rapid growth in liquidity seems to have been a 49·8 per cent rise in the liabilities of the monetary authorities, due to a rapid growth in Banco do Brasil loans (+ 62 per cent), large Central Bank emergency and ordinary rediscounts and the net inflow of foreign exchange.

Import control measures were tightened during the course of 1976. Public sector non-petroleum imports were planned to be cut back by 25 per cent (in US$) in 1976, and it seems that, so far as direct imports are concerned, the overall target was effectively enforced. An even stricter target was established for 1977 with an across-the-board reduction of 12 per cent in nominal terms (i.e. even greater in real terms), with exceptions being granted to the steel and petroleum enterprises. In spite of substantial price increases, decreed for petroleum, the 28 per cent rise in oil imports in 1976 encouraged the government to close petrol stations at night and at weekends and to raise the price of diesel, fuel oil and petrol yet again. In February 1976, quantitative import restrictions were applied to a wide range of non-essential imports, and this measure was extended in 1978 by a complete prohibition on the import of a much wider range of manufactured goods. Lastly, late in 1976, a compulsory one-year, non-interest-bearing cash deposit was required of Brazilians travelling abroad, amounting to about US$ 1100.

For 1976 as a whole, industrial output grew very rapidly as a response to measures taken in 1975; towards the end of the year, there was, however, a significant fall in retail sales (see *Conjuntura Econômica*: 'Termometro de vendas'), though its causes may have had more to do with the corrosive effects of accelerating inflation (in excess of 40 per cent in 1976) on real disposable income and *direct* intervention in the HP credit market than with overall monetary policy.

Monetary and fiscal policy in 1977

Following the sudden recovery in activity in 1976 and the sharp acceleration in the rate of inflation (some indices showing a rate of inflation of almost 50 per cent for that year as a whole), the government attempted to implement restrictive monetary and fiscal policies again.

The Federal Treasury account moved into a small surplus from a small deficit in 1976, but it played essentially no role as a source of monetary expansion in 1977. The monetary authorities appear to have been much more successful at controlling the lending programmes of the official financial institution: in nominal terms, loans to the private sector by the Banco do Brasil, the BNDE, and the National Savings Bank (Caixa Econômica Federal) were much less in 1977 than in either 1975 or 1976. But the authorities had to contend with a large rise (US$ 460 million) in foreign exchange reserves and with the fact that the special import and foreign travel deposits were nothing like as important as a source of monetary contraction as in 1976 – the year of their imposition. In this situation, the authorities resorted to freeing interest rates *throughout* the whole financial system (as a means of discouraging the growth of credit), increased commercial banks' compulsory deposits (from 35 per cent to 40 per cent) and raised Central Bank discount rates. Raising interest rates, however, was a double-edged weapon, since it *increased* foreign capital inflow and made government debt less attractive, with the result that the government was a net purchaser on the open market to the tune of 1·4 billion cruzeiros. In a further effort to control liquidity, the government de-monetised foreign capital inflow between December 1977 and January 1978 (though still paying interest on these deposits). The net effect of all these measures was that monetary policy appears to have been just as expansionary as in 1976: the money supply (M_1) grew by 37·6 per cent against 37·2 per cent in 1976 (and a forecast of 25 per cent) and loans to the private sector grew by 54·4 per cent as against 57·3 per cent (against a forecast of 34 per cent). Since, as measured by certain indices, there was something of a fall in the rate of inflation, the data seem to indicate that *real* private sector liquidity may even have expanded in 1977. Yet again, the control exercised by the monetary authorities seems to have been severely limited.

Nevertheless, despite the apparent failure of this contraction-ary monetary policy, the industrial sector moved into a deep recession, manufacturing output grew by only 2·3 per cent. The main sources of deflationary pressure appear to have been a deceleration in the rate of accumulation and a fall in demand for passenger cars. The preliminary national accounts data indicate that the investment/GDP ratio fell from 26 per cent in 1975 to 22·6 per cent in 1977, and this was reflected in large (−30 per cent) reductions in machinery and equipment imports and a 7·2 per cent fall in domestic engineering industry output. Cuts in public sector investment plans, reflecting international pressures on the government, and the economy's failure to keep to the targets set by the second National Development Plan, played a role in this; road and railway construction programmes seem to have been most affected and there was also a downward revision of steel investment plans. It is not so far clear, however, whether private sector investment also tailed off, as a growing volume of idle capacity, inherited from the investment bonanza of 1972–3, made itself felt. Passenger car output declined by 12 per cent (the first in its history) and the vehicle sector's output by 6·7 per cent. The main causes of this seem to have been a reduction in HP terms from thirty-six to twenty-four months, a rise in the size of initial down-payments, much higher interest rates and the erosion of real disposable income due to the adoption of a less liberal earnings policy.

The country's export performance was exceptionally good, with some classes of manufacturing exports experiencing quan-tum increases of 20 or 30 per cent. Coffee prices also continued to soar, so that despite a 50 per cent cut in volume, export receipts increased by 10 per cent (see Table 7.10). Imports declined in real terms, with the aggregate import coefficient down to 8·1 per cent by 1977 from 11·6 per cent in 1975: it is rather too early to distinguish between the success of the policy of import controls linked to import-substitution or the effect of the severe industrial recession.

The effect of the recession on the rate of inflation is also open to question. The evidence is quite ambiguous as to whether there ever was a reduction in inflation between 1976 and 1977: the general and wholesale price indices indicate that there was – with the impact of the recession showing up in the monthly figures for the second half of the year. On the other hand, cost-of-living indices for some of the major metropolitan areas (São Paulo, Porto Alegre, Belo Horizonte, Belém and Curitíba) indicate a quite significant increase in the rate of inflation between 1976 and 1977. Extensive indexation (despite a small fall in real earnings in 1977), the liberalisation of interest rates, continued import-repression and the effect of the sharp recession on unit costs in manufacturing must all have played a role in preventing deflationary demand pressures from having a more substantial effect on the rate of inflation.

To conclude, it appears that, in 1977, the Brazilian economy experienced the severe recession which policy-makers had hitherto attempted to avoid. However, it is by no means clear that this was the outcome intended by policy-makers, and monetary restriction again appears to have been largely ineffective. As in the early-to-mid-1960s, we appear to be witnessing a cyclical downturn in private sector investment spending, to which short-term macroeconomic management was largely insensitive; indeed, the slowing-down of the public sector investment programme was almost certainly a contributory factor in the recession.

INFLATION, STABILISATION AND INDEXATION

The main factors responsible for reversing the trend in the rate of inflation since 1974 were, first, the sharp deterioration in the terms of trade and, in particular, the rapid rise, in 1974 and 1975, of the price of imported semi-manufactures, capital goods and, of course, oil; and, second, the severe import constraint and accompanying import controls, the former contributing to demand pressures and to reducing the elasticity of supply of the economy as a whole and the latter to cost pressures, both directly (due to the effect of import deposits and increased protection) and through their effect on competitiveness; a third factor was an apparent increase in the overall savings-investment gap of the total public sector (see above); in addition, there were large year-on-year fluctuations in agricultural output and periods of acute shortage of foodstuffs for domestic consumption; finally, the attempt (at least to mid-1976) to extend 'indexation' to both the urban minimum wage and the wage increases permitted for workers earning above the urban minimum contributed, along with other 'indexation' mechanisms (affecting the exchange rate and some financial assets), to re-feeding the inflationary process and preventing any fall-back from achieved rates of inflation.

The rising trend in the rate of inflation since 1974 would seem to indicate that the stabilisation policies pursued were singularly unsuccessful. In an economy experiencing such a powerful import constraint, characterised by a substantial degree of 'indexation' and a considerable degree of oligopoly throughout manufacturing industry, there are certainly limits to the effectiveness of demand management in reducing inflation. The lesson drawn from the stabilisation policies pursued in the mid-1960s appeared to be that, while a sharp contraction in demand was reasonably successful in bringing the economy out of hyper-inflation, wage cuts also played a not insignificant role; furthermore, recession-induced rises in average costs placed a limit on the extent to which demand-contraction could bring about further reductions in the rate of inflation. A judgement on whether a really sharp contraction in demand might have succeeded in reducing inflation is clouded by the existence of a 'stop-go' cycle in the level of activity, partly as a result of the government's failure to apply demand-constraint consistently and its failure (or inability) to implement a really severe monetary squeeze. However, the inflation 'ratchet' in operation might indicate that some role should be attributed to changes in activity levels, years of recession (1975 and 1977) being associated with some stability in the rate of inflation (as compared with the year before), while the recovery in activity in 1976 took the rate of inflation to a significantly higher level. It is, therefore, not possible to demonstrate unambiguously that the rate of inflation has been insensitive to the control of demand, and this has permitted the IMF and the World Bank to call for the adoption of more consistently applied fiscal and monetary policies of a deflationary character to bring down the rate of inflation from the extremely high (though apparently stable levels) of 1976 and 1977.

Faced with such stubbornly high inflation rates, the government has increasingly been forced to admit that 'indexation' is a powerful device for 'feeding' the inflationary process and for stabilising any achieved *rate* of inflation. The policy has, therefore, been modified in several important ways, which might eventually have a favourable effect on inflation. Firstly, since September 1975, the price index used to correct financial assets has failed to reflect the effects of so-called 'fortuitous' factors, which are beyond government control, such as harvest conditions or oil price rises. Also, since June 1976, the formula used to compute correction factors takes into account anticipated inflation – which has been consistently underestimated. To give an example of the effect of these modifications, while wholesale prices rose by 46·8 per cent in the twelve months to May 1977, the index of monetary correction in the same period amounted to 37·4 per cent. Further, the application of monetary correction to loans made by the BNDE and other official development institutions has been quite substantially modified in recent years. Secondly, wage policy suffered an important modification from mid-1976 onwards: whereas government-imposed wage settlements implied a 7 per cent rise in real wages in 1975 (reflecting the adjustment of the 'wage formula' in November 1974 and the incorporation of a productivity component), there has been a steady decline in real terms since July 1976, due to the introduction of a so-called 'terms of trade' factor, designed to reflect changes in the terms of trade between industrial product prices, on the one hand, and prices of agricultural products and imported raw materials, on the other. Similarly, while the real urban minimum wage (decreed by the government) rose by 3 per cent between May 1975 and May 1976, it remained unchanged between May 1976 and May 1977.

To conclude, in the face of such a variety of cost-push factors and the renewal of import-substitution activities in an overall situation of severe import constraint, it is perhaps not surprising that high rates of inflation have persisted.

CONCLUSIONS

There is no doubt that Brazil has largely succeeded in escaping from some of the worst consequences for the rate of GDP growth which might have been expected following the emergence of an acute payments disequilibrium in 1974, whose causes lay in rapid import-penetration and a serious deterioration in the terms of trade. Brazil's continued ability to borrow from official institutions and the international private capital market, thus avoiding resort to the IMF, and the substantial foreign exchange reserves which had accumulated by 1973, must be counted as the main factors responsible for this. In addition, a large cut in import-volume (due to import controls and import-substitution activities), the great degree of diversification of the export structure and favourable coffee prices also contributed to a growing relief of the trade imbalance.

In view of the substantial scale of foreign capital inflow, it must be presumed that foreign bankers are reasonably optimistic about the country's ability to repay indebtedness in the 1980s, as the result of the maturation of several resource-based investment programmes and the modernisation of the agricultural sector. And the official Brazilian view is that, following a period of adjustment similar to the mid-1960s, domestic capacity will grow and the balance of payments strengthen so that, by 1980, the economy will be able to resume rapid growth, based on a high elasticity of supply and the absence of a foreign exchange constraint. Nevertheless, the burden of recent borrowing has been high, in terms of the rates of interest being paid, the deteriorating maturity structure of the external debt and rising debt-service obligations. Lending to Brazil is undoubtedly good business, but, given that equilibrium had been attained on the trade balance by 1977, the prospect of annual debt-service in excess of US$7 billion must make default – or at least a moratorium on debt-service – a very tempting option for the Brazilian authorities.

Nevertheless, despite the achievement of keeping growth going, short-term economic management can hardly be accounted as enormously successful. In particular, the authorities have completely failed to achieve a reduction in growth to a lower, steadier level, the economy lurching through a 'stop-go' cycle. The causes of failure here would seem to lie in a virtual ignorance of the short-run behaviour of the 'real' economy and the apparent failure of the authorities to be able to implement any desired monetary policy. The continued upward-ratchet movement of the rate of inflation must also be counted a failure, though fortunately (due to the political factors outlined above and growing political mobilisation), the urban poor and working-class have not borne the burden of adjustment as in the mid-1960s. While import controls and government-induced import-substituting investments have been somewhat successful in promoting some adjustment to the external disequilibrium, the continuing need for large capital inflow (even during the recession of 1977) indicates that further adjustment is necessary. Moreover, despite a few innovations in social policy, nothing significant has been done to utilise the opportunity presented by Brazil's growing wealth to restructure the economy in order to satisfy the basic needs of Brazil's poor in terms of a stable supply of cheap foodstuffs, acceptable social service provision and a civilised level of urban infrastructure. These are the principal factors which lie behind Brazil's continuing political crisis.

NOTES

1   At least up until the time of writing – April 1978.
2   This paper will not attempt to cover the period of the 1960s: for a discussion of the stabilisation policies embodied in the *Plano Trienal* (1963) and their effects, see J. Wells, 'Growth and Fluctuations in the Brazilian Manufacturing Sector during the 1960s', unpublished Ph.D thesis, Cambridge University, 1977. For an excellent account of stabilisation policies pursued between 1964 and 1967, see A. Fishlow, 'Some Reflections on Post-1964 Economic Policy', in A. Stepan, *Authoritarian Brazil*, Yale University Press, 1972.
3   See J. Wells, 'The Diffusion of Durables in Brazil and its Implications for Recent Controversies Concerning Brazilian Development', *Cambridge Journal of Economics*, 1977, vol. 1, pp. 259–79.
4   See R. Bonelli and P. Malan, 'The Brazilian Economy in the Seventies: Old and New Developments', *World Development*, 1977, vol. 5, pp. 19–45.
5   Ibid.
6   Ibid.
7   See J. Wells, 'The Distribution of Earnings, Growth and the Structure of Demand in Brazil in the Sixties', *World Development*, 1974, and Wells, 'Growth and Fluctuations . . .'
8   See J. Wells, 'The Role of the State and The Brazilian Economic Miracle', mimeo, 1976.
9   See E. L. Bacha, 'Issues and Evidence on Recent Brazilian Economic Growth', *World Development*, 1977, vol. 5, pp. 47–67.
10 Judged by the available social indicators, the performance was, of course, much less impressive. The distribution of earnings and of total personal income appears to have deteriorated throughout 1967–73, and there is precious little hard evidence of any significant positive 'trickle-down' effect on the absolute income levels of the most impoverished urban and rural groups. It is not possible to demonstrate that there was any reduction in urban unemployment or under-employment, and while the market for durables may have deepened, there is some evidence of deterioration in urban nutritional standards; see J. Wells, 'Recent Trends in Brazilian Nutrition', mimeo, 1978.
11 It is worth noting that official manipulation of the Rio cost-of-living index produced a further decline in inflation, from 16·4 per cent (1972) to 12·6 per cent (1973) – in line with official targets! An independent estimate for the City of São Paulo suggests the rate accelerated to 26 per cent in 1973 (DIESSE – Departamento Intersindical de Estudos Socio-Económicos).

12 There was, of course, greater recourse to the more costly source of foreign currency loans; these had been of the order of US$3·2 billion in 1972/73, but rose to more than US$5 billion in 1974. Euro-dollar interest rates also rose sharply in 1974 and the need to finance such a large external deficit in a somewhat tighter international capital market forced Brazil to lower the minimum acceptable maturities on foreign loans (in September 1974) from ten years to five years – thus bringing about a deterioration in the maturity structure of the foreign debt.

13 See *Diário Comércio e Industria*, São Paulo, January 1978. It should be emphasised that this was not wholly a technical problem, but more a question of the monetary authorities' failure to control supposedly subordinate institutions.

14 Output of domestic electrical appliances rose by only 2 per cent during 1974 and that of electronic equipment actually fell by 11·1 per cent; these declines in output were also accompanied by rapid stock-building. Producers pointed to the credit squeeze and the effect of accelerating inflation on personal disposable income as the principal causes (see *Conjuntura Econômica*, February 1975). Passenger car output increased by 13·1 per cent, but this was accompanied by substantial accumulation of stocks and a rise of 127 per cent in exports.

15 See S. A. Morley, 'Inflation and Stagnation in Brazil', *Economic Development and Cultural Change*, January 1971.

8 A Comparative Perspective

LAURENCE WHITEHEAD and
ROSEMARY THORP

As we stated in the Introduction, the consequences of stabilisation policies appear to fall into three categories. These were defined as, first, the reduction of disequilibria in the balance of payments, the public sector deficit and the inflation rate, in accordance with programme targets; second, the establishment or reinforcement of a particular system of economic accumulation and distribution; and third, the consolidation of the social and political bases of the resulting economic system, so that it can operate effectively over a long period. Clearly we are in no position to make firm judgements about the success under the second and third headings of the stabilisation policies reviewed here. Nevertheless, these require just as much attention as the first consequence, which is the only one given systematic consideration by orthodox monetarists and the only type of result with which IMF conditionality is directly concerned. In this final section we shall therefore draw together themes from the Introduction (concerning the current international situation and the problems it poses for the IMF and for Latin American policy-makers, and the difficulties of legitimising dependent capitalism in the region) and attempt to relate these general issues to the varied circumstances of the six countries under review, as they emerge from their recent stabilisation experiences.

The first section summarises the underlying political and economic situation in the six countries and contrasts the policy response to crisis. The second takes up our main preoccupation: the consequences of stabilisation policies.

264

THE NATIONAL CONTEXT

Two of the cases studied stand out immediately as extreme examples of liberalisation and return to the market – Chile and Uruguay. Both significantly reduced protection as a deliberate attempt to internationalise and rationalise the economy, as well as achieving a major cut in consumption to the same end. Chile relied heavily on deflationary monetary and fiscal policy – more so than any other country – as well as a restraint on wages. Uruguay achieved rather little by way of orthodox demand-restraint but because of her highly urbanised and factory-based workforce was able under a harsh dictatorship to use wages policy to implement a cut in consumption and in unit costs.

During 1975 Argentina also represented an attempt at a return to market signals, with a massive and chaotic relative price adjustment, combined with attempted fiscal restraint, which was ineffective, and monetary controls, which were far more severe than planned. However, following the fall of the Perón government (the point at which Di Tella's chapter terminates) much more sweeping policies of return to market forces were adopted in Argentina as well.

It is almost certainly no accident that the three countries (out of our six case studies) which reverted most fully to liberal economic policies were those which experienced annual inflation rates of more than 100 per cent – Chile (over 500 per cent in 1974), Argentina (over 400 per cent in 1976) and Uruguay (107 per cent in 1974). The first two of these were countries in which the political authorities had previously shown the least inclination or ability to contain public pressures for expenditure and consumption. They had both experienced three years of civilian governments, under elected Presidents whose organised support derived above all from the trade union movement (Allende 1970–3, the Perón duo 1973–6).[1] Although in each case significant inflationary pressures came from abroad, and although inflationary expectations inherited from previous years may also have contributed to the intensity of the crisis, our analyses here have reached the conclusion that the character of these governments accounts for a large proportion of the total inflation. The contrasts between these two governments and the other four must not, however, obscure the differences between Allende and Perón. Chile's

Marxist government aimed to replace a largely market-dominated economy by one in which central planning would play the leading role. The labour unions and the central planners maintained a fragile alliance based on the presidency and implacably opposed by the majority in Congress, not to mention domestic and foreign propertied interests and the US government. For a political scientist, therefore, the proximate cause of the Chilean inflation was the inability of these warring executive and legislative branches of government to harmonise their spending and revenue-raising decisions; but by itself this would be a misleadingly formalistic explanation.[2] The deeper political cause was the ideological conflict, and the competing mass mobilisations in which the whole of Chilean society was involved. For most supporters of the Allende government the recruitment of popular support had to take precedence over any coherent strategy of economic management, and for many of its opponents currency speculation, black marketeering and even economic sabotage became legitimate instruments of political struggle. By contrast, General Perón was no Marxist and those of his supporters who thought otherwise were quickly disabused. The Peronist executive commanded an overwhelming majority in Congress and was initially viewed by many elements of the propertied classes as the only hope of containing social disorder. General Perón apparently believed he was pursuing a coherent strategy of economic management and one likely to appeal to business interests as well as his labour following: by controlling prices he could stabilise the level of wages and provide easy credit to enterprises wishing to expand. Three factors rendered this approach unviable, however. By the time of Perón's death (July 1974), the level at which wages were supposed to be stabilised had become unsustainably high in real terms, since this was the only way for the government to reinforce the authority of the official CGT leadership; in any case real wage levels that might have seemed sustainable in the international boom conditions of 1973 could not be considered viable the following year, when the world recession developed, eroding Argentina's foreign exchange reserves; as for other counter-inflation policies, the government increasingly relied on price controls and exchange rate fixity as an effective substitute for either monetary or fiscal restraint. After eighteen years in opposition many of the diverse currents of Peronist support expected the new government to reward them for their loyalty. Increased public expenditure, over-high real wages, and an artificially pegged exchange rate may make an unwise combination, but they could be the understandable biases of a labour-based civilian government and need not of themselves have led to the extremes of economic dislocation experienced by Argentina in 1976. They were, however, compounded by further policy decisions that made for an explosive situation: public sector revenues were allowed to fall, as subsidies and price controls were used to repress artificially the underlying inflation, and an exchange rate correction was delayed until long after its inevitability was apparent, thus stimulating contraband and black marketeering on a massive scale. It would have required the deployment of all Perón's personal authority to rectify this unviable combination of short-term expedients but, knowing his poor health, he chose not to worry about the long-term, or even to arrange a responsible succession. His death left the Argentine government no better able to manage the economic situation than Chile's embattled Marxists, and with less excuse.

Although in retrospect the economic policy adopted in Uruguay since 1972 seems to anticipate later measures adopted in Chile and Argentina, both the political and the economic contexts were rather different. Inflation peaked at a level much lower than the other Southern Cone countries, but much higher than in Brazil and Peru, let alone in Mexico (30 per cent in 1976). All these four regimes were much more well-entrenched than the governments of Allende and Perón, which may help explain why they were able to contain inflation at lower levels. All four could count on a loyal public administration and judiciary, a restrained or docile press, and no effective veto-power exercised either by Congress or by the labour movement. Of the four, the Uruguayan economy seemed the most vulnerable to the international recession and also suffered the added disadvantages of a long history of severe inflation (so that destabilising expectations were widespread) and of economic stagnation. In fact Uruguay had been experiencing progressively more acute stabilisation crises and shrinking levels of *per capita* output for well over a decade before the oil price rise. Its productive system was probably the most vulnerable (a negligible domestic market, a very limited range of export possibilities, dependence on imports for nearly all its most essential inputs) and was required to support the most extensive and ambitious welfare system. By 1970 the degeneration of this situation had already reached an advanced stage, with various attempts to concentrate political power in the hands of the President and to withdraw long-standing rights and privileges from labour and welfare beneficiaries (in 1968 inflation had already surpassed 100 per cent). By the time of the 1973 boom three different types of challenge to conservative/authoritarian government had all been defeated: the guerrilla movement, the labour movements, and the liberal/parliamentary movement. This explains why Uruguay embarked on a policy of severe economic orthodoxy and military dictatorship before either Chile or Argentina, and indeed before the oil crisis.

Up to the time of writing Peruvian responses to the stabilisation crisis have not replicated the extremes of liberalisation practised in the Southern Cone, and it seems apparent that such a course would meet some fierce resistance. However, the Peruvian crisis remains very severe and unresolved, so that further measures remain quite possible. So far Peru's policies have been highly orthodox in intention, with monetary and fiscal restraints and the removal of subsidies and price controls. But there has as yet been no question of wholesale conversion to the restoration of market forces and to the reduction of protection. The restrictive measures actually implemented have provoked such severe reactions that the authorities have wavered between attempts at deflation and suspended agreements with creditors, while the crisis deepens. This is partly because the external shocks that precipitated the present crisis hit an economy that was already facing a critical long-run crisis in its model of accumulation, resulting from a combination of stagnating prospects on the supply side in exports and a partially related fall-off in domestic investment. Thus, containment of pressures for consumption was particularly crucial to economic policy-making. In certain respects the Peruvian situation looked rather favourable to this end: there was no change of President for almost seven years (1968–75), and when the change finally occurred it was the Finance Minister from the previous government who took over, thereby preserving a certain degree of continuity. The Peruvian labour movement has, if anything, grown in independence and combativity during the 1970s, whereas unions in the other three countries have been crushed.

But even at its most assertive, Peruvian labour does not yet constrain economic policy-making to the extent that used to be customary for the Southern Cone labour movements. Indeed, for the first half of the 1970s the Peruvian military regime was relatively well insulated from the pressures of immediate consumption demands, stressing instead the high rate of investment it was able to allocate to long-term development projects mainly in the public sector, and able to operate in a context of near price stability.

But it seems evident that some time before the actual removal of General Velasco from the presidency (August 1975), there was already a significant change in the character of the regime. The early momentum of the revolutionary government had been eroded by late 1973, with events in neighbouring Chile probably contributing to the change in mood. More specifically, the margin of manoeuvre for the economic policy-makers was considerably reduced by the changed international outlook following the oil price rise, by the accumulating consequences of the regime's previous economic decisions, and by the growing pressures it faced to produce concrete benefits for specific groups in order to live up to its previous rhetoric of reform. The international difficulties were nothing like as severe as those that confronted Uruguayan policy-makers, and the internal pressures were far more manageable in military-run Peru than in civilian-ruled Chile and Argentina. Nevertheless, real wages and salaries in Lima were reportedly 33 per cent higher in 1973 than in 1968, by which time the short-term economic pressures had greatly increased. The problem was compounded by increased concern in military circles about the country's national security, especially in relation to Chile (see Table 8.1, which gives estimates of the huge increase in Chilean military expenditure that occurred in 1974 and the Peruvian response in 1975). The dollar value of Peruvian imports nearly doubled in 1974 and a whole range of public enterprise, built up under the patronage of the military government, launched into spectacular investment projects.

TABLE 8.1   Military expenditure of the six countries as a percentage of GNP

	Argentina	Brazil	Chile	Mexico	Peru	Uruguay
1970	1·81	2·31	2·54	0·67	3·27	1·96
1973	1·48	2·12	3·11	0·71	3·73	2·43
1974	1·65	2·05	5·28	0·70	3·53	2·66
1975	2·32	2·21	4·32	0·88	4·80	2·40

Source: US Arms Control and Disarmament Agency (1976).

The conclusion seems unavoidable that by 1974 the authority of the executive had weakened to the point where substantial central control over spending decisions had been lost. Despite the enormous power formally concentrated in the leadership of the military regime, some combination of national security fears, labour and popular pressures, and the proliferation of autonomous bureaucracies, had severely undermined its capacity for coherent economic management well before the downfall of President Velasco.

Mexico's famously stable and resilient political system appears on the surface to have contained the shocks of inflation and stabilisation far more successfully than any of the four countries discussed above. Partly this reflects the character of the post-revolutionary political institutions themselves, and partly the fact that the disequilibria in the economy were in some sense less severe. (Table 8.1 shows how little of her resources Mexico wasted on military expenditures in comparison with the Southern Cone republics.) In contrast to Peru, Mexico's oil discoveries of the early 1970s have proved genuine and of fundamental importance. Their existence may have somewhat cushioned the consequences of the postponement of stabilisation policies. Mexico has also benefited from the relatively indulgent provisions of the IMF's three-year Extended Fund Facility, and has so far experienced only a fairly slight slowdown in public borrowing and monetary conditions. But one should not underestimate the severity of the shocks recently experienced. After twenty-two years of free convertibility with the dollar at a fiscal parity, the collapse of the currency in the last months of the Echeverría presidency produced considerable traumas, even though a degree of normalcy may subsequently have been restored without necessitating the most severe extremes of austerity. The whole financial system was predicated on free convertibility and close integration with the US economy, so that Mexico operated none of the adjustment devices that make 30 per cent inflation rates reasonably tolerable in most South American republics. Social tensions and conflicts are no less acute in Mexico than in any of the other countries included in our study (as Mexican policy-makers were clearly aware, for example, during the upheavals of 1968), and the long-term stresses inherent in the growth strategy adopted in the 1950s are described in FitzGerald's chapter. However, successive Mexican governments have proved unusually adept at containing or dispersing social tensions and managing the stresses of the growth strategy. After the successful repression carried out by the government in 1968, the Echeverría administration (inaugurated in 1970) felt the need to re-establish popularity and legitimacy by increasing the distribution of benefits. At the same time it aimed to expand the public sector to compensate for deficiencies in the preceding patterns of investment. Attempts to achieve this coincided with a slowdown in the economy, partly caused by the downturn in the US economy of 1971, so that the incremental resources available for distribution shrank just when the political necessity for increased distribution had increased. The attempt to escape from this dilemma by rapidly expanding the domestic economy tended to push internal prices up out of line with those prevailing in the USA, thus putting the exchange rate in jeopardy. For a while these problems could be disguised by increased government borrowing, both on the domestic credit market and from private international sources, and by increased subsidies on consumer goods and in public sector pricing policies, which had the effect of disguising the degree of internal inflation. By 1973/4, however, imported inflation became a major problem and forced policy changes that involved 'catching up' on the accumulated domestic inflation as well. In the light of these developments the established parity with the US dollar clearly could not be sustained over the longer-run, and yet the Echeverría administration determined not to devalue, at least during that presidential term. There may have been strong political reasons for this decision, but it led to an even greater build-up of foreign indebtedness, without enabling the government to master the inflation or achieve structural change in the economy. Instead it created an irresistible climate for private speculation against the currency, speculation that was bound to mount as the presidency entered its lame-duck phase and that added a significant further twist to the inflationary spiral.

Brazil, alone of the six countries studied, has not experienced a single year since 1968 in which its growth rate has fallen below its population rate, nor has the exchange rate for the cruzeiro at any point required sharp realignment. In three crucial respects the Brazilian government has succeeded where the others failed in maintaining firmer control over three strategic and interrelated economic variables: wage pressure, and mass consumption pressures more generally, have never acquired sufficient autonomy to undermine centralised policy-making; the demand for imports has not been allowed to outrun what the administration could coherently finance; and public sector finances have also remained basically under control.

Several features of the domestic political context may have contributed to the inflation. Although successive Presidents have maintained the broad continuity of the military dictatorship since 1964, the difficulties of orderly presidential succession have certainly not been entirely overcome. In 1973 the outgoing presidential team sought to increase the popularity and influence of their faction by promoting unsustainably fast growth, undeterred by the physical bottlenecks and monetary difficulties that this might bequeath to their successors. They even manipulated the price index, with the result that the incoming administration had to take responsibility for some inflationary catch-up (quite a serious consequence considering the Brazilian indexation system). Beginning in 1974 the Geisel presidency sought to consolidate its hold on power by correcting some of the worst distributive inequalities produced by the previous period of profits-led growth. Higher minimum wages were to precede more open tests of electoral opinion, from which a 'liberalised' regime hoped to emerge with enhanced authority. All this was to be accomplished in association with a controlled slowdown in the rate of economic expansion.

We are now in a position to draw some conclusions about the short- and long-run results of the six stabilisation efforts discussed in this book. It can be seen that the external shocks of 1974−5 were quite as serious for Brazil as for Mexico, Argentina, or Peru. Yet they have been more successfully absorbed. There are, of course, many features of Brazilian economic policy and of the country's political life that offset this positive record, and even in terms of narrowly defined economic success the record is far from optimal, as we see in the next section. The strains of adjustment would have been considerably worse had not Brazil been so greatly favoured by foreign investors and international bankers and by the price of coffee. Also, it has certainly not been through orthodox 'free market' policies that the government has achieved its major successes in regulating consumption or curbing the growth of imports. On the contrary some of its most effective policy instruments have involved distinctly more state interventionism than is fashionable elsewhere: notably increased import controls and extensive but by no means automatic indexation. Monetary policy has been moderately restrictive, but in the sector of the economy where market freedoms have been more liberally extended, namely banking and finance, economic policy-makers have suffered damaging setbacks, with less success in controlling the monetary aggregates than they had hoped.

THE RESULTS OF ATTEMPTED STABILISATION

It should be noted at the outset that not even the 'first level' consequences of stabilisation (those most directly monitored and specified by the international agencies) are as unproblematic as they might appear at first sight.

If we take first the question of stabilisation of domestic prices, we find that not one of the programmes which we have considered here has actually stabilised the price level. Chile proves to be the nearest thing to an exception, with inflation currently running at under 50 per cent in 1978, compared with levels of 400–500 per cent at the height of the disequilibrium. Reviewing the different case studies, this result is easily explicable: the actual amount of deflation successfully achieved was sometimes less than intended, but, more importantly, deflation was typically accompanied by strong cost-push inflationary factors. These were in part the result of relative price adjustments, but in part a consequence of the deflation itself, as, for example, the rise in unit costs which accompanied falling output. The short-term goal with greater priority has been the improvement of the external balance. Here there has admittedly been some success in every case, though in the case of Mexico this was due mainly to an exogenous rise in exports (oil and coffee), and in the case of Brazil in part to coffee, and in part to unorthodox measures (import controls), with domestic deflation playing a relatively minor role in both cases. The other case studies suggest that only certain types of export structures permit the easy stimulation of exports by curbing domestic consumption – i.e. where the traditional export products are also consumed at home, as in Argentina and Uruguay – and then there may still be a market problem to be faced. The hoped-for stimulation of non-traditional exports may require a very large (and continuing) cut in real wages, as in Uruguay, and may even then run the risk of protectionism in developed countries as the amount exported increases. Where the structure of the economy provides little chance of export promotion, 'success' is achieved only by an enormously costly squeezing of investment and industrial activity, to economise on imports. Peru shows the limits and the costs of such a process.

But there is still a further problem, even with regard to short-term goals. Suppose that an internationally vulnerable economy, like that of Uruguay, undergoes a severe bout of deflation and austerity in accordance with orthodox prescription. If major disequilibria exist in the world economy at large, the attempts by a small vulnerable economy to correct its internal disequilibrium by following internationally approved 'best practices' of orthodoxy may be repeatedly thwarted by shocks from outside.

This prospect of successive cycles of deflation in a continually frustrated attempt to adjust to shocks from outside may seem very hypothetical (although Uruguayans might be more inclined to recognise its plausibility). The same point can also be made in a different way, that may command more acceptance. Orthodox stabilisation measures are more likely to produce quick results and therefore command political and intellectual support when it is a healthy and buoyant international system on behalf of which discipline is being exerted. If we are correct in the contention we set out in the Introduction, that the dollar-based international economy is experiencing fundamental long-term strains, then we may anticipate growing scepticism about the assumption that acceptance of orthodox policies must after a painful interlude lead to subsequent economic recovery. There may be no better alternative available, but at least for some of the more vulnerable countries the typical orthodox stabilisation package offers no reliable guarantee even that the short-term disequilibria will be effectively corrected.

These considerations have already suggested how far even measures which are effective in terms of first-level goals run the risk of failing in terms of our second and third levels. Repeated deflation in response to unstable international conditions means high costs in terms of capital formation; even short-run success with non-traditional exports may not imply a new motor of accumulation and growth, if it in fact represents largely the offloading of surplus products unsalable at home. Although it is possibly premature to judge either the Uruguayan or Chilean experience, we would argue that so far the record of IMF-approved stabilisation policies in Latin America gives no firm basis for assuming that short-term adjustment will necessarily be followed by sustainable long-term growth.

Chile, for example, was the first Third World country to receive adjustment assistance from the IMF, back in 1947. (Indeed it was in relation to this Chilean application that the IMF first elaborated the practice of 'conditionality', a system of involvement in the economic policy-making of member states not envisaged in the original articles of association.) Over the next thirty years the Chilean economy was subjected to a wide variety of major stabilisation efforts (1955–6, 1962–3, 1965–6 and 1974–6), each of which involved resort to a further IMF 'standby' arrangement to correct the 'temporary' disequilibrium, whilst on average income per head rose little more than 1 per cent per annum. Undoubtedly the most recent stabilisation programme has been the most doctrinaire and the most drastic, and has been accompanied by sweeping political changes designed, once and for all, to clear the way for a private-enterprise system of capital accumulation. Defenders of the latest (Chilean) stabilisation policy will therefore deny that the results of previous attempts show that such policies fail to promote long-term growth. They will argue instead that previous policies were not applied with sufficient determination and persistence to prove their worth.

Argentina and Uruguay have similarly experienced a series of attempts at economic stabilisation since the mid-1950s, none of which (with the possible exception of Argentina in 1966)[3] showed much sign of paving the way for sustainable long-term growth. In those countries, too, the most recent stabilisations have been the most drastic and have been accompanied by sweeping institutional changes, designed to eliminate all the democratic impediments held responsible for frustrating earlier capitalist growth strategies. The historical evidence from the Southern Cone does not, therefore, suggest that there is anything easy or automatic about the association between short-term stabilisation and the resumption of long-term economic growth. Nevertheless, the current generation of policy-makers firmly assert that this time, with the prospect of an indefinite concentration of power in their hands, more systematic economic policies will produce the desired long-term effects on the growth rate.

Although we must not attempt to anticipate the future, some observations can be made about these three cases of ruthless stabilisation that may help assess their prospects of establishing a more successful new model of accumulation. (Similar observations can also be expected to apply to Peru, although the eventual outcome of her current stabilisation crisis is not yet known to us.) First, the international economic environment is less favourable than in the 1950s or 1960s, so that if recent policies *do* pave the way for a successful resumption of growth they will have proved their efficacy in particularly adverse circumstances. Second, however, in the cases of Uruguay and Chile (admittedly the most fragile economies) we already have the experience of three or four years of stabilisation attempts to judge by. At the end of this period the success in terms of some of the short-run stabilisation aims (especially balance-of-payments equilibrium) is considerable, although not perfect. Something like the kind of equilibrium that existed between previous stabilisation crises has been restored. But over the same period very little net investment has occurred, so that there has been little improvement in the underlying productive capacity of the economy. Drastic shifts of resources have occurred from one sector of the economy to another (e.g. from import-substituting industries to exporters, from debtors to creditors, from welfare services to the agencies of repression), but in aggregate the domestic resources available for savings and productive investment have not risen to a level sufficient to generate self-sustaining growth. Third, therefore, the success of the currently favoured accumulation model appears to rest on the ability of these four governments to attract sufficient inflows of foreign savings and investment on appropriate terms, and with the desired effects on the overall allocative efficiency of their economies. It would be erroneous to claim that such a strategy can never succeed in producing rapid material growth, or to disregard the fragmentary evidence of its effects in the Southern Cone. However, the evidence suggests that from short-term stabilisation to long-term economic recovery on private enterprise lines there remains a vast distance to be covered, that the time lags may be painfully long, and that at least the more fragile or severely disrupted economies will find themselves depending very heavily on external capital flows to speed their recovery, since the domestic consequences of drastic stabilisation measures do not tend to favour a rapid restoration of internally generated growth.

A prolonged display of economic orthodoxy and ruthlessly repressive government may serve to attract foreign capital, but as yet even this remains more a hope of the policy-makers than an accomplished fact. In the current political and economic climate, and after the recent experiences of inflation, nationalisation and political troubles in many Latin American countries, most foreign investors will hesitate before committing large amounts of capital to any but the largest and most secure countries of the region. Geography may be another factor: Mexico, with its long border with the USA, is a far more interesting market than Chile or Uruguay could ever be. Whitehead suggests in his chapter on Chile that 'marginality' in respect of the world market is itself a reason for extreme policies, since only such could be expected to yield dividends in terms of external aid and trade preference: the point would apply equally to Uruguay. At any rate if substantial resources are to be tied up in a country for a long period of time, they may require a government that is not only firmly in control and strongly committed to orthodoxy, but also one that seems to be capable of legitimising itself. The third level of 'consequences of stabilisation' therefore seems quite closely related to the second. A stabilisation programme will only be a lasting success if it paves the way for a system of economic accumulation capable of averting future stabilisation crises. However, the most recent and most drastic stabilisation programmes being undertaken in Latin America seem hardly designed to transform the internal capacity for accumulation of these economies. Their best prospect of success would seem to be if they can attract in long-term foreign capital, but in that case lasting success may well depend on the consolidation of the social and political bases of the economic system. However, these are not the type of consequences which orthodox monetarists or IMF advisers are particularly well-equipped to understand nor do they receive particular attention in those quarters.

We shall conclude this comparative survey by briefly considering what lessons our six country studies offer concerning the possibilities of 'legitimising' the new economic order after a stabilisation crisis. Brazil is widely quoted as a long-established and convincing demonstration that this can be done. During the early 1960s a weak civilian government presided over a process of rising inflation and growing disequilibrium quite similar to those of the 1970s studies in this volume. Following the military seizure of power in 1964, a stabilisation policy was implemented which, by the late 1960s, had completed the process of short-term adjustment and cleared the way for a sustained period of economic growth at least according to this interpretation.[4] The new political order was quite repressive and dictatorial (although less severe than the recent Southern Cone regimes) and was based very explicitly on close co-operation between the military and major domestic and foreign business interests, to the virtual exclusion from political life of the other sectors of society. In Brazil this formula has proved resilient enough to endure for fourteen years and ride out the economic shocks of 1974–5 with more success than any of the other countries under review. We cannot, however, say that even in Brazil the formula has been fully legitimised. Indeed, one of the major political problems for the military regime has been its repeated inability to secure an adequate degree of electoral support for its candidates. Nevertheless, the various forms of opposition which the Brazilian model has inspired have not yet commanded sufficient support to destroy business confidence in the regime, which private enterprise continues to regard as a satisfactory example not only of economic stabilisation and subsequent growth, but also of political stability and guarantees.

Underlying this question of international confidence, however, is another and deeper factor: the enlistment of a solid basis of class support. The Brazilian regime, relying on support from the business classes, has – at least until very recently – obtained remarkably effective support, enabling it to preserve its autonomy of economic management and to escape the damaging dictates of IMF orthodoxy, whereas the regimes which attempted to govern with labour support, or on the basis of a state machine trying to govern in splendid isolation from the underlying social forces, have found the task of economic management far more intractable.

Does the conclusion follow that in future Latin American governments that wish to remain outside the clutches of the IMF and avoid acute problems of economic management should rule in closer alliance with business interests? Argentina, Chile and Uruguay certainly seem to be acting in accordance with this view and it also seems to have growing influence on the governments of Mexico and perhaps even Peru. Although the IMF and the World Bank avoid being too explicit on such highly political questions, the practical import of their policy recommendations is to point in the same direction. However, perhaps it is fitting to conclude by pointing out that there are grounds for doubting whether this prescription would prove all that reliable.

First, Brazil's relative success is not entirely solid, as current pressures on her to change her trading practices makes clear.[5] Second, even in Brazil the close alliance between government and business interests encounters enough resistance to raise some doubts about its permanence, especially if there is a climate of continuing international recession. Third, regaining the support and confidence of domestic and foreign business interests after the stabilisation traumas of the mid-1970s in the Southern Cone will be a very different matter from the Brazilian government's task of simply preserving an established level of support and confidence. In countries like Chile and Peru, for example, the policies of the early 1970s drastically affected the private sector, so that an alliance with such a group would require reconstruction rather than just reassurance. Even in Argentina or Mexico, where business interests have been under far less severe threat, the political and social price of attempting to imitate the Brazilian model could well turn out to be prohibitive. Finally, although deliberate policies chosen by a restructured Brazilian state have much to do with that country's relative success in coping with the international crisis over the past few years, one must not overestimate the degree of freedom available to ruling élites in individual Latin American republics. International conditions (both economic and political) were very favourable to the consolidation and success of the Brazilian formula, at least for the first decade of its existence, but those conditions seem distinctly less likely to prevail in the coming decade as pro-business dictatorships attempt to consolidate themselves, for example, in Argentina, Chile and Uruguay.

NOTES

1 For a comparative survey of inflation and stabilisation in Argentina, Brazil and Mexico in the 1950s and 1960s see Skidmore (1975).
2 For a general and comparative discussion of 'The Political Causes of Inflation', see the forthcoming review article of that title, Whitehead (1979).
3 On this, see Juan C. de Pablo (1972), which identifies four previous stabilisation programmes – in 1953, 1959, 1962 and 1965. IMF standbys were arranged in 1959, 1962, 1967 and 1976.
4 See Chapter 7 above, by John Wells.
5 E.g. on 10 May 1978 the Assistant Secretary to the US Treasury, Mr C. Fred Bersten, told the Brazilian-American Chamber of Commerce in New York that some Brazilian trading practices were directly contrary to US

countervailing duties laws, and that the US was likely to retaliate unless subsidies to exports and the protection of domestic industries were both diminished before the end of 1978. Brazil's Foreign Minister replied by telling a meeting of the OAS, a month later, that Latin America's foremost trading partner 'uses GATT to promote its exports, and its trade act to limit its imports'. Nevertheless Brazil subsequently announced a phased withdrawal of its trade controls and export subsidies.

REFERENCES

de Pablo, Juan C. (1972), *Política Anti-inflacionaria en la Argentina (1967 – 70)*, Ediciones Amorrurtu, Buenos Aires.
Skidmore, T. (1975), 'The Politics of Economic Stabilization in Latin America', *University of Winsconsin Discussion Paper in Economic History EH 75 – 27*, Madison, Wisconsin.
US Arms Control and Disarmament Agency (1976), *World Military Expenditures and Arms Transfers 1966 – 75*, Government Printing Office, Washington.
Whitehead, Laurence (1979), 'The Political Causes of Inflation', *Political Studies*, Clarendon Press, Oxford, forthcoming.

Index

281